From One Beggar to Another

Nathan Kaspar

WALDORF PUBLISHING

Published by Waldorf Publishing
2140 Hall Johnson Road
#102-345
Grapevine, Texas 76051
www.WaldorfPublishing.com

From One Beggar to Another

ISBN: 978-1-64467-178-8
Library of Congress Control Number: 2019951783

Copyright © 2019

Design by Baris Celik

This book is dedicated to Jesus Christ, the only way to heaven and my Lord and Savior. His love, truth, grace, and mercy are never-ending and He reaches His hand out to all!

Acknowledgements

Thank you, Katie, for supporting me and this book, having my back, and always loving me incredibly well. You are my soulmate and love of my life. Thank you, mom and dad, for never giving up on me and sacrificing so much out of love for me and Jonathan, and now our families. Thank you for pointing us all to Jesus. Thank you, Jonathan and Maggie, for being an awesome brother and sister-in-law, always being there, and for your love and joy. Thank you, Nancy, Bob, and Heather, for being wonderful parent-in-laws and sister-in-law. Thank you to all my family and friends for your love and support. Thank you, also, to Towne for your support and for serving God's people with love. Waldorf Publishing, thank you for your help and patience during the process of editing and publishing. There are many people through the years that have impacted my life, and to you, I also say thank you.

1/1

Good Greetings!
Where in the name of jingle bells and candy canes did this past year go?!

Let me begin by saying there is nothing magical about this New Year's Day. In a sense, it can be symbolic of a clean slate and hope for a new beginning. However, I urge you to not place your hope in this symbolism, but in the One who created day and night!

"But as for me, I will look to the LORD; I will wait for the God of my salvation; my God will hear me." (Micah 7:7)
The God who saved you will guide you through this New Year, and always. He hears you and though He may not answer in accordance with your human desire, trust that His answer is the one you need. Place this verse on your mirror, on your phone, on a card in your car, or somewhere your eyes will often read these words from God!

Know this verse, know the truth of this verse, know the power of this verse, and know the One whom this verse is about.

Will you choose to be a warrior for Christ Jesus this year? Will you choose to grow in Him?
Will you choose to actively serve Him in your church and be involved beyond Sunday morning? If you already are, will you choose to continue to serve and be involved?

I beseech and implore you to answer yes!

And as you travel through this upcoming year, hear Jesus as He says to you, "And behold, I am with you always, to the end of the age." (Matthew 28:20b)

Go forth this New Year in Jesus Christ!

1/2

Hello and Greetings,

What causes your soul to stir within you? Hearken back to moments when you felt within your heart a passion bubbling up in such a way that made you feel that there was a cause greater than yourself worth giving your last breath for. Was it a real-life event, a scene in a movie, a passage from a book, or a speech you heard?

There are moments in life where a person must choose if he or she will stand in the safe zone, or venture into the battle zone.

"Jonathan said to the young man who carried his armor, 'Come, let us go over to the garrison of these uncircumcised. It may be that the Lord will work for us, for nothing can hinder the Lord from saving by many or by few.' And his armor-bearer said to him, 'Do all that is in your heart. Do as you wish. Behold, I am with you heart and soul.'" (1 Samuel 14:6-7)

This young man believed and followed Jonathan with fiery courage and passion. He was not choosing to venture out with 50%, 75%, or even 99% of his heart and soul. He was all in!

Do you follow Jesus with that sort of self-abandonment of laying aside your earthly safety and comforts? Does your soul stir with passion at the thought of following after God and standing with Him in the midst of spiritual warfare? Does your heart swell with love for your God to the point that you find joy at the thought of standing with Him even though it may cost you your reputation, job, friends, or very life?

May your heart's cry to Jesus Christ be, "Do as you wish. Behold, I am with you heart and soul."

Venture forth today and every day with and for the One who ventured forth to Earth for you.

1/3

Hello to You,

How many directions does prayer hold? How many streets does it go down? It must, not should, be multi-directional and be a two way street of communication with God Almighty, your Father.

Don't just speak to Him, but listen intently. It's hard to not get distracted during the listening part. Ask God to take away distractions. Don't think about what you have to do, the challenges waiting for you, or the last few Oreos waiting for you to eat.

Any good relationship has communication both ways. Your relationship with God is no different--and is actually more important.

Listen!

1/4

Hello,

Have you seen the movie, *The Patriot*? It's a good one, and you can even learn something from the dialogue between two characters in the movie, Charlotte Selton, and Benjamin Martin.

Charlotte: "You have done nothing for which you should be ashamed."

Benjamin: "I have done nothing. And for that, I am ashamed."

My intent is not to shame you by any measure or degree. My intent is to spur you on!

Benjamin was reflecting at his decision to not fight for his country during the raging war.

Don't share Benjamin's regret or let the same be said about you in the spiritual war that is waging! Jump in the fray with Christ as your general!

1/5

Good greetings everyone,

David was a man that had a very easy life. You could really describe it as a life of ease and luxury. The man never faced heartache, never committed many sins, and really did not have a passion for the things of God.

Completely kidding. Those are all false descriptions about the man of which God described as a man after His own heart. David did not live a life that was always at ease. His life had heartache, troubles, and treacherous sins. But David had a heart that was passionate about serving his King, a heart that was truly repentant after he committed sinful acts.

"Have mercy on me, O God, according to your steadfast love; according to your abundant mercy blot out my transgressions. Wash me thoroughly from my iniquity and cleanse me from my sin! For I know my transgressions, and my sin is ever before me...Create in me a clean heart, O God, and renew a right spirit within me." (Psalm 51:1-3, 10)

When you falter, and you will (as we all do), let this be your prayer. Let David's prayer become your heart's cry--your soul's cry to your Heavenly Father.

"If seven times a day we offend him and repent, does he forgive? Ay, that he does. This is to be unfeignedly believed, and I do believe it: I believe that, often as I transgress, God is more ready to forgive me than I am ready to offend, though, alas, I am all too ready to transgress. Hast thou right thoughts of God, dear hearer? If so, then thou knowest that he is a tender father, willing to wipe the tear of penitence away, and press his offending child to his bosom, and kiss him with the kisses of his forgiving love." (Charles Spurgeon)

Don't take God's grace for granted or appraise it cheaply. His grace does not grant us free reign to sin. But dwell in the promise of His forgiveness, grace and mercy; beseech Him to guide you into honoring

Him with all you've got!

    God is loving.
    God is forgiving.

    Go and run to Him.

1/6

How for art thou doing?

Remember those eraser pens and how the ink was not completely erased when you used the eraser? Good thing that's exactly what happens when you confess your sins to Jesus and ask for His forgiveness!

Just kidding. Good think His blood washes away all our sins and God the Father sees no blemish!

Take time each day to remember that Jesus washed all of your sins away and that no sin is greater than His blood…and not sin of another is greater either.

Buy an eraser and let it stand as a reminder that the world's way of dealing with sin to get to heaven is not enough. God's way is. He erased your sin and stands ready to for another that would but believe.

Remember erasers!

1/7

Hi Everyone,

I would like to begin by sharing a dream I had recently. During the dream, Papa Jack (my mom's dad who passed away in 2009) and I saw each other. As we were looking at one another, I pointed up to Heaven which was communicating to him that I would see him one day up in Heaven.

You may be suffering from the loss of someone you loved dearly. Or, you may know someone who is suffering. Or both.
In Christ, there is hope...sweet and powerful hope.

"But now he is dead. Why should I fast? Can I bring him back again? I shall go to him, but he will not return to me." (2 Samuel 12:23)

In this passage, David had just lost his young son and he explains that though his son cannot come back to life, he will one day see him again after he himself dies. For non-Christians, death is an eternal separation from God. Whether your loved one was a believer or not, Jesus will be your comfort and uphold you. Yet as Christians, death is not a permanent separation. Death is... well, let's allow J.R.R. Tolkien to illustrate death for us from *his Lord of the Rings: Return of the King* book:

PIPPIN: I didn't think it would end this way.
GANDALF: End? No, the journey doesn't end here. Death is just another path, one that we all must take. The grey rain-curtain of this world rolls back, and all turns to silver glass, and then you see it.
PIPPIN: What? Gandalf? See what?
GANDALF: White shores, and beyond, a far green country under a swift sunrise.
PIPPIN: Well, that isn't so bad.
GANDALF: No. No, it isn't.

Remember David's words that you too will be reunited with those who believed in Jesus Christ.

For this reason, hope.
For this reason, share Jesus with anyone who will listen.

Until we reach that heavenly reunion, press on in Jesus Christ.

1/8

Good Greetings,

Yoda I am not. Carry a light saber I do not. But take a look at this quote from Star Wars: "In my experience there is no such thing as luck." (Obi-Wan Kenobi)

Such is truth though. There is no such thing as luck from a biblical perspective. There are no coincidences with God, and nothing catches Him by surprise!

Wish someone God's best or Godspeed instead of good luck!

Godspeed!

1/9

Everyone Hello,

Don't worry, I did not write that when I was half asleep or in a dream state. No, I'm not trying to invent a new language either! That was intentional.

"The heart of the righteous ponders how to answer, but the mouth of the wicked pours out evil things." (Proverbs 15:18)

The placement of words is extremely important, not only in the greeting of an email, but also in our daily conversations with others. We need to utilize wisdom and discretion in where we place certain words and the timing with which we bring up certain topics. We may need to bite our tongues and not bring up something until a later time. Or, we may need to say one thing first, discuss it, then bring up the second item. When you need to approach someone regarding a critique, confront someone on an issue, or simply bring up a conversation that has the potential to not go smoothly, try to first mention something positive about the person you are speaking with. Then, move to the next item.

"Let your speech always be gracious, seasoned with salt, so that you may know how you ought to answer each person." (Colossians 4:6)

Ask God to guide your words today and always. Use the Bible and prayer to season your heart, mind, and speech. Jesus said, "For out of the abundance of the heart the mouth speaks." (Matthew 12:34b)

Have a wonderful day, everyone! Go forth in Christ to use your words and their placement wisely today and every day!

1/10

Whom do you claim to believe in?

It may seem like a trivial question as you think to yourself, "Jesus of course!" But do you really believe? Do you truly live with the confidence and belief that the God of everything lives in you, that He can do anything He desires through you, that He is bigger than any problem? Do you?

"And when he got into the boat, His disciples followed him. And behold, there arose a great storm on the sea, so that the boat was being swamped by the waves; but He was asleep. And they went and woke Him, saying, 'Save us, Lord; we are perishing.' And He said to them, 'Why are you afraid, O you of little faith?' Then He rose and rebuked the winds and the sea, and there was a great calm. And the men marveled, saying, 'What sort of man is this, that even winds and sea obey Him?'" (Matthew 8:23-27)

The God you claim to believe in has the power that makes the winds and sea obey Him. There is nothing going on in your life, now or in the future, that is not subject to His power. Trust Him to handle it as He sees fit, for your own good and His glory.

"Then Moses stretched out his hand over the sea, and the Lord drove the sea back by a strong east wind all night and made the sea dry land, and the waters were divided. And the people of Israel went into the midst of the sea on dry ground, the waters being a wall to them on their right hand and on their left." (Exodus 14:21-22)

That same God lives in you! There is nothing He cannot do! He wants to use you for His glory and to show you more of Himself to grow you closer to Him.

Have faith to follow Him.
Be joyful in submitting to Him.
Truly live for the One you claim to believe in!

Ask Him what He wants you do to.
Believe that He is, really is, who you claim He is (because He is).
Stand in sheer awe of what He does.

Sail with Him out into the God-known (because what is unknown to us has always been known to God)!

1/11

Good Good Greetings!

"It's a dangerous business, Frodo, going out your door. You step onto the road, and if you don't keep your feet, there's no knowing where you might be swept off to." (J.R.R. Tolkien)

The world we live in is a battlefield of the mind, heart, and soul. When you step foot on the ground each and every day, the enemy is seeking to spiritually sweep you off your feet! Many ideas and beliefs are presented to you throughout the day through different mediums such as the internet, billboards, social media, TV, movies, music, books, and anything else you can imagine!

Our society dwells within an atmosphere of moral relativism which is the belief that whatever pleases you, whatever you feel is the truth, whatever is right for you, is correct. There is no absolute truth.
This is incorrect from a biblical perspective because God's Word is absolute truth!

"See to it that no one takes you captive by philosophy and empty deceit, according to human tradition, according to the elemental spirits of the world, and not according to Christ." (Colossians 2:8)

But moral relativism is also incorrect from a logical perspective. If someone states that there is no absolute truth, they have just stated an absolute, therefore, contradicting themselves.

Always turn to the Bible to find truth, to test what is presented to you from the world, and to make your stand with. God's Word is never-changing and will guide you always. Pray to God that He would help you to not be deceived by all the false-messages and false-truths that the enemy will send your way. God is truth, absolutely!

Go forth today and every day standing on and resting in the absolute truth foundation of God!

1/12

Greetings!
"SFT"
See God's face
Feel God's presence
Trust His love

I can't take credit for this, for it comes from "7 Days in Utopia." It is rich and powerful. Remember this today, and always!

Next, I would like to share with you a portion of thoughts written down by a very dear friend of mine, Kirk Oliver. He and his family have journeyed through an extremely deep valley, beginning in the fall of last year. The long of the short is that they have four children, two of which are male twins born this past October. One of the boys, Joshua, had open heart surgery right before Christmas. Dwell upon these words that were given to Kirk from God and the Bible verses. Ask God to speak to you through them.

"I wouldn't wish the last three months of stress, pain or sleepless-ness on anyone. But I also wouldn't trade it for anything. My faith, my marriage, my family have never been stronger. It's funny how open-heart surgery puts perspective on things I used to think were a big deal. God saved my little boy."
(II Corinthians 1:9-11, II Corinthians 4:8-9)

He also listed these references, which are indeed powerful:

"Indeed, we felt that we had received the sentence of death. But that was to make us rely not on ourselves but on God who raises the dead. He delivered us from such a deadly peril, and he will deliver us. On him we have set our hope that he will deliver us again. You also must help us by prayer, so that many will give thanks on our behalf for the blessing granted us through the prayers of many." (II Corinthians 1:9-11)

"We are afflicted in every way, but not crushed; perplexed, but not driven to despair; persecuted, but not forsaken; struck down, but not destroyed;" (II Corinthians 4:8-9)

I leave you with this quote by Corrie ten Boom: "There is no pit so deep, that God's love is not deeper still."

1/13

Well, Good Hello!

To what or to whom do you turn to in times of distress or desperation?

An article recently published in the Wall Street Journal discussed how exercise helped certain individuals cope with the ending of relationships. Describing one individual, the article stated, "But once she signed up for this new challenge [obstacle course race], she says training became like church or therapy. She joined a new community that had nothing to do with her old life."

Please hear me...I have nothing whatsoever against obstacle course races! In fact, I completed my first 200-mile obstacle course race this past week!

Completely kidding (on the part about me).

Again, to what, or to whom, do you turn to in times of distress or desperation?

Exercise is a healthy stress-reliever, but it cannot come before Jesus Christ and His Word, the Bible. For every season of life, good and bad, we must turn to Him and dive into His Word. He is, and will always be, your sustainer.

Do you stray away from church, or do you make an intentionally concerted effort to be with the body of Christ, your family? God desires for you to run to Him and stay connected with the church body. Doing so, your church family can walk with you through the valley, you can serve Christ, and ultimately in order that Jesus Christ may be glorified!

"I lift up my eyes to the hills. From where does my help come? My help comes from the Lord, who made heaven and earth. He will not let your foot be moved; He who keeps you will not slumber. Behold, He who keeps Israel will neither slumber nor sleep. The Lord is your keeper; the Lord is your shade on your right hand. The sun shall not strike

you by day, nor the moon by night. The Lord will keep you from all evil; He will keep your life. The Lord will keep your going out and your coming in from this time forth and forevermore."
(Psalm 121)

Where do you lift your eyes up to? God or the world?

Lift them up to Jesus!

1/14

Hello and Hi,

God is good. All the time.
All the time. God is good.

Situations surrounding your life and my life do not dictate His goodness. He's good because He's God.

Our relationship with God can tend to be like a chameleon. In our minds, the character of God blends into our surroundings. When in reality, we are actually the ones whose character has blended in with our surroundings. His character does not change...and thank Him that it does not!

"Jesus Christ is the same yesterday and today and forever." (Hebrews 13:8)

Trust that all the promises of God's Word will not change.
"For all the promises of God find their Yes in Him [Jesus]." (2 Corinthians 1:20)
Trust that all of the character traits of Christ will never change.

Though your circumstances may change, though God's promises may appear to falter, though your life may appear to be forsaken by God, God does not change. His promises are forever certain and true, and He will never leave you.
"And behold, I am with you always, to the end of the age." (Matthew 28:20b)

Remember, Satan is a chameleon, for he seeks to deceive you.
God is a lion, and the darkness trembles at His roar!

Follow the Lion of Judah!

Because He roars!

1/15

Top of the...
Let's go a different route...
Merry Day to You!

Christmas season has come and gone
But not so must its generously cheerful song
For whether or not the Christmas season is here
Christ the Savior's birth transpired to squelch man's fear
So, sing joy to the world and oh holy night!
For because of that moment your future is bright!

There is a story of a man who was once blind. Then Jesus came to him. We pick up in verse 25b of the 9th chapter of the book of John:
"One thing I do know, that though I was blind, now I see."

Though this man was speaking from a physical standpoint, this was your story from a spiritual standpoint.
Your eyes were blinded by your sin. Your future was hell.

But now your eyes have been opened if you have accepted Jesus Christ as your Lord and Savior. Your future is bright! This doesn't mean tough times won't transpire in your life. But your future has hope! Your future is heaven!

How has your life changed since coming to know Jesus? Don't dwell on the "how do I fully explain such and such" questions. Dwell on the fact that you now see spiritually!

What about your current life does the Holy Spirit desire to change and develop? Ask Him. Surrender your life each day, every moment to Him.

Go forth today and every day echoing what this man said thousands of years ago...
"One thing I do know, that though I was blind, now I see."

1/16

Hello and Good Greetings!

Have you ever felt that your self-esteem was at rock bottom? You've journeyed through the valleys and enjoyed the mountaintops, but you just don't feel that you have enough juice in the tank to continue. Or maybe you've tried to build someone else's self-esteem up. You do so with the best of intentions, not desiring anything in return just with the hope of seeing that person shine again.

Parents desire to build up their children's self-esteem. Friends, family, teachers, coaches, etc. desire to build up one another's self-esteem.

According to Merriam-Webster: self-esteem is "a confidence and satisfaction in oneself" Synonyms for self-esteem: "ego, pride, pridefulness, self-regard, self-respect." Constructively critique the norm and what is comfortable.

If we strive to build up our own, or someone else's self-esteem... we are actually striving to build up the view of self, the idea of self-sufficiency, and in turn we are pursuing the glorification of self over Jesus (even if that is not our intention). We are wretches saved by God's grace...why should we desire to build up our self-ability?

John 3:30 says, "He must increase, but I must decrease." Thus, replace the concept of self-esteem with Christ-esteem. Direct your heart and the hearts of others off of self and onto Jesus. For example: "Therefore, if anyone is in Christ, he is a new creation. The old has passed away; behold, the new has come. All this is from God, who through Christ reconciled us to Himself..."
(2 Corinthians 5:17-18a)

When you encourage someone, encourage them not with the mindset of what they did in and of themselves, but what Christ did through them and helped them accomplish. "But exhort one another every day, as long as it is called 'today,' that non or you may be hardened by the deceitfulness of sin."

(Hebrews 3:13)

Feasting upon God's Word will decrease the time one thinks about themselves (self-esteem) and increase the time one thinks about their wonderful Savior (Christ-esteem). Ask Jesus today and every day to build up and increase your Christ-esteem! Because He esteemed us, He died for us! He loves us greatly!

Esteem Him today and every day!

1/17

Good Greetings,

Today's devotional will be about snow, but not snow at the same time. You may be thinking, "It finally happened. He has lost it! He's going to be writing about and not about snow simultaneously. Poor soul, the cold temperatures must have finally impacted his ability to write."

Fret not, I shall explain. Oh...and you can't lose what you never had!
I digress...

The snow that fell this weekend created a beautiful landscape. In the past when we let our dogs out in the backyard after it had rained, their paws became muddy and they tracked mud into the house. But when it snowed, their paws were not muddy, which was nice for our carpet!

In the same way, the blood of Jesus Christ allows you to not have "muddy paws." You can enter into the throne room of God Almighty through the great High Priest, Jesus Christ!

"Come now, let us reason together, says the Lord: though your sins are like scarlet, they shall be as white as snow; though they are red like crimson, they shall become like wool." (Isaiah 1:18)

Your past, present, and future sins have been forgiven and washed clean. Guilt is not more powerful than Jesus. Your sins are never too great for Jesus. Jesus is greater still!

I also noticed this morning up at church how the sunlight reflects off of the snow. Let this be a reminder to us all that when we are covered by the blood of Jesus Christ, we are to reflect His light to a lost and hurting world, just as the snow reflects the physical sunlight!

Lastly, my wife Katie and I built a snowman yesterday. You know, it's kind of like how the Christian can be a snow-man or snow-woman (as a symbolic reminder) for as the snowman is made of snow, the Christian is made of the blood of Jesus Christ. Let the snow remind you of Christ's blood!

Go forth today, knowing your sins are covered by the blood of Jesus Christ as the snow covers the ground!

Be a snow-man or snow-woman today!

1/18

Hello and Hi!

Giving is the easiest thing in the world. There is absolutely nothing easier than giving your hard-earned money to the church and other causes of God. In fact, it's easier to do those things than to buy something for yourself!

While I'm on a roll (Hawaiian rolls are awesome by the way), it's always easy to eat healthy, and begin and maintain an exercise routine! The above paragraphs demonstrate time travel into the world of sarcasm/joking!

None of those above actions are easy. They are difficult to begin and difficult to maintain. Why? We believe the money is ours. We are prideful of the hard work we demonstrated to earn the money. We forget that we don't even deserve the money in the first place and that God was gracious and loving to give us the money. We are stewards of His gifts. Money is also not the most fun subject for our ears to hear. I don't write this out of crisis or desperation, but as a reminder. The Bible contains God's words on the subject, and we must take heed!

"Honor the Lord with your wealth and with the first fruits of all your produce." (Proverbs 3:9)

We need to give God the best, not the scraps of our money (it's not ours in the first place!). He is the giver; we are the stewards!

"The point is this: whoever sows sparingly will also reap sparingly, and whoever sows bountifully will also reap bountifully. Each one must give as he has decided in his heart, not reluctantly or under compulsion, for God loves a cheerful giver." (2 Corinthians 9:6-7)

Give with joy! Give generously! God gave and continues to give generously!

There is a phrase that says to give until it hurts. God would say to us, "Don't give until it hurts and then stop giving. Give and continue giving through the hurt. My Son did."

This doesn't mean we aren't wise with the money God gives, but that we give with a joyful heart, a generous heart, and not with a heart that has limits. Let God guide your giving!

Give as He gave!

1/19

Good Good Greetings to You All,

Knock-knock!
Who's there?
Cash!
Cash-who?
No thanks, but I will take a peanut!

I know, I know. I should have been a stand-up comedian. It's never too late.

Anyway, where were we? Oh yes...that was a joke and though it may not have caused you to laugh, laughing in general is good medicine.

At the same time, sometimes laughter is not a good response.
"They said to him, 'Where is Sarah your wife?' And he said, 'She is in the tent'" The Lord said, 'I will surely return to you about this time next year, and Sarah your wife shall have a son.' And Sarah was listening at the tent door behind him. Now Abraham and Sarah were old, advanced in years. The way of women had ceased to be with Sarah. So, Sarah laughed to herself, saying, 'After I am worn out, and my lord is old, shall I have pleasure?' The Lord said to Abraham, 'Why did Sarah laugh and say, 'Shall I indeed bear a child, now that I am old?' Is any-thing too hard for the Lord? At the appointed time I will return to you, about this time next year, and Sarah shall have a son.'" But Sarah denied it, saying, 'I did not laugh,' for she was afraid. He said, 'No, but you did laugh.'" (Genesis 18:9-15)

Don't laugh in disbelief at the promises and blessings God has for your life. God is serious about His joyous blessings and serious about His promises!
C.S. Lewis even said, "Joy is the serious business of heaven." Joy is what Christ died to give us! He takes it seriously and gives it freely!

Don't ever feel a promise or blessing of God is impossible! God doesn't have impossibilities. Now, the prosperity gospel is a lie from hell. Just because you follow Jesus, that does not mean you will be given a new car, home, etc. But also know and believe that again, no promise or blessing of God is impossible!

Find joy today in Christ! Enjoy a good laugh!
But don't laugh in disbelief.
Cling to His promises and thank Him for His blessings, today and always!

1/20

Good Hello Y'all,

Would you describe yourself as a servant or consumer? Don't quickly answer!

"What is going on?" you might be asking yourself. "What does he mean?"

Do you take time each day to come to Jesus and thank Him for healing you from your sin? You are not perfect and still sin, but He has healed you from a sin-stained soul through the blood of His sacrifice.

"On the way to Jerusalem he was passing along between Samaria and Galilee. And as he entered a village, he was met by ten lepers, who stood at a distance and lifted up their voices, saying, 'Jesus, Master, have mercy on us.' When he saw them, he said to them, 'Go and show yourselves to the priests.' And as they went, they were cleansed. Then one of them, when he saw that he was healed, turned back, praising God with a loud voice; and he fell on his face at Jesus' feet, giving him thanks. Now he was a Samaritan. Then Jesus answered, 'Were not ten cleansed? Where are the nine? Was no one found to return and give praise to God except this foreigner?' And he said to him, 'Rise and go your way; your faith has made you well.'" (Luke 17:11-19)

Interesting how these folks were calling out to Jesus when they were desperate, verbalizing that they desired healing from Him. They also verbalized high esteem towards Jesus as they called Him 'Master.' But when they were healed, all but one didn't want anything to do with Jesus. The nine had a consumerism faith--one that just wants to verbal-ize Christ, but not internalize Him.

Oh, how you and I are just like the nine! We come to Christ when we are desperate and in need. But we forget we are in need of Christ every second!

One came back and thanked Jesus, knowing the position of Jesus versus himself; He did not forget his Healer. Jesus recognized this man's faith. This man not only verbalized Christ but internalized Him too. In other words, his faith was not one of consumerism, but servant-ism.

Choose today to be like the one that came back to thank Jesus. Thank Him every day and be specific in your thanksgiving! Have it be said of you that you were not a consumer-Christian, but a servant-Christian--you had servant-ism faith and not consumerism faith, you verbalized and internalized Him!

1/21

Hello!

"How are you and the family doing?"
"We're doing awesome, thanks for asking! God is good and we're enjoying life! How are y'all doing?"
"Same here, doing wonderful!"

How often do conversations like this occur in and out of churches? Often. Often times too often.

Now, such conversations can be truthful, but often times they are cover-ups for what is really going on.

Too often.

We condition ourselves to give cookie-cutter answers, without depth of soul, without the raw and unabridged, matter-of-fact truth. Why is this? Fear of being judged. Fear of being un-friended. Pride in not wanting to come to a point of admittance. Impatience in not wanting to slow down and talk about life's struggles. Settling for life as it is and not having hope things could change. Lack of faith and not being willing to admit we are struggling with our faith.

Often.

"Bear one another's burdens, and so fulfill the law of Christ." (Galatians 6:2)

"A friend lives at all times, and a brother is born for adversity." (Proverbs 17:17)

The body of Christ is meant to walk together through life's jubilations and life's treacherous valleys. Bear means "to accept or allow oneself to be subjected to especially without giving way; to support the weight of; to hold above."

This is how we all as the body of Christ (here or around the world) need to respond to each other. We must share the raw truth with one another, knowing that these verses will be the response from our brothers and sisters in Christ.

No longer simply often, but every single time! Be the church. Live it out.

Share what's really going on. Listen to others when they share what's really going on. Bear each other's burdens.

Be the church! Go forth today and every day with this heart every single second!

1/22

Good Greetings,

Have you given the ministry of presence lately? No, not presents, but presence!

There are times in life when we do not need to, and even should not, say anything to others. We need to minister to them simply with our presence. There are undoubtedly times where we need to, and should, say something to others. But not every time.

Ecclesiastes 3:7b states that there is "a time to keep silence, and a time to speak."

Ask God for discernment on when to speak and when to simply hold your tongue. There are times to listen while the other person speaks. And when you listen, truly listen. Don't spend that time dwelling on what you are going to say afterwards. There will also be times where you just need to be with that person, neither of you saying a word. But they know you are there, and they know that you care.

Be present when you are present. In other words, as Jim Elliot stated: "Wherever you are--be all there."

Give your presence as a present to others. Through your presence, God will be present and reveal His presence as a present to the other person.

Thank God He came to be present with us and give us the present of salvation!

Only because of His present of presence, you live!

1/23

Hello Freed-Ones in Christ,

"We've learned to fly the air like birds. We've learned to swim the seas like fish. And yet we haven't learned to walk the earth like brothers and sisters." (Dr. Martin Luther King Jr.)

On this day, Dr. King is remembered for the struggle he undertook and led for racial equality in America. But the struggle must carry on-- both inside and outside of the church. Paul, inspired by the Holy Spirit, writes in Galatians 6:26, "For in Christ Jesus you are all sons of God, through faith."

There is no room in Christianity for racism, prejudice of any kind, or hatred. Let me be very clear, THERE IS NO ROOM. Now also let me be clear, racism takes many forms: white towards black, black towards white, and any other race towards another.

We must strive towards unity in Christ and share this with those who we come into contact with (Christian or non-Christian). Dr. Jerry Vines has said before that a Christian does not have the luxury of being unkind. Such truth.

Let your faith be lived out through your words and actions. Love others with the love of Christ. Stand firm in biblical convictions, but with love. Treat everyone equally, for we are called to live in love. No person's color, or anything else, should be reason for discrimination. If someone is homosexual or identifies as another sex than what they were born, love them in Christ. Let me be clear, do not condone homosexuality or any form of unbiblical sexuality. But do not condemn either. Stand firm in love.

Go forth today and every day in bold love, unflinching courage in God's Word, and unwavering kindness!

1/24

Top of the day to you,

There were two NFL playoff games this weekend and in one of them, a play took place where multiple penalties were not called. This was a pivotal play of the game. The penalties were obvious yet went unchecked and unattended.

Was this wrong? Yes. Does this describe our personal and spiritual lives? Yes!
We see what is in front of us, but decide (for whatever reason) to not take action as we should. Inaction is still an action!

"But someone will say, 'You have faith and I have works.' Show me your faith apart from your works, and I will show you my faith by my works." (James 2:18)

We must take God's Word, stand upon it and live it out. We must.
We must see what is happening and then take action. We must.
We must live it out towards people, towards societal issues, within our families and work environments, and within any other situation we may find ourselves.

As the character Anne Howards says in the movie *The Patriot*: "Will you now, when you are needed most, stop at only words? Is that the sort of men you are? I ask only that you act upon the beliefs of which you have so strongly spoken, and in which you so strongly believe."

I urge you to not stop at words or cease because of fear or lack of acceptance. May your life reflect the God you profess to believe in no matter how hot of a political issue you may be dealing with or approaching. Seek His Word regarding what your stance must be and ask Him for strength to hold the ground. Such issues include the sanctity of life, marriage, and sexuality. God's Word is the final authority on these issues, as well as other issues. Abortion is unbiblical, marriage is between one man and one woman for life, and a person is born either male or female and in the image of God.

Approach each issue in love and in such a way that honors Jesus Christ. God's truth is eternal, His grace is unfaltering, forgiveness is all-encompassing, love is never-ending, mercy is undeserved, and peace enduring!

Throughout your day, week, and life, have eyes to see and hearts to act, no matter what the issue, through the power of the Holy Spirit!

1/25

Good Greetings!

Tomatoes are my favorite food! I love having them with my burger, on a sandwich, or by themselves. They are just so refreshing, and I really enjoy the... wait just a second there, kemosabe! I actually am not a fan of tomatoes. My wife, Katie, loves them, but I prefer onions on my burger!

I may or may not have had a nice, juicy burger for breakfast. Just kidding.

Anyway, someone says something is their favorite if it is elevated in value above the rest. Do we do that to people? Do we do that with our family? Do we do that with our church family?

"Now Israel [Jacob] loved Joseph more than any other of his sons, because he was the son of his old age. And he made him a robe of many colors. But when his brothers saw that their father loved him more than all his brothers, they hated him and could not speak peacefully to him." (Genesis 37:3-4)

As we see above, favoritism by a parent towards children is sinful and creates strife amongst the siblings. Though there may be people we naturally get along with easier or have more in common, we must fight against the urge to play favorites...us showing favoritism. This sort of behavior is very harmful and creates disunity, which is precisely what the enemy desires. Fight against it with the power of the Holy Spirit!

Now, I am not saying we cannot have friends with which we are closer to than others. But we must not isolate ourselves to just those friends. Enjoy branching out at gatherings! Enjoy branching out at church to fellowship with those that you are not as close or familiar with!

Seek out others this week that you are not as close with and begin building bonds where there were none before!

Go forth today and every day in His power!

-39-

1/26

Greetings Everyone,

Thanksgiving Eve. That's the day one might have thought it was this past Saturday at the grocery store. It was rocking and rollin'! And yes, I purposefully left off the "g." But at the same time, store employees were in the process of stocking items. Though the employees were not rude in any sense of the word, this stocking added to the crowdedness.

How many times do we wait until the crowdedness of life caves in upon our lives to begin "restocking" our relationship with Christ? We desperately desire for God's help during the valleys of life, but often times forget Him during the mountaintop times!

"Everyone then who hears these words of mine and does them will be like a wise man who built his house on the rock. And the rain fell, and the floods came, and the winds blew and beat on that house, but it did not fall, because it had been founded on the rock. And everyone who hears these words of mine and does not do them will be like a foolish man who built his house on the sand. And the rain fell, and the floods came, and the winds blew and beat against that house, and it fell, and great was the fall of it." (Matthew 7:24-27)

Don't wait until the waters rise to seek God. Seek Him during the good times and the bad. Pursue Him with every fiber of your body! Build your foundation upon Him, and Him alone!

Digging into the Bible, fellowshipping with believers, attending Sunday school and Sunday worship service, and getting plugged into a ministry to serve at your church are all ways God will use to build your life upon His foundation!

Stock your soul's shelves now with the grandest of spiritual nour-ishment. God is the best chef and His ingredients are eternally satisfy-ing.

Eat today!

-41-

1/27

Hi!

God has never left you...even in the midst of lonely times. He. Never. Has. And. He. Never. Will.

"Now Samuel was offering up the burnt offering, and the Philistines drew near to battle against Israel. But the Lord thundered with a great thunder on that day against the Philistines and confused them, so that they were routed before Israel. The men of Israel went out of Mizpah and pursued the Philistines and struck them down as far as below Beth-car. Then Samuel took a stone and set it between Mizpah and Shen, and named it Ebenezer, saying, 'Thus far the Lord has helped us.'" (1 Samuel 7:10-12)

Quick note, this doesn't mean that God had been their help up unto this point and then would abandon them. Samuel set up a reminder that God's hands, not human hands, had been their provider, sustainer, and protector.

Don't fall into the trap of believing that you carried yourself, that you provided for yourself, that you made a way where there seemed to be no way. Daily remind yourself that it was and always will be Jesus! Do this by seeking Him in prayer, reading His word, and dwelling with His people. Even set up an "Ebenezer" to keep your memory on Him. Sticky notes, items on your desk, messages on your refrigerator, pictures...whatever it takes to remember daily that it's Him... then, now, and forever!

Go forth today and everyday remembering Him!

1/28

Hello Everyone,

Enslaved Freedom or Freed Freedom:
Are you enslaved by the idea of freedom or freed by the reality of freedom?

I have never used a movie reference in a sermon that I have ever preached! Well...that's about as true as saying that an Italian does not like pizza, or a Czech does not like a kolache! (I have both in my blood and definitely like both those types of food!)

Thus, without further ado, the following is a quote from the movie *Braveheart*:
"There's a difference between us. You think the people of this land exist to provide you with position. I think your position exists to provide those people with freedom. And I go to make sure that they have it."

Do we view others in the light of what can they do for us?
Do we use our freedom for selfish purposes?

"For you were called to freedom, brothers. Only do not use your freedom as an opportunity for the flesh, but through love serve one an-other." (Galatians 5:13)
- What does it mean that you were called to freedom?
- What are some of the ungodly ways we use our freedom...both the action and the mindset?
- How are we to use our freedom to serve one another?

You are enslaved by the idea of freedom if you simply do what you want, when you want, how you want, and to the extent you want. You think you are free, but in reality, you are still a slave to your fleshly desires!

You are freed by the reality of freedom when you submit what you want, when you want it, how you want it, and to what extent you want it to Jesus Christ. You believe in Him and experience the true freedom

He gives as you look to serve others in and through the freedom He has given you!

Go forth using your freedom to set others free by serving them and telling them the truth of the Gospel of Jesus Christ!

FREEDOM!

1/29

Good Good Greetings,

2.5 hours...on average...for a year. The perfect amount of sleep for the body per night! Seems like paradise, right?

Wrong. Not like paradise. Not. At. All.

But that's what my dad endured years ago in order to provide for his family.

Gracious! I can only say that I have some large boots to fill when that day comes that I become a dad.

Love. He did it all out of love. He was living out Jesus' commandment:

"This is My commandment, that you love one another as I have loved you. Greater love has no one than this, that someone lay down his life for his friends. You are my friends if you do what I command you." (John 15:12-14)

Now although my dad was not called upon to give up his physical life (he would have in an instant if he was called upon), he gave of himself, not out of enjoyment or because it felt good, but because he loved my mom, brother and me.

Love. It must be an action, not just a feeling. Why? Because love is deeper than a mere feeling. Jesus proved that. The cross demonstrated it.

Who do you need to love? Remember what love is and what it requires.

Who do you need to love? Dwell upon this question.

Who do you need to go out of your way at home, church, work, during the day-to-day moments of your life to love?

Is there a person that gets on your nerves? What person seems to require extra patience to deal with? Who do you need to lay aside your own feelings, desires, and wants, to love, serve, and truly give of your time to?

Dig deep for the answer, really deep. I'm not talking about a mere text or 'hello.' But truly giving of yourself to love another person.

Remember what Jesus gave for you! Remember the patience He has with you! When you remember what Jesus did, there is no amount of love, sacrifice, or patience that is too great for you to give and show to another!

Go forth and love others in the name, for the name, and by the name of Jesus Christ!

1/30

Good Greetings,

Celebrity crushes. Yep, I said it. Celebrity crushes. Are they healthy for a single person or a married person to have?

When a married person thinks or speaks about a celebrity (or any person for that matter) in such a way as to convey how good they look, which one is better looking, or if they could, which one they'd rather go on a date with, this conveys unfaithfulness.

"However, let each one of you love his wife as himself, and let the wife see that she respects her husband." (Ephesians 5:33)

You may be thinking, "But it's just in good fun and would never happen." Affairs begin in the mind and even thoughts, and as Jesus said, are adulterous if they are lustful. It's emotional adultery and adultery of the heart and mind.

Having eyes for only your spouse is, frankly speaking, not a joking matter.
It's serious business according to Jesus.

"But I say to you that everyone who looks at a woman with lustful intent has already committed adultery with her in his heart." (Matthew 5:28)

When you're together with just the guys or hanging out with just the girls, don't loosen your lips and begin talking in such a way that dishonors your spouse and does not convey your love and devotion towards them.

"Many a man proclaims his own steadfast love, but a faithful man who can find?" (Proverbs 20:6)

I'm not saying that a single person can't speak about the attractiveness of another person, but be very careful that that slippery road does not lead to one of sexual thoughts or speech. Begin growing solid habits now for when you do become married and practice faithfulness now towards your future spouse. Even if you never become married, you are honoring God with your mind.

It's not the way the world does it, but that's an indication of which way is God's.

Go against the current for the sake of your spouse and your God!

Go forth today practicing faithfulness in word, deed, and thought!

1/31

Hello!

This upcoming Sunday two teams will line up and play against each other. They will prepare mentally and physically prior to the game. They will endure fatigue, physical punishment, and mental stress all for the goal of winning the Super Bowl. A goal that spans back before the season even began.

Paul writes:

"Not that I have already obtained this or am already perfect, but I press on to make it my own, because Christ Jesus has made me his own. Brothers, I do not consider that I have made it my own. But one thing I do: forgetting what lies behind and straining forward to what lies ahead, I press on toward the goal for the prize of the upward call of God in Christ Jesus." (Philippians 3:12-14)

There are many earthly goals we set and sometimes achieve. Some of these, depending on what they are and our motive behind them, are good. But what about your eternal goals? Do you press on each day toward heaven (the prize)? Do you set your goals and live your life to hear, "Well done, good and faithful servant?" You cannot earn your salvation but strive to live in a manner that puts action to what you verbalize to believe and honor Jesus in all you do! Press on!

Realize that you are not perfect, and perfection will only be reached in heaven. Also, realize that Jesus took hold of you through His death and resurrection. Remember to forget the past as Christ has forgiven you. Press on each day closer to Jesus, strain ahead with His strength and grace, and relish the fact that you have the opportunity each moment to serve and glorify Him!

Press on today and every day in Christ!

2/1

Greetings,

They need to get their act together!
Can you believe what she said?
Man, oh man, I can't comprehend the fact that he actually did that!

We tend to elevate certain sins above others.
We also tend to elevate the sins of others above our own.

Paul wrote in Romans 3:22-24, "the righteousness of God through faith in Jesus Christ [is] for all who believe. For there is no distinction: for all have sinned and fall short of the glory of God, and are justified by his grace as a gift, through the redemption that is in Christ Jesus."

Always remember that every single one of our sins are on equal ground before a perfect, righteous, and holy God. The child molester, the rapist, the abuser, and even the terrorist, have committed no greater sin than you or me. Tough message to stomach, but it's biblical truth. Yes, there are varying consequences for different sins here on earth, but all of us have equal guilt!

"For there is no distinction: for all have sinned and fall short of the glory of God, and are justified by his grace as a gift, through the redemption that is in Christ Jesus."

Remember it is only because of God's great grace that you are forgiven!
Speak of others with this truth in mind.
Treat others with this truth in mind.
Love others with this truth in mind.

Go forth knowing in His grace and with His mercy in mind!

2/2

Hello and Greetings,

How are your ears doing?
What?!
Exactly.

That was a joke! But in all seriousness, how are your ears? Your spiritual ears that is...
"My sheep hear My voice, and I know them, and they follow me." (Jesus, as recorded in John 10:27)

Jesus is the Great Shepherd and you are one of His sheep as soon as you accept Him as your Lord and Savior. We, like sheep, are foolish when left to our own vices. When we follow the voice of Jesus, we are walking in truth and obedience!

But does He speak audibly? It's not past His ability to do so, but often times He does not. He speaks through His Word, the Bible. An important, but tough, question to ask yourself is, "Am I spending time reading and dwelling upon His Word as I need to?

Cochlear implants--what are they and what do they have to do with what I'm talking about? "A cochlear implant is an electronic medical device that does the work of damaged parts of the inner ear (cochlea) to provide sound signals to the brain."1 The devices focus the individual on what is important to hear.

We are damaged by sin from conception. God's Word, through and by the power of the Holy Spirit, guides a Christian and allows them to hear God's voice. The Holy Spirit will focus you on what you need to hear.

---

1   (https://www.cochlear.com/au/home/understand/ hearing-and-hl/hl-treatments/cochlear-implant)

Are you listening? God gives each believer spiritual ears to hear!

Do you want to hear what He has to say? Do you really, truly, want to?

God is speaking! The Lion is roaring! You are His sheep...will you listen and follow your Shepherd's voice?!

2/3

Hello and Greetings,

Life is a gift from God, and it is precious. Now, we must not put our hope upon things of this life...people, events, places, abilities. He does not want us to waste one iota of a second we have here on earth!

Because of this powerful truth, eat fruit every single day!
No, no, no, I'm not speaking about beginning a diet.

Well, what are you talking about then!?
I just told you. Eat fruit every single day!
We heard you. But what in the name of Jiminy Christmas do you mean?!
Ah, yes...

"But the fruit of the Spirit is love, joy, peace, patience, kindness, goodness, faithfulness, gentleness, self-control; against such things there is no law. And those who belong to Christ Jesus have crucified the flesh with its passions and desires." (Galatians 5:22-24)

Spiritual fruit is sweet to your soul, to the souls of others, and honoring to your Father in heaven. Have you ever seen a fruit basket? God has and continues to give you the biggest fruit basket possible. He demonstrates and shows each of the fruits of the Spirit to you.

Eat of His fruit and give a fruit basket to everyone. Yes, everyone!
Even him? Yes.
And her? Yep.
No way you could mean them!
You better believe it.
Even- Let me politely interrupt you and answer yepper-doodle-do.

Through your verbal communication, your non-verbal communication (letters, texts, emails), and your body language. Dig deep and think about how you can do that by asking the Holy Spirit to teach you. By doing this, you will not waste the time God has given you, you will honor Him, and you will reflect Jesus.

Thank God for the fruit He consistently gives you!
Give a fruit basket to everyone you come into contact with!

-54-

2/4

Good Greetings,

Unity. According to Merriam-Webster 'unity' means: the quality or state of not being multiple: oneness; a condition of harmony: accord; the quality or state of being made one: unification.

There are not different sects here and different sects over there. There are no cliques. NONE!
Unity means playing the same music with different instruments, for a symphony is composed of different types of instruments, but when combined, they play wonderful music to the enjoyment of the audience's ears.

The church must have an audience of One and be unified!

"I appeal to you, brothers, by the name of our Lord Jesus Christ, that all of you agree, and that there be no divisions among you, but that you be united in the same mind and the same judgment." (1 Corinthians 1:10)

Think (but be careful as you do so as to not sin) of a person at church that is difficult for you to deal with. A person that irritates you, tests your patience...a person that you really would rather just see and say hello to, but not spend any sort of extended time with.

Now, ask God to throw those feelings into the pit of hell. Right now!

Those are human thoughts. Those are fleshly thoughts. Those are sinful thoughts. Those are thoughts we as fallen human beings have, but must surrender them to God Almighty, for they are not honoring to Him and not thoughts of unity!

Ask God to give you a mindset and spirit of unity, and a desire to love everyone you come into contact with. Ask God to help you to desire to spend time and talk with those that you, according to your flesh, would rather not.

God chose to dwell with you!
Who are you to ostracize someone else because they annoy you?!
All struggle, but none have the right to deem those actions as acceptable!

Unity! Go forth today and every day with a mindset of unity in Christ!

2/5

Greetings,

"You shall love the Lord your God with all your heart and with all your soul and with all your might." (Deuteronomy 6:5)

From one football fan to another, a piece of food for thought for the both of us to chew on:

How many of us desire to watch the Super Bowl for the things that accompany it (such as the festivities, hanging out with others, and the tasty food), versus for the pure pleasure of the game?
[Either way is a right way.]

Comparably...

How many of us desire Jesus for the things we hope to be given from Him (such as a better job, improved health, more money, a new home, etc.), versus for the pure pleasure of the relationship?
[One way is the right way, by which we must pursue with the help of Jesus.]

"You shall love the Lord your God with all your heart and with all your soul and with all your might." (Deuteronomy 6:5)

Love Him because of who He is, not for what He can do, or what you hope He will give you.

Enjoy watching tonight's game and the accompanied festivities!
Enjoy your relationship with Jesus even more!

2/6/19

Good Greetings,

Take a moment to read and dwell upon this, written by James Allan Francis:

"Here is a man who was born in an obscure village, the child of a peasant woman. He grew up in another obscure village, where He worked in a carpenter shop until He was thirty, and then for three years He was an itinerant preacher. He never wrote a book. He never held an office. He never owned a home. He never had a family. He never went to college. He never put his foot inside a big city. He never traveled two hundred miles from the place where He was born. He never did one of the things that usually accompany greatness. He had no credentials but Himself. He had nothing to do with this world except the naked power of His divine manhood. While still a young man, the tide of public opinion turned against Him. His friends ran away. One of them denied Him. He was turned over to His enemies. He went through the mockery of a trial. He was nailed to a cross between two thieves. His executioners gambled for the only piece of property He had on earth while He was dying—and that was his coat. When he was dead, He was taken down and laid in a borrowed grave through the pity of a friend. Nineteen wide centuries have come and gone and today He is the centerpiece of the human race and the leader of the column of progress. I am far within the mark when I say that all the armies that ever marched, and all the navies that ever were built, and all the parliaments that ever sat, all the kings that ever reigned, put together have not affected the life of man upon this earth as powerfully as has that One Solitary Life."

Jesus said, "Blessed are the meek, for they shall inherit the earth." (Matthew 5:5)

Remember the biblical Jesus, not the one modern society would have you to believe. Following Jesus does not guarantee wealth. Following Jesus guarantees peace and joy unbeknownst to the world.

Remaining humble, as Christ was, also guarantees that you will one day inherit Christ's rule when all is made right.

Know who Christ is, who He really is, and glean joy and contentment from His example. Pursue Christ and don't get all caught up in pursuits and recognitions of this world!

Because of One Solitary Life, you have life!

2/7

Hello and Greetings,

Jesus said, "Blessed are the poor in spirit, for theirs is the kingdom of heaven." (Matthew 4:7)

Wait a quick second (yes a second is already quick and it does not need me to tell it to hurry up)! Why should I be poor in spirit? Doesn't that mean I'm weak or lacking?

Yes!

But, not as you may think. We are all weak and poor apart from Christ. We must come to a point that we realize we have nothing of redeeming value in and of ourselves, and we need Jesus for salvation and the gift of heaven!

Every day, and I do mean every day, we must have this same attitude of the heart!

Every moment of every day remember from whence you came and from whence He came, in order that you might one day go to where He is!

Remember and go forth!

2/8

Greetings Everyone,

What is one thing God has given you that you take for granted?
What's another?
And another?

Take time right now and thank Him for these things. Write them down and remember them!

Granted no more…may it be your cry!

Enjoy His blessings in thankfulness!

2/9

Hello and Hi,

Don't you always feel blessed when you're down and out, crying, weeping, sad, and just downright grief-stricken?

Why yes, yes, I do…don't you?
No.
Really?
Yes.
Yes?
No.
That's what I thought!

Wait a mere morsel of a centa-second. You do? Do I?

Ok, ok…enough of all those shenanigans. No, not in our flesh do any of us feel blessed. But that's because we are not remembering Christ's promise:

"Blessed are those who mourn, for they will be comforted." (Matthew 5:4) Now, He's not saying that it will be a jolly fun time going through all those seasons of life. But He is saying that you will be comforted in and through His grace-filled mercy. There is hope…a right grand amount of it!

So, know that no matter the tumultuous time you go through, the times that seem to nearly rip your very heart from your chest, Jesus promised you would be comforted and not left to cope with loss on your own.

No, we are not exempt from suffering.
Yes, we are promised comfort from and by Christ!

Enjoy every morsel of this truth in Christ, today and every day!

2/10

Howdy,

Are you hungry this morning? If you eat now, it will be good for you as I have heard that breakfast is the most important meal of the day. How about some flap jacks with syrup and a side of sausage and bacon?! Then you can wash it all down with a cold glass of freshly squeezed orange juice. Ahhhhhhhhhh!

As I'm writing this, it is actually afternoon and I have not consumed any flap jacks today. I would like to ask for sympathy at this moment, but I digress.

"Blessed are those who hunger and thirst for righteousness, for they shall be satisfied." (Matthew 5:6)

A person hungers after God and is made righteous immediately upon receiving Jesus as his or her Lord and Savior. He makes a person right with God by the covering of His blood, which was shed upon the cross.

Do you continually hunger to be more like Him?

Do you hunger for the character of God in your life like a hearty meal?
Do you thirst, like a cold and refreshing glass of orange juice, to be a reflection of Jesus to a lost and dying world?

Reading His Word, getting plugged into your local church, sharing Christ with others and praying to God are all ways you can hunger and thirst after God's righteousness. God will honor you as you do.

Hunger and thirst today…and be satisfied by Jesus!

2/11

Good Howdy,

"Gosh, would I like to slug him!"
"Gee-wiz, would I like to throw a couple pies in her face!"

Yep, we have all thought those or similar thoughts. They are not right, but we must admit we have them.

Why do we like the idea of vengeance? Is it because we ourselves have forgotten the fact that we have been shown mercy? We love to impute what was not imputed to us.

Jesus says, "Blessed are the merciful, for they shall receive mercy." (Matthew 5:7)

But golly, would I like to…
Stop right there, citizen!

Remember what was imputed to you? God's mercy, not wrath, because of Jesus Christ's sacrifice on the cross--He took your place!

Show mercy towards those that you "feel" don't deserve it. Now, I am not saying that there are not consequences to actions. But what I am saying is that there are moments where a consequence does not have to be dealt or a certain action can be withheld. Love on people and show them mercy.

Impute what was imputed onto you!

2/12

Hello,

Who are you?
My name is…wait, am I asking you, or are you asking me?

Anyway…who are you, whose are you, and what are you doing with your life?

It's a question each of us asks at different points in our lives.
It's a question the world is all too quick to give us an answer.

But the world's answer would seek to write a false narrative for your life.
God's Word provides truth and when you allow Him to write your story, He will compose an epically wonderful story that will last into eternity!

God says, "Fear not, for I have redeemed you; I have called you by name, you are Mine." (Isaiah 43:1b)

Do you want to know what each of us should be doing with our lives? Here it is!

"And Jesus came and said to them, 'All authority in heaven and on earth has been given to me. Go therefore and make disciples of all nations, baptizing them in the name of the Father and of the Son and of the Holy Spirit, teaching them to observe all that I have commanded you. And behold, I am with you always, to the end of the age.'" (Matthew 28:18-20)

That is your purpose, no matter what season of life you find yourself in or what profession you find yourself in. God will use you for His kingdom.

Who are you?
You belong to God Almighty!

You are His child because Jesus Christ is your Lord and Savior!

You have purpose to tell others about Him and help them grow closer to Christ!

Boom!

Now get out there and go forth in His power today and every day!

2/13

Good Evening,
I mean Good Afternoon,
Good grief…Good Greetings!

Don't you just love tasting a rotten apple? Or, isn't sour milk delicious?! Ok, Ok. Maybe you just enjoy some good ole' fashion stinky cheese!
(There is a point to today's devotional, I cross my heart.)
Of course you don't!

You may like all of those, but in their pure state. You don't want them entering your mouth when they are rotten.

In the same way, our sin makes us rotten and we are unable to enter God's presence on our own accord (not the car, ha). We need Jesus.

No, not Jesus plus something or someone else. Just Jesus!

He said, "Blessed are the pure in heart, for they shall see God." (Matthew 5:8)

When you accept Jesus as your Lord and Savior, He takes away your sin and makes you white as snow. You are pure. Because of this, you now see God with spiritual eyes! He reveals His character to you and teaches you His ways.

Then, because of His transformation of your heart, you now desire to be pure and be in pursuit of what honors Him. Your heart and mind have been transformed to pursue purity in thought and action.

He reveals more and more of His character and will to you. You grow in your knowledge and understanding of Him!

Jesus grants you the purity to see the Father!

Pursue purity in thought and action today, that you may grow closer in your walk with Jesus Christ!

   Pursue Him because He pursued you!

-68-

2/14

Good Morning and Happy Chocolate Day!
Hehehe, oh alright…Happy Valentine's Day!

Truth be told, this is a holiday that many people celebrate their love for one another. Many use it to celebrate what is actually lust. On the other hand, this day can be a very lonely, burdensome, and a sad day for others: those who have lost a loved one, those who have gone through a broken relationship, those who have a deep longing for a relationship while not being in one at this time, or those who have other reasons for this not being a day they look forward to.

Yet, this day is, and continues to be, associated with the idea of love.

There is still purpose for each person that can be gleaned from a discussion on love. But what is love? It's that mushy-gushy feeling that makes you want to climb mountaintops, makes you feel as if you could fly, gives you the strength to swim across the oceans! Now, let us all come back to reality…

Not that love cannot make a person feel this way, but true love is not based upon emotions! Real love, not lust or infatuation, does not flee at the onset of trouble. It does not abandon another when the fight comes knocking that the door. Love does not give way to fear when surrounded by the enemy.

"Greater love has no one than this, that someone lay down his life for his friends." (John 15:13)

Love is not, at its core, a feeling or an emotion. Love in a friendship or romantic relationship. For feelings and emotions fluctuate. Feelings or emotions are not what kept Jesus from saying, "I don't want to remain on this cross for them."

He chose to out of love for His Father and us!

"For God so loved the world, that He gave His only Son, that whoever believes in Him should not perish, but have eternal life." (John 3:16)

"See what kind of love the Father has given to us, that we should be called children of God; and so, we are." (1 John 3:1)

Take time today and ask God to show you how you can love others in the name of Jesus Christ--through self-sacrifice, through deed and through word.

Celebrate more than human love, celebrate the love God has shown and continues to show you!

2/15

You To Greetings Good

I appear discombobulated, don't I?!

Do you sometimes feel like that after a heated discussion, argument, or some other un-peaceful moment?

Jesus said, "Blessed are the peacemakers, for they shall be called sons of God." (Matthew 5:9)

He doesn't mean that there isn't a time for a government to go to war (justly I may add). He also doesn't mean that your life will never experience conflict.

What He does mean is that a sign of you being a Christian will be that you seek peace in the midst conflict. You strive to talk, instead of yell. Listen, instead of only talk. Seek compromise (where biblically acceptable). Strive to imitate Jesus in the midst of strife.

Seek God's help to be that person. Don't set out to win. Set out to serve, as Christ did. Ask God to help you remain calm, ask questions, listen, share, and set your pride aside for the sake of the cross.

Don't be someone that is characterized by being discombobulated when conflict arises. Don't seek to cause disorder. Seek peace through the peace of Christ. This will be a sign that you are a Christ-follower.

Jesus won you peace with God.
Jesus gave you His peace.
Seek to tell others about His peace as well as be a peacemaker amidst conflict.

Peace!

2/16

Good Persecuted Day!

What in Sam hill?!
Before I venture forth, allow me to take a pause to ask, how did this phrase come to be? Who is Sam and where is his hill? Is it an important place? Was Sam well know too? Who's on first? Or actually, who's on the hill? Wait, what?!

I digress back to less confounded matters…

Do you feel like this is a day you will face persecution? Have you faced persecution before and if so, why? We all love persecution! Not really.

But Jesus has an important statement for Christians regarding persecution:
"Blessed are those who are persecuted for righteousness' sake, for theirs is the kingdom of heaven. Blessed are you when others revile you and persecute you and utter all kinds of evil against you falsely on my account. Rejoice and be glad, for your reward is great in heaven, for so they persecuted the prophets who were before you." (Matthew 5:10-11)

Being a Christ-follower in this world guarantees you that you will face persecution. But why? The world aligns itself against the principles of Christ.

If you stand upon the foundation of the righteousness of your Savior and stand for biblical principles, know you will face persecution. But Jesus will be with you! He and His followers before Him all faced persecution!

Rejoice in persecutions! This doesn't mean it's fun to be persecuted, or that you have to fake a smile during it. Suffering for our sins wasn't fun for Jesus, "who for the joy that was set before Him endured the cross…" (Hebrews 12:2b) He knew He and His would be glorified and people would come to know Him, which was His joy!

Joy through Jesus is the soul smiling in the midst of a frowning world.

And heaven is waiting for you! Oh, glorious shores! Take heart! Believe what awaits you and press on, knowing that Jesus walks with you!

Press on through the persecution!

2/17

Hello and Hello,

Take a moment and think of someone you can send an encouraging text, email, or phone call to. Use this as an opportunity to share a verse, a truth from God's Word, or let them know you prayed for them (make sure you pray before you tell them though!).

We are all called to encourage one another, but sometimes we become too busy or self-indulgent in our own little worlds.

Be intentional in encouraging others.

Do it now…please!

2/18

Greetings and Good Greetings,

"Of old You laid the foundation of the earth, and the heavens are the work of Your hands. They will perish, but You will remain; they will all wear out like a garment. You will change them like a robe, and they will pass away, but You are the same, and Your years have no end." (Psalm 102:25-27)

Remember His truth in the midst of a changing and unsettled world. As you remember and dwell upon this truth, share it with whoever will listen!

Jesus' truth is eternal
Jesus' grace is unfaltering

Jesus' forgiveness is all-encompassing
Jesus' love is never-ending

Jesus' mercy is undeserved
Jesus' peace is enduring

Remember, and tell the world!

2/19

Good Hello,

We live in a safe world, don't we?!
We live in a world free from mourning and heartache as well right?!
This world is one where we always want to be men and women of action, standing for the truth of God's Word and we never become distracted!

Maybe we should just stick to the truth.
The truth is that all of the above are: No, no, and false!

But there is One who is able in the midst of an unable world!

Rise up today and be of good cheer
Each day, for the Christian, one knows Jesus is near

Rise up today and be of action
Not bound by fear and deceiving distraction

Rise up, rise up, for the battle is God's
It is He who will prepare the path which you trod

"The LORD will keep your going out and your coming in from this time forth and forevermore." (Psalm 121:8)

This does not mean necessarily that no physical harm will ever befall you, or that you will never face hardships. It does mean that your heart and soul are in the palm of God's hands. It does mean that He will forever see you and care for you through it all. Through. It. All.

Rest on in this promise as you go forth today!

2/20

Greetings on a day that God may have such a time as this task for you to accomplish.

Come again!?
What in tarnation do you mean?!

"For if you keep silent at this time, relief and deliverance will rise for the Jews from another place, but you and your father's house will perish. And who knows whether you have not come to the kingdom for such a time as this?"
(Esther 5:14)

Ah ha, eureka! Wait…
What in tarnation do you still mean?!

Esther was at a crossroads in her life where she faced a difficult decision. Did God have her at this point for a specific reason, one grander than she could possibly imagine?

Yes!

God had ordained her to be the instrument by which He would save His people from death. She could not see clearly at the time, but she would soon.

Through every season of life, God is at work. He is in the past, present, and future. What may seem like a crazy, confused, whacky, trying, perplexing, you name it period of your life is precisely a period when you need God to give you spiritual eyes and spiritual discernment to know what action He wants you to take. When you ask the "why" questions in life, remember to seek God's will.

With God, there are no coincidences. Nothing in His will happens by chance. There is no luck. Maybe God wants you to accomplish _________________ right now, which is why He brought you to this situation, place, challenge, etc.

You may not see, but He does. Who knows why you are at this moment in your life to accomplish _______________?

Let God fill in the blanks and guide you!

2/21

Give or Get Greetings!

Yes, that was on purpose.
Yes, my fingers and brain were on the same page.

Will this be a morning, day, week, month, year, lifetime where you are a giver or a taker? Don't, I urge you, be quick to answer that question.

Paul said in Acts 20:35, "In all things I have shown you that by working had in this way we must help the weak and remember the words of the Lord Jesus, how He Himself said, 'It is more blessed to give than to receive.'"

There is nothing wrong with enjoying receiving a present, nothing at all. Jesus is not saying that. But He is saying that it's better to give. Generally, we are in agreement when we hear this. "Of course, I love giving more than receiving!"

But do we really and truly?
Do we give only when it's comfortable or convenient?

Until giving interferes with eating out, until it comes between my coffee/soda/snacks, until it's between giving and going on a vacation, until it's buying the new outfit or toy, until it's between buying the new TV, until it interferes with our savings or retirement, until it comes between us seeing a movie, sports event, or other types of entertainment/ recreation?

We give until giving comes between my desires and the needs of others, the church, and causes of God but we often choose our desires!

We must be wise in our giving, but also generous! Enjoy all of the above mentioned, but don't allow them to come before giving to your church, other platforms God is working through, and others that are in need.

God would say to us, "Don't give until it hurts and then stop giving. Give and continue giving through the hurt. My Son did."

Because He gave, go forth and give in His name!

2/22

Howdy,

Pull yourself up by your own bootstraps! That's a saying that many people do and have long abided by. Do it yourself and find a way to accomplish it by your own strength, right?

But is that really biblical?

God says, "Trust in the Lord with all your heart, and do not lean on your own understanding." (Proverbs 3:5)

Now, I am in no way, shape, or form advocating that the government should just take care of us so we would have no responsibility. As much as it is in a person's control, each man and woman should strive to work hard and diligently to provide.

But, not at the expense of believing that God is not the reason and power by which you accomplish such things. Not at the expense of self-sufficiency instead of Christ-sufficiency!

Trust and seek God.
Rely upon Him to provide and direct you.
He will not fail you.

So, yes…lace up your bootstraps and be diligent in working for the Lord. But all the while, relying upon Him and not having a heart-stance of self-sufficiency, but Christ-sufficiency!

"BLT"
Believe
Lean upon
Trust

Remember to consume your BLT today and every day!

2/23

Greetings on this day that God All Merciful has given,

"And God spoke all these words, saying, 'I am the LORD your God, who brought you out of the land of Egypt, out of the house of slavery… You shall not make for yourself a carved image, or any likeness of anything that is in heaven above, or that is in the earth beneath, or that is in the water under the earth. You shall not bow down to them or serve them, for I the LORD your God am a jealous God, visiting the iniquities of the fathers on the children to the third and fourth generation of those who hate me, but showing steadfast love to thousands of those who love Me and keep My commandments.'" (Exodus 20:2, 4-6)

Let today's devotional be simple, but eternally impactful: there is not a plurality of ways to heaven. There is no other god but God. There are tons of false gods, but only one true God. In a society that believes god is who you choose him, her, or it to be, hold fast to God's truth!

As Jesus said Himself, "I am the way, and the truth, and the life. No one comes to the Father except through me." (John 14:6b)

Hold fast and do not be moved.

Christ is your anchor!

2/24

Pray tell, good greetings to thee!

Mixing the greetings up a bit. But, know that God is with you and loves you deeply…that never changes, no matter what.

"And God spoke all these words, saying, 'I am the LORD your God, who brought you out of the land of Egypt, out of the house of slavery…You shall not take the name of the LORD your God in vain, for the LORD will not hold him guiltless who takes His name in vain.'" (Exodus 20:2, 7)

YHWH (Yaweh) was and is God's name, but the Israelites regarded this name of God so highly and reverently that they would not say it aloud. When you see "LORD" in the Bible (all caps), you are reading the translation of YHWH in Hebrew.

Do you, do I, hold God's name in such a high reverence? If not, why?
Do we feel that He's our buddy or the man upstairs?

He is closer to you than the air you breathe. He's not your buddy-buddy or the man upstairs. That way of thinking does not ascribe the awe, respect, and reverence that we must approach Him with. He is due it!

Also, we must be mindful and careful using His God's name, not solely in such a phrase as, "Oh my ______." If we are lightly using the name God, Jesus, etc. we are not obeying this commandment. If you say, "So help me God," and do not hold to your word, you are not holding God's name in reverence.

Bottom line is be like the Hebrews in how they revered their God and His name. We can say His name aloud but should still hold the same level of reverence. There is no amount of reverence that is too great for us to show Him!

He's worthy!

2/25

Good Greetings Everyone,

"Certainly, work is not always required of a man. There is such a thing as a sacred idleness, the cultivation of which is now fearfully neglected."   (George Mac Donald)

Our culture pushes individuals to and encourages them to be anything but idle. We may feel if we are idle, then we are lazy, weak, but missing out on something. Music, movies, phones, they all are good things, but are conduits of constant stimulation. We are able to be "connected" at all times through social media at the touch of a button on our computers, tablets, or phones. They are considered "smart" phones but are they really?

I don't hate technology, I promise!
But we must be careful and wise with our use of it.
And it does not encourage sacred idleness.

"And God spoke all these words, saying, 'I am the LORD your God, who brought you out of the land of Egypt, out of the house of slavery…Remember the Sabbath day, to keep it holy.'" (Exodus 20:2, 8)

God Himself commands us to rest…rest! Your Sabbath may be on a Sunday, but your profession may not allow that and guess what? That's okay! But the commandment to still honor the Sabbath remains. This means having a day that you relax, rejuvenate, commune with God and worship Him (this part should be every day too), and be idle to an extent. Rest, rest, rest! God commands it because He created us and knows it is essential for us and brings Him honor!

Side note--working on a Sunday does not give you the excuse to not become involved with a church. It does throw an added challenger into the ring, but this will reveal your character and true desire to make God, church, and the fellowship of believers a priority in your life.

Follow this command, to both honor God and reap the benefits that

He desires for you!

2/26

Howdy,

Have you ever heard it said that some things you never outgrow? Like gummy bears in ice cream! Well, maybe that's just me, but I shall continue onward.

"And God spoke all these words, saying, 'I am the LORD your God, who brought you out of the land of Egypt, out of the house of slavery…Honor your father and your mother, that your days may be long in the land that the LORD your God is giving you.'" (Exodus 20:2, 12)

Notice the result that is mentioned as well: "that your days may be long in the land that the LORD your God is giving you." This does not mean that everyone who honors their mom and dad will live long lives. They may or may not, but that is not the point. The point is that God commands us to honor our parents and God's blessing upon our lives is a direct God-given result!

We never grow too old to not honor our parents any longer. We age to a point where we are no longer underneath their authority but are always under command to respect them and honor them. Ways this is lived out are: caring for them, being patient with them, listening to their advice (although you may choose to go decline it, do it respectively and lovingly), calling them to talk and check on them, taking them to appointments…and any other way you can think of!

What if parents abused their children when they were younger or were just outright terrible parents? First, this is not an abnormality unfortunately and a very sad reality. Don't feel you are less in God's eyes.

But also realize that they are no less in God's eyes as well in the sense that their sins are no greater than your sins. You don't have to like them or spend all your time with them. You are called to love and respect them, no matter what.

You can only do this with the help of Jesus Christ. Rely on Him.

Remember the grace and love He has and continues to show you.

If you don't have parents alive, carry out this command to those who, by age, could be your parents and the elderly you know, and come into contact with.

Obey His command.
Reflect His grace and love.
Always--for He does!

2/27

Hello!

Short and sweet! Like a s'more: it's short in height, and a tasty, delectable treat! Anyways, sometimes short and sweet is the best way to communicate and all it takes for a point to stick.

So, without further ado…

"And God spoke all these words, saying, 'I am the LORD your God, who brought you out of the land of Egypt, out of the house of slavery…You shall not murder.'" (Exodus 20:2, 12)

Biblical understanding of this commandment is critical to our approach of worldly issues and to how we approach other aspects of the Bible.

This command is not saying that killing is wrong, but that murder is wrong.

Killing is necessary at times such as in self-defense, defending another, or wars that are just. However, murder is always wrong.

The heart motive is the issue. Murder contains a selfish, evil motive, not with the cause of good at the forefront. Killing, when justified, contains a selfless and righteous motive, with the cause of good at the forefront.

"The true soldier fights not because he hates what is in front of him, but because he loves what is behind him." (G.K. Chesterton)

"You have heard that it was said to those of old, 'You shall not murder; and whoever murders will be liable to judgment.' But I say to you that everyone who is angry with his brother will be liable to judgment; whoever insults his brother will be liable to the council; and whoever says, 'You fool!' will be liable to the hell of fire.'" (Matthew 5:21-22)

Jesus expands upon the commandment in Exodus to say that unjustifiable anger in your heart, insulting another, and being rude to another has committed murder in his heart. Jesus is concerned about your heart's posture towards Him and others!

Ask your Father to develop a heart of love towards others, reflecting Him, and living out what has been shown to you!

Go forth today and every day holding onto the truth of God's Word and seeking to know more and more!

2/28

Greetings and Hello and Hi,

Be reasonable!

That's a rude way to begin the devo.

I apologize.

Thank you.

But, in all seriousness, please be reasonable.

With who?

Sorry again. I'm saying that to the person reading this, not you.

Oh, okay cool.

Now…

Emotions and selfish desires can wage war against reasonableness. Then, we seek our way above all else. If our way is not chosen, then we toss the other person's idea into the raging sea, shackled with a billion-pound weight to ensure it does not rise ever again.

"Let your reasonableness be known to everyone…" (Philippians 4:5)
Merriam-Webster defines reasonable as "fair" and "possessing sound judgment."

Be that type of person in order to reflect Jesus to a lost and dying world! Don't compromise on the truth as often, you can create middle ground with a person to make fair compromises. Be just and wise in the decisions you make, not showing favoritism.

Seek God and He will not fail to help you in this.

Be reasonable!

3/1

Good Greetings,

Have you ever thought to yourself, "What have we done as a society? We have taken what God created as a gift and distorted it!"

Sex is one of those gifts. A beautiful, beautiful gift.
The enemy, Satan, likes to pollute such gifts and deceive mankind.

"And God spoke all these words, saying, 'I am the LORD your God, who brought you out of the land of Egypt, out of the house of slavery…You shall not commit adultery.'" (Exodus 20:2,14)

At this very moment, you may be thinking to yourself, "Now I know I haven't broken this commandment! I may have had unjustifiable anger in my heart, but this one I'm safe on!"

Wrong! (Yes, that may have come across as harsh.)
"But I say to you that everyone who looks at a woman with lustful intent has already committed adultery with her in his heart." (Matthew 5:28)

I would venture to say that most every person has lusted at some point in their life. Once again, Jesus expands upon a commandment.

Don't place yourself in situations that may lead to the physical or mental breaking of this commandment. Be drastic in your precautions. Why? Is it better to be drastic in precautions, or pay the price for infidelity towards your spouse or future spouse, and most importantly, God?

Stay clear of movies, TV shows, and music that even hint at lustful scenes.
Steer clear from restaurants or other places that would do that same (like Hooters and such places).
Don't even think about a strip club as an outing with the girls or guys, or to go to a bachelor or bachelorette party.
Don't talk about other women's looks (if you're a husband), or

about guys (if you're a wife). That's not honoring, loving, or faithful to your spouse. If you're single, be careful that talking doesn't lead to sexual talk or thinking.

Be drastic in your precautions for the reward for obeying Jesus is worth it!

3/2

Good Greetings and Hello!

Just don't do it! Ya, hear--just don't steal! Don't take what ain't yours!
Okay, devotion over and complete for today.

Not so fast, citizen!

"And God spoke all these words, saying, 'I am the LORD your God, who brought you out of the land of Egypt, out of the house of slavery…You shall not steal.'" (Exodus 20:2, 15)

This may seem simple but dive further. Yes, don't take what you haven't paid for from a store. But, how about stealing by not taking, or actually by not giving, which in turn is taking without payment because you are not giving.

Yep.

What I mean is, for instance if you're working and waste a lot of time, if you take an hour lunch break when you are only allotted 30 min, or taking a 30 minute break when you are only supposed to take 15 minutes, then you are stealing money from the company you work for. Period, or end of report as my grandpa used to say! Not trying to be harsh, but it's the truth and what God would demand of us as His children.

Other ways of stealing include falsifying your expense report, not being completely truthful to the IRS, plagiarizing, burning DVDs, games, or music, or using any copyrighted items without permission.

God desires much of us, but in reality, it's nothing compared to what is there for us to enjoy. His grace makes all things possible that may seem difficult for us but completely worth it!

Go forth and steal not, but give freely!

-96-

3/3

Greetings Y'all,

I was born in Texas, played football growing up, almost played for the Dallas Cowboys, and my brother almost played basketball for the Dallas Mavericks.

There are parts from the above sentence that are true and some that are not. I didn't almost play for the Cowboys and my brother didn't almost play for the Mavericks. I did play for the Chicago Bears and my brother played for the Chicago Bulls.

Ok, well, maybe…not. But I wrote that to illustrate the following commandment:

"And God spoke all these words, saying, 'I am the LORD your God, who brought you out of the land of Egypt, out of the house of slavery…You shall not bear false witness against your neighbor.'" (Exodus 20:2, 16)

Plain and simple, don't go around lying. Be truthful. Don't make up falsities about others to put them down and bring yourself up. Don't do it! Don't bolter your life's resume with false information to puff out your chest.

Gossiping is alright though because it's just fun and doesn't really cause pain.

No way is that a correct statement! Negative, no matter how you spin it!

Don't make postings on Facebook that you know, or suspect are incorrect.

TRUTH--PURSUE IT AND PRACTICE IT!

For the sake of keeping God's commandment and honoring His holy name. He bought your soul with truth.

Live in truth!

3/4

Hello Everyone,

Gosh, I wish I had that, or this. He doesn't really deserve it, and I do! No way she should have those things! I. Deserve. It. All.

Have you ever found yourself wanting something with an unhealthy desire or to an unhealthy level?

Merriam-Webster defines covet as, "to desire (what belongs to another)…"

"And God spoke all these words, saying, 'I am the LORD your God, who brought you out of the land of Egypt, out of the house of slavery… You shall not covet your neighbor's house; you shall not covet your neighbor's wife, or his male servant, or his female servant, or his ox, or his donkey, or anything that is your neighbor's.'" (Exodus 20:2, 17)

It's an easy commandment to break and fall prey to our fleshly longings. To be clear, it is not a sin to desire things, so long as they line up with God's desires for your life.

When you desire something that belongs to another person, not as in "I hope to be able to have a house like them one day if God allows it," but in a way that reflects an ungrateful heart and a heart that depicts selfishness. In doing so, you break this commandment. Or if you are feeling that they do not deserve it and you do (in a way, mind-stealing from them).

Be content with what God has given you. Work hard, not to out-do others, but to glorify Him and to reflect Him to a lost and dying world!

Be content, for He has lavished grace upon grace, love upon love, hope upon hope, and mercy upon mercy onto and in your life!

3/5

Greetings on this day that God has made,

People are never irritating, are they? Ha.
But then again, we are never irritating to others, right? Ha!

When someone irritates you today, use it as an opportunity to pray.
Thank Him for specific things He's given you, including the forgiveness
of your sins.

Focus on Him and turn your eyes away from the irritation!

3/6

Good Greetings,

Remember, oh soul, remember this truth!
Remember that when life's trials grow and expand in might…

Sometimes God lifts one hand to allow suffering and trials. But forget not that He has two hands. Believe and remember that He is holding you with the other.

God said, "fear not, for I am with you; be not dismayed, for I am your God; I will strengthen you, I will help you, I will uphold you with my righteous right hand." (Isaiah 41:10)

When trials hit, we all can lose heart and sight of simple, yet powerful truths and foundations of our faith.

Remember and pass this remembrance along to others! For His sake and His glory.

You are held in His two hands!

3/7

Hello and Hi,

Death is a subject that is not necessarily enjoyable to discuss, but one that must be for it is inevitable for us all.

I know, I know. This is simply and exactly what, and precisely the topic you were hoping would be brought forth this morning.

But keep reading (please).

I saw you but for a moment in a dream one night
Gone from this world with white shores in your sight

Your Savior and Friend had called you home to be with Him
Christ's blessed assurance brought face to face as your favorite hymn

And looking at each other where no words were spoken
Pointed upward did I that I would join you one day for death's sting was broken

Paul writes that Jesus "abolished death and brought life and immortality to light through the gospel." (2 Timothy 1:10b)

Death is not a subject that we as Christians need to fear. Yes, it is saddening for those left behind. But it is not a 'goodbye', but a 'see you later'.

It does not make the passing of a loved one easy, but it does add hope as an ingredient to what would otherwise be a recipe for hopelessness.

Remember this and share such hope amongst a dying and lost

world!

Jesus won over death!

3/8

Hello Everyone,

"Man, I did it again."
"I just feel like I'll never beat this habit!"

If you have ever felt like this or are feeling this way, take heart.

Free on the outside, yet shackles within
The soul begins to wonder, "How did this happen again?"
Temptations and pulls of the world seem unfair
As attacks by the enemy consistently lead to despair

For this side of heaven sin shall remain
Fair exists not and the fall has led to pain
Dear soul, take heart, and remember His Name
The Name above all Names took upon Himself your blame

Jesus, Jesus, Jesus Christ your Savior is He
Who rose from the dead wherefore, grace, you to see
Take hold of His hand, outstretched towards your soul
You no longer need be shackled by the bondage of sin's toll

"No temptation has overtaken you that is not common to man. God is faithful, and he will not let you be tempted beyond your ability, but with the temptation he will also provide the way of escape, that you may be able to endure it."
(1 Corinthians 10:13)

Soak your soul, heart, and mind in this verse. Ask God to guide you into the avenues of escape and to lead you to a Christian support system within your church to build a steady foundation in order to withstand the attacks that will come.

Temptations are real.

Jesus is stronger!

Take heart!

3/9

Goods Greetings Tos Yous,

I know that seems confusing. And you're right.
Shame, regret, and guilt can do the same to our lives. Those three feelings, and others, have the ability to make life seem confusing

With tears for profit and pride for gain
The enemy thought you were condemned by your name
For through the years you were now known as shame

The guilt and the anguish had long come to bear
The weight and the pressure seemed to poison hope's air

With joy for profit and humility for gain
Jesus Christ came to adopt you and give you a redeemed name
For now through eternity you shall tell of how He bore your blame

Freedom and solace have now come to bear
The mercy and grace of God have now freshened hope's air

"There is therefore now no condemnation for those who are in Christ Jesus." (Romans 8:1)

Through and in Jesus Christ, trust His promise and look to Him for your name, not your past, and not the world.

Confusion ceases in Him!

3/10

Greetings Everyone,

Can you be a part of something, go to that same something, and take action within the same thing at the same time? If you can, should you? Must you? Will you?

"For as in one body we have many members, and the members do not all have the same function, so we, though many, are one body in Christ, and individually members one of another." (Romans 12:4-5)

You were saved not only to go to church, but to be the church!

Yes, have faithful attendance at your church.
But…
You are called to do more than merely attend.

Each person of the body of Christ has been given gifts to use as they function as part of the whole.

God has given you gifts that He desires and commands you to use! This will bring you great joy and purpose!

If you are not sure what your gifts are, talk to a trusted Christian friend or church staff member.

Be a part of, attend, and take action through serving your local church body!

Go forth in Jesus and with His power!

3/11

Merry…he's not really going to say it is he?
Christmas!

I, contrary to my above greeting, realize it's not Christmas! Though, as I write this, I have a Christmas candle lit and a small, artificial Christmas tree (minus ornaments and lights) in front of me. Yes, I may be odd in that manner!

But take a moment to proceed…

Christmas season has come and gone
But not so must its generously cheerful song

For whether or not the Christmas season is here
Christ the Savior's birth transpired to squelch man's fear

So, sing joy to the world and oh holy night!
For because of that moment your future is bright!

"These things I have spoken to you, that my joy may be in you, and that your joy may be full." (John 15:11)

Through Christ, you can have the joy that is associated with Christmas, today! But His joy is deeper than decorations or presents. His joy is rooted in His death and resurrection for your soul's freedom!

In that joy, give, and give, and give. Of your time. Of your money. Of your words.

For the renouncement of His name, for the sake of His sacrifice, and for the glory of Christ!

Merry Christmas!

3/12

Goooood Hello,

"The narrowest road is always the most fun, enjoyable, and easiest!" -Said no one ever.

It's tough, plain and simple. The road that is most travelled has the path beaten down and is safer; the narrow path is dangerous--most certainly dangerous.

But that is precisely the path Jesus calls His followers to tread and journey on through this adventure called life.

"Enter by the narrow gate. For the gate is wide and the way is easy that leads to destruction, and those who enter by it are many. For the gate is narrow and the way is hard that leads to life, and those who find it are few." (Matthew 7:13-14)

He did.
He knows the trials of that path.
He will never leave you on that path.

We must be willing to take an unpopular path in order to popularize the name of Jesus Christ.

This path will fly in the face of what is considered sane, normal, popular, or successful.

Take it anyway.
Jesus did.
He knows the trials of this path.
He will never leave you on this path.

On the path, your goal is to beckon out to a dying world, the saving grace, and unfathomable love of Jesus Christ!

Take the path.

Jesus did.
He knows the trials of this path.
He will never leave you on this path.

This path filled with trials and tribulations…but endless joy, hope, and peace with heaven as your eternal home.

Take the path!

3/13

Hi,

"I…uh…I just…I wish I had the words to say."

Have you ever been in that position where you just have the words to say for the situation you found yourself in?

I know what you're going through. I've been there myself.

Words, words, where are the words?
What once seemed secure now feels insecure
Grief, grief, how heavy the grief
What once seemed so joyous now feels sorrowful
Hope, hope, oh where is the hope?
What once seemed so promising now feels all but lost

Words, words, where are the words?
Let Jesus quiet your soul and rest on His ground secure
Joy, joy, how life-lifting the joy!
What joy is known now remains though times may be sorrowful
Hope, hope, oh what blessed hope!
What once appeared lost is not found in the Lord!

"You keep him in perfect peace whose mind is stayed on you, because he trusts in you." (Isaiah 26:3)

Let Jesus quiet your soul as you focus upon His Word, verses in the Bible. He will give you the words to say when He wants you to. Wait on Him. Trust Him. Through Jesus, you have joy in the midst of grief, and hope in the midst of sorry.

Look to Him and He will help you communicate as He desires. When He doesn't, trust Him to understand that sometimes words aren't needed, just your presence to a person that's hurting. Either way, His presence is always sufficient for you and each person you come into contact with.

Rely on the Word for your words!

3/14

Good Greetings,

I have a few questions for you:

Why are you here?
Why do you exist?
Do you feel that your purpose is all but dismissed?
Trudging along for temporary gains
Existing but not really
How do you survive through the emotional pain?

Take heart, all ye burdened of soul
Take heart, all ye who seek purpose
Have you forgotten Him who died and rose again?
Him who defeated death?

Jesus, Jesus, Jesus is He!
Forget not the plan and purpose He has for thee!
So, come to His table and you will find
Joy, peace, strength, and purpose divine!

"But you are a chosen race, a royal priesthood, a holy nation, a people for his own possession, that you may proclaim the excellencies of him who called you out of darkness into his marvelous light." (1 Peter 2:9)

Jesus' purpose is found in the fact that when you are saved by Him, you tell others about Him and proclaim His glorious salvation! That is your purpose and it may be carried out through different avenues.

You may be called to be a construction worker, a teacher, an artist, a computer programmer, a nurse, or a salesman. Those are all noble professions. Those are all professions by which God uses to proclaim His salvation to a lost and dying world.

Look to Him when you forget or lose sight of your purpose!

You've been called, go forth, and proclaim!

3/15

Hello and Hi,

Does the morning ever hit you--and boom! You feel just blahhhh.
You're not alone. Yet, don't accept that through the power of Jesus!

Life remains a tremendous gift
Don't allow your actions to send such a gift adrift

Intentionally remember
Intentionally commit
That each moment is a gift and your actions must not send His gift
adrift

Through every avenue of your day
Through the interactions that tend to keep your joy at bay

Intentionally remember
Intentionally commit
That each moment is a gift and your actions must not send His gift
adrift

Thus, eat of the fruit, the fruit of the Spirit
Beseeching Jesus to feed you, His character to inherit

Intentionally remember
Intentionally commit
That each moment is a gift and your actions must not send His gift
adrift

"This is the day that the Lord has made; let us rejoice and be glad
in it."
(Psalm 118:24)

God made this day!

Thus, He has a plan!
You are a part of that plan!
So, each day is a gift of God!
Rejoice in that truth!

Rejoice!

3/16

Hi and Howdy,

Sweet and short!

Remember from whence you came and from whence He came, in preparation for when you go to where He is!

"And such were some of you. But you were washed, you were sanctified, you were justified in the name of the Lord Jesus Christ and by the Spirit of our God." (1 Corinthians 6:11)

"In my Father's house are many rooms. If it were not so, would I have told you that I go to prepare a place for you?" (John 14:2)

Remember the way you used to live before coming to know Jesus. Remember who you were.
Remember what Jesus has done for you.
Remember to live in such a way as to reflect such a remembrance, knowing your destination is heaven.

Live to hear God's words to you: "Well done, good and faithful servant."
(Matthew 25:21a)

Go forth!

3/17

Good Hungry Greetings!

Hungry?

Have you had a BLT today?

You may be thinking, "Why is he asking me if I've had a BLT in the morning? Who has a bacon, lettuce, and tomato sandwich in the morning?"

Valid question. Although, *I* would eat a bacon and lettuce sandwich in the morning. I'll give my tomato to my wife, Katie. She loves those suckers! (Yes, I know it's not a sucker, but I digress)

No, I don't mean an actual BLT. I mean:

Believe…in Him
Lean…not on your own understanding
TrustHim, and Him alone for wisdom and life

"Trust in the Lord with all your heart, and do not lean on your own understanding. in all your ways acknowledge Him, and He will make straight your paths." (Proverbs 3:5-6)

Look to Him in prayer and through the Bible. Ask Him to also lead you to godly people for advice and wisdom as He speaks through them!

Eat heartily!

3/18

Good Good Greetings Everyone,

J.R.R. Tolkien wrote, "You can trust us to stick to you through thick and thin - to the bitter end. And you can trust us to keep any secret of yours - closer than you can keep it yourself. But you cannot trust us to let you face trouble alone, and go off without a word. We are your friends, Frodo."

This is a wonderful depiction of how Christians are to go through life with one another. Paul writes in Galatians 6:2, "Bear one another's burdens, and so fulfill the law of Christ."

Are we truly living this vital and unnegotiable aspect of Christianity? We must. Jesus did. He calls us to do the same.

Are you truly there for others? Truly there? Will you walk through the hellacious times of life with others? Will you sacrifice for the sake of another? Will you vow to come alongside your friends, family, and brothers and sisters in Christ to face trouble with them?

Will you?

3/19

Hello Everyone,

May I share something that I'm not the best at, but I believe is vital for the Christian life?

Listen in order to discuss
Discuss in order to understand
Understand in order to grow
Grow in order to reflect
Reflect in order to glorify
Glorify in order to love
Love in order to die
Die in order to live
All for the sake of Jesus Christ!

"I have been crucified with Christ. It is no longer I who live, but Christ who lives in me. And the life I now live in the flesh I live by faith in the Son of God, who loved me and gave himself for me." (Galatians 2:20)

Ask God to help kill your fleshly desires and replace them with His desires. It is not easy and not always fun, but it is worth it in light of what he has, and continues to do for you!

Because of Him, you can do it!

3/20

Good Morning,

Nouns, adjectives and verbs! Don't you just yearn for a grammar lesson right now?!

I dont' and thats' why Im' not going to attempt to give one…
Anyway…

Love is a noun
God it is He

Love is a verb
An action that must be carried out by you and by me

Love is an adjective
A word that must describe
All who profess belief in the Trinity

All for the sake of reflecting Christ Jesus
Who came, suffered, died, and rose again
Out of love for His Father

"Beloved, let us love one another, for love is from God, and whoever loves has been born of God and knows God." (1 John 4:7)

God is love.
If you believe in Him, you must be described as a person of love.
Why? Because you love others in His name!

Pray now, and ask God to tell, and show you now, and throughout the day ways you can show others His love.

From one loved by God to another, pray!

3/21

Hello and Greetings,

Our mere mortal words fall into an inadequacy chasm
For how can we express thanks for a love we cannot fathom?

Our souls were sentenced to eternal damnation
For we were enemies of God's heavenly nation

Our Christ, He came and dwelt among men
For to pay our penalty for our sin He left heaven

Our hearts He calls to and desires to live in
For thus let us forever give thanks for our salvation He did win

"Oh, give thanks to the Lord, for He is good, for His steadfast love endures forever!" (Psalm 107:1)

Forever!
Be of good cheer!
Be of a thankful heart!

For mere mortals He came!

3/22

Greetings on this day that God is in control over.

A reminder to you and something you can share with others that you come across. Be that beacon of hope that points to the ultimate Beacon of Hope!

For those…
Who endure never ending toil
For those…
Who believe their soul could never be royal

Listen, listen closely!

Know that…
The devil desires to destroy you
Believe that…
Jesus' sacrifice proves He loves you

Jesus desires to end your toil
Rest in knowing your Jesus-saved soul is royal

"Come to me, all who labor and are heavy laden, and I will give you rest. 29 Take my yoke upon you, and learn from me, for I am gentle and lowly in heart, and you will find rest for your souls." (Matthew 11:28-29)

For those, for you, for me!

3/23

Good Morning, Afternoon, or Evening,

Do we actually realize and comprehend the horrendous nature of our own sin and the grace of Jesus Christ? Do we categorize sin and sinners according to our feelings, or according to God alone?

God alone is holy and perfect. All of us are objects of wrath apart from Jesus Christ.

Therefore, the sinful heart, sinful nature, and need for God's grace and forgiveness through Jesus Christ are all equally necessary for everyone. This includes the following: the robbed and the robber, the abused and the abuser, the murdered and the murderer, and the raped and the rapist.

We all, each one of us, are in need God's grace and love.

"The gospel is this: We are more sinful and flawed in ourselves than we ever dared believe, yet at the very same time we are more loved and accepted in Jesus Christ than we ever dared hope."
-Timothy Keller

"Surely, He has borne our griefs and carried our sorrows; yet we esteemed Him stricken, smitten by God, and afflicted. But He was pierced for our transgressions; He was crushed for our iniquities; upon Him was the chastisement that brought us peace, and with His wounds we are healed. All we like sheep have gone astray; we have turned—everyone—to his own way;
and the Lord has laid on Him the iniquity of us all." (Isaiah 53:4-6)

Realize your sinfulness and recognize His sacrifice!

Today, and every day!

3/24

Good Greetings,

God says to you and to all believers:

"And your ears shall hear a word behind you, saying, 'This is the way, walk in it,' when you turn to the right or when you turn to the left." (Isaiah 30:21)

On life's journey, our ears hear from whom our heart delights in!
To whose voice are your ears tuned in to hear?

Do you delight in God and His ways for your life?
If so, you will hear His voice guiding you moment by moment.

Tune in closely!

3/25

Hello Everyone,

If Jesus had a Facebook page, He would have lots of "friends," but few "followers."

But as we see, Jesus didn't come to be liked or have people say, "There's a really nice guy with feel-good things to say." Jesus came to be loved, worshipped, and have people say, "There is the Son of God!"

Don't be concerned about being liked. Be focused on serving Jesus Christ and bringing a smile to His face.

"But the Lord said to Samuel, 'Do not look on his appearance or on the height of his stature, because I have rejected him. For the Lord sees not as man sees; man looks on the outward appearance, but the Lord looks on the heart.'"
(1 Samuel 16:7)

Be concerned about your heart's posture towards God.

Also, don't judge a person by his or her looks either, demonstrate Jesus' love to all!

Follow Jesus!

3/26

Good Afternoon, Morning, or Evening,

Maybe this describes what you have thought, are thinking, or will think:

Though I do not know what my entire story shall entail, the various chapters that shall make up my life's book, nor what my final sentence shall be, I know Jesus holds the quill and takes the time to write each word.

"'For I know the plans I have for you,' declares the Lord, 'plans for welfare and not for evil, to give you a future and a hope. Then you will call upon me and come and pray to me, and I will hear you. You will seek me and find me, when you seek me with all your heart.'" (Jeremiah 29:11-13)

This does not mean that for your life, God will necessarily give you wealth. It does not mean He will give you all the material possessions you dream of or desire.

It does mean He has plans for your life. He has and continues to write your story with His pen of love, grace, and mercy. He desires for you to pursue Him with everything you've got. It means He desires good for your life. It means He gives you hope and a future that rests in His hands, a future you can look forward to.

Walk in His truth!

3/27

Good Greetings Everyone,

How do you feel this morning? Now, although that's not a bad or sinful question to ask, one cannot base, and should not base, his or her life upon feelings. One cannot base what God's Word says base upon feelings of self or culture.

Suggestions, not commandments, our hearts do prefer
Many teach, "It's about you," and our feelings concur

Yet, Jesus did not leave a list of suggestions
His way, not our feelings, must fill our confessions

Jesus loves and He saves, for He showed us the way
To obey His commandments, waiting for that glorious day!

"And by this we know that we have come to know Him, if we keep His commandments." (1 John 2:3)

His commandments, not suggestions, are for our good and His glory!

Follow Christ, not your feelings!

3/28

Hello,

Do you like boats? Have you ever built a boat? Would you like to? Would you have liked to have been on the ark with Noah and his family? Do you like to go on cruise boats? How about hunting fish on a boat?

Side note: the hunting part was a joke.

Maybe you don't like boats at all!

Either way, where you look in desire, you will steer towards your goal.

"Therefore, since we are surrounded by so great a cloud of witnesses, let us also lay aside every weight, and sin which clings so closely, and let us run with endurance the race that is set before us, looking to Jesus, the founder and perfecter of our faith, who for the joy that was set before Him endured the cross, despising the shame, and is seated at the right hand of the throne of God. Consider Him who endured from sinners such hostility against Himself, so that you may not grow weary or fainthearted." (Hebrews 12:1-3)

Keep your eyes on Jesus. Know those that have gone before you in order to keep the legacy strong. When you remember what He did for you, you will be motivated and strengthened to press on.

Desire Him above all else!
Steer towards Him!

Until we reach heaven's shores!

3/29

Hello and Greetings,

Those you are closest to can often be the ones you are harshest with.
I, myself, am guilty of this.

Take time and ask God for help showing His love that was shown
to you.

Don't take close relationships for granted. Don't!

No, no, no!
Don't do it!

Seriously, don't. Show your appreciation and don't be so harsh.
Remember how much you love them and act like!

Go for it!

3/30

Good day to you,

Do you like making shadow puppets? Well, maybe not anymore, but did you? Do you enjoy seeing them? If nothing else, do you know what a shadow is?

(Just having some fun, laugh out loud, haha!)

The shadows of life doth exist to reveal
Lessons and memories our hearts twill feel

Reminding, remembering, the past in the future
Prevents, instructs, and thus, shadows nurture

Shadows are but a reflection of something. It is not the thing itself as it is with our past. There are sweet memories we like to, and should, think back upon, though the memory is not currently taking place any longer. It brings a smile to the soul.

Past mistakes are shadows as well. These shadows are ones we must not dwell upon, but learn from and remember, lest we make the same mistakes again. They are shadows, but they are in your past and do not hold sway, in and through the power of Jesus Christ, over your life any longer. There are consequences to pay for past actions, but God's grace will strengthen and uphold you!

Ask God for wisdom to learn from the past for His glory in the present and future!

"Blessed is the one who finds wisdom, and the one who gets understanding." (Proverbs 13:13)

Go in His wisdom for the sake of His name!

3/31

Hello Everyone,

Jesus is God: full of love, grace, mercy, and forgiveness.

He is not a mystical genie in a bottle, granting our every wish. Facebook is not His platform where He brings monetary wishes to fruition based on what we share.

He did not promise us that we could escape every tribulation. We are not guaranteed wealth, promotions, or any materialistic increases for following Him.

Jesus did promise us
Eternal life if we would but repent, believe, and confess that He is our Lord and Savior, the one and only way to heaven.
He would never leave us--ever.

The sun will shine
The clouds will rain
But only the umbrella of truth, the truth of Jesus Christ, will remain.

He shall protect thee from harm
From rays and from rain
For the armor of God
The Holy Spirit promises to ingrain

"I am with you always, to the end of the age." (Jesus)

Know and believe, truly, who Jesus is and what He's all about!

4/1

Good greetings to you on this day God has created,

God has not forgiven every sin, just some of them that you have committed. Did you know that?

April Fools!! Completely kidding. It's great that that's not the truth, right?!

'Twas hurt, 'twas pain, that marked my way
My soul remained shackled day by day

For another's actions and words did wound
My heart's trust and affection now lied hewn

But God, yes but God, those two words oh so precious
Crashed upon and broke down my walls so tenacious

He said, "Oh child, I see, and I know
All the hurt, all the pain, that has brought your soul low"

"Even now I will heal you and comfort you still
Yes, I will show you my graciousness as a part of my will"

"And through My great graciousness ye shall abide
As My Holy Spirit teaches you forgiveness by My side"

"For remember at Calvary I did recompense
And for your soul's sin I did offer complete forgiveness"

"Unforgiveness' yoke you are now free from!
Go now and forgive with My grace that has come!"

"…forgiving each other; as the Lord has forgiven you, so you also must forgive." (Colossians 3:13b)

Go forth because of Him and forgive others!

4/2

Good Good Evening, Morning, or Afternoon,

Do you realize that you are a person that flees?
Yep, you are.
Me too.
Yes, yes, we both are.

But God pursues!

I desired to flee Him
But He constantly pursued me

I strove to direct my own path
Yet He constantly pursued me

I esteemed Him not and valued cheaply His grace
Still He constantly pursued me and valued me greatly

Jesus Christ took the nails for my sin
As He submitted to the Father and valued Him greatly

Jesus Christ compels His children
To constantly pursue Him and value Him greatly

"What man of you, having a hundred sheep, if he has lost one of them, does not leave the ninety-nine in the open country, and go after the one that is lost, until he finds it? And when he has found it, he lays it on his shoulders, rejoicing. And when he comes home, he calls together his friends and his neighbors, saying to them, 'Rejoice with me, for I have found my sheep that was lost.'" (Luke 15:4-6)

Remember that He pursued and rescued you to give you salvation.
Remember He still pursues you as you traverse life's path, not to re-gift salvation, but to guide and direct you.

Pursue Him.

Be a person that pursues others as well, telling them of Jesus, and never giving up on the hope that they will come to Christ.

Go forth!

4/3

Good Morning,

Carpe Diem!
Translated from Latin, this means, "Seize the Day!" Are you truly living each day to the fullest, regardless of the circumstances you find yourself in, or the challenges you find yourself facing?

Our days are passing, twill soon be time
To enter eternity as death's bell doth chime

Hope we have in the name of Christ Jesus
He defeated death and shall never leave us

Thus, while on this side of heaven's splendor
Seize the day, serve Jesus, in joyous candor

"The thief comes only to steal and kill and destroy. I came that they may have life and have it abundantly." (John 10:10)

This offer is not solely for when life "appears" good or when the seas are calm. Jesus came so that you could live each day to the fullest, and have life abundantly here, as well as eternally in heaven. How? By living in the will of God and choosing to seek Jesus no matter what!

Carpe Diem in Jesus Christ!

4/4

Greetings Selfish Self,

What?! Who are you calling selfish? Wait one Christmas second! I'm actually a very giving person.

Are you? Am I?

At our root, we are all selfish individuals and, whether we verbalize it or not, love our self-interests.

John the Baptist said, "He must increase, but I must decrease." (John 3:30)

Fight for the death
That doth give breath

Self's death does gain
Jesus' breath of heavenly gain

Yet mighty is sin's pull
For thine enemy seeks to rule

But Jesus, yes but Jesus
Mightier than the enemy is He

Conquered sin, won the war
Jesus gave thy soul victory forevermore

Ask Jesus for help as you seek to submit to Him and not your sinful flesh. Ask Him to be lifted up and your desires minimized, erased! He will aid you in this battle!

Go forth in Him!

4/5

Good Selfish Day,

Wait, are you trying to just repeat yourself from yesterday?!
Why, pretty much yes, yes I am.

Why?

We all need it is why!

"He must increase, but I must decrease." (John 3:30)

The flesh, it shall plead, to serve only me
My hopes, my dreams, I value above Thee

Calvary speaks of the God-Man's desire
Of His submission of will that did transpire

How can I not surrender my all to my King
To Him, my service, I wholeheartedly bring

Continue pressing on and forward toward submitting your desires to those of God through prayer, Bible study, fellowshipping with believers, and serving in your church!

Press on for Him!

4/6

Howdy,

Have you ever felt that you're just running in a circle, and somehow, all your purpose and joy seems to be evading you?

When we aren't pursuing the things of God, this will be the resulting feeling.

Unsatisfied striving, contentment eluded
Gaining worldly bliss, true joy excluded

Deceived soul, lift thine weary eyes to Jesus
Rest in His promise that He will never leave us

Worldly strivings shall cease, contentment Jesus will give
Heavenly bliss thee shall find in the new life ye now live

"I have seen everything that is done under the sun, and behold, all is vanity and a striving after wind." (Ecclesiastes 1:14)

Everything, when not centered in Christ, is a vain pursuit.
Make sure you're pursuing Christ in all you do, think, say, and dream of doing!

Pursue Christ today and every day!

4/7

Hello and Hi,

Ready for poetry this morning?!

Maybe? Maybe not?
Ok, here we go!

'Twas Christ that brought peace to earth
And caused our hearts to give rebirth
Do not fret for what today may bring
For you know Christ, Who is the King

My body and mind began to grow weary
How would or could I continue this journey?
Then my soul heard a voice from up on high
My child, I shall renew thee; I heard thy cry

God pursued them with relentless love
Yet they chose below rather than above
Surrender, surrender! I heard Jesus say
Enter my joy and rest for I AM The Way

"And do not be grieved, for the joy of the Lord is your strength."
(Nehemiah 8:10b)

Attack the darkness today in that truth!

4/8

Good Morning,

God may purposefully give you more than you can handle today!

Wait a jolly second…I thought God wasn't like that?

As you go through life, God will never tempt you, but He will test you. These tests are to strengthen your faith in Him, deepen your love relationship with Him, prepare you to tell others about Him, and bring glory to Him.

"Count it all joy, my brothers, when you meet trials of various kinds, for you know that the testing of your faith produces steadfastness." (James 1:2-3)

When you are challenged today and face trials, ask God to give you joy and His perspective. Ask Him to teach and sharpen you.

For His glory and to reflect Him to a lost and dying world!
To give bread to beggars!

Accept the challenge for His namesake!

4/9

Good Greetings,

"From the days of John the Baptist until now the kingdom of heaven has suffered violence, and the violent take it by force." (Matthew 11:12)

This verse is not saying we should go around slugging people to get them to believe in Jesus or to get them to go to church.

But we are not to be weak or cowardly Christians. There is a spiritual battle waging even as we speak, and we must get into the fray.

I would like to share a quote from a WWII veteran, Ed Pepping.

"A doctor determined I had a severe concussion and had cracked three vertebrae in my neck…that was all I needed to know. Five of us decided to go AWOL, left the hospital, and went back to the 506th."

Wow. No wonder they have called this generation 'The Greatest Generation'. This man left safety to return to battle even with the high possibility of death.

Why? Because he loved his buddies and his country, wanted to return to them, and desired to continue fighting alongside them in their just cause.

Let the same be said of you in your walk with Christ as you fight against darkness, alongside fellow Christians.

Fight!

4/10

Good Hello and Hi,

"Gracious words are like a honeycomb, sweetness to the soul and health to the body." (Proverbs 16:24)

My brother, Jonathan, wrote a note many years to me when he was in elementary school that read:

"Dear Nathan,

You played an eccellent, most fabulous game ever. I am sorry I couldn't be there to tell you that. Have a good day tomorrow, I may see you in the morning.

Your one and only brother,
Jonathan
Joseph
Kaspar"

It had smiley faces all around it.

Those words are like a honeycomb. Think of words now, and throughout your day that you can give to others that are sweet to their souls.

Give others honeycomb today and every day!

4/11

Good Unknown Day,

Yes, this day is unknown. You may think you know what is going to transpire today, but you really don't--neither do I.

Corrie Ben Boom said, "Never be afraid to trust an unknown future to a known God."

She faced many uncertainties when she was imprisoned in a Concentration Camp by the Nazis during WWII. Take a lesson from someone who suffered this side of heaven and is now walking the shores of heaven with Christ, her King.

"May the God of hope fill you with all joy and peace in believing, so that by the power of the Holy Spirit you may abound in hope." (Romans 15:13)

Be not afraid of the unknown!

4/12

Howdy Y'all,

Get ready to sing!

A one and a two and a…
I don't hear you!

Just…
Wait, was that a soft note of song?!
Kidding...

Let's look at the book of Psalms for the remainder of the month, from chapters 100-123.

Why? Because that's the empirical and scientific biblical method of devotion!

Kidding again. Anyway, if you've read some of these before, read them again. We can never read them enough!

Psalm 100
Make a joyful noise to the Lord, all the earth! Serve the Lord with gladness! Come into his presence with singing! Know that the Lord, he is God! It is he who made us, and we are his; we are his people, and the sheep of his pasture. Enter his gates with thanksgiving, and his courts with praise! Give thanks to him; bless his name! For the Lord is good; his steadfast love endures forever, and his faithfulness to all generations.

There is much to be gleaned from this chapter, but take a moment to medicate on each part, each sentence, each word.

Give thanks!
Remember that you belong to the God of all things!
God is good and His goodness is not dependent upon circumstances!

Whoo-hoooo!

Make a joyful noise!

Greetings and Hi,

Good Morning,

"As part of Christ's army, you march in the ranks of gallant spirits. Every one of your fellow soldiers is the child of a King. Some, like you, are in the midst of battle, besieged on every side by affliction and temptation. Others, after many assaults, repulses, and rallyings of their faith, are already standing upon the wall of heaven as conquerors. From there they look down and urge you, their comrades on earth, to march up the hill after them. This is their cry: 'Fight to the death and the City is your own, as not it is ours!'" (William Gurnall)

We must always remember we are in a battle, in a war. It is spiritual and the cost is eternity. Be encouraged and strengthened and inspired to press on in the name of Jesus, through the hellacious times of life!

"And they have conquered him by the blood of the Lamb and the word of their testimony, for they loved not their lives even unto death." (Revelation 12:11)

Choose to not love yourself. Choose to not love the things of this world. Choose, this day and every day moving forward, to love Jesus and to fight with His Word and through prayers, alongside the saints in the battle against the devil! Make sharing the Gospel a priority in your life!

May the cause of Christ be yours as well!

4/13

Good Greetings and Happy Day,

Have you sought out one wiser than you?

"Ha! There's no one wiser than me!"
Why on this earth did you just say that?
"I didn't. *You're* the one writing this," you may be thinking.

And you would be right. But is there a hint of truth to the statement above?

Do you feel as though there isn't anyone wiser than you? If not, have you sought out someone that can mentor you?

Even Billy Graham, [quick recap of who he is], had a mentor. Yes, that's right.

David wrote, "he who walks in the way that is blameless shall minister to me." (Psalm 101:6b)

Find someone that is a mature Christ-follower and ask them if you can meet with them on a regular basis to help you grow in your walk with Christ.

In the New Testament, Timothy had Paul. Who will your Paul be?

Be a Timothy!

4/14

Hello and knock knock,

Who's there?
Wait, how can someone be knocking when there is no door, and this is a message?

Why am I spoiling the joke, you may be asking?

You may not be asking that at all, but actually questioning why you are reading this when it seems like the writer has become delirious.

But do you feel sometimes as if you're knocking on the door of God's room and not receiving any reply? Do you feel as if your prayers are going unheard?

"Hear my prayer, O Lord; let my cry come to you! Do not hide your face from me in the day of my distress! Incline your ear to me; answer me speedily in the day when I call!" (Psalm 102:1-2)

Truth be told, it may seem sometimes that your prayers are not reaching the ear of God. Or if they are, He does not seem to be answering you.

It may feel…

Don't base it off of feelings!

God hears your prayers, though He many not give you the answer you desire. His timing may not be what you had hoped for, but that doesn't mean He hasn't heard or responded to your prayer.

His answer can be 'yes', 'no', or even 'wait'. The waiting will result in a 'yes' or a 'no'.
It may seem or feel otherwise, but rest in the foundation He hears and answers.

He loves you! Rest in that truth!

He loves you! Rest in that truth!

4/15

Greetings,

I love dust, don't you?! Yes, dust…I simply, without a doubt, love dust!

Kidding,   am   I?
Yes, yes, I am.

But, guess what? Dust is a good reminder to us!

"For He knows our frame; He remembers that we are dust." (Psalm 103:14)

God knows that because of the fall in the garden, our lives quickly come and go.
He loves and grants us His mercy and grace in the midst of our frailty.

When you see dust, thank God for showing you love, grace, mercy, and compassion in the midst of your frailty. Remember that you are not some superhuman that will never die. Remember to live each moment of every day for Jesus!

Yes, clean the dust when you see it. And use that as a reminder to ask God for forgiveness for the dust in your life (sin) and as a reminder to now let your Bible or your prayer life become dusty!

Use dust as a reminder today and every day!

4/16

Let's just jump right into it…

"Bless the Lord, O my soul!
O Lord my God, you are very great!
You are clothed with splendor and majesty,
covering yourself with light as with a garment,
stretching out the heavens like a tent.
He lays the beams of his chambers on the waters;
he makes the clouds his chariot;
he rides on the wings of the wind;
he makes his messengers winds,
his ministers a flaming fire.
He set the earth on its foundations,
so that it should never be moved.
You covered it with the deep as with a garment;
the waters stood above the mountains.
At your rebuke they fled;
at the sound of your thunder they took to flight.
The mountains rose, the valleys sank down
to the place that you appointed for them.
You set a boundary that they may not pass,
so that they might not again cover the earth."
(Psalm 104:1-9)

Simply dwell upon those verses that describe the greatness of God, the God you believe in, the only true God. Just dwell and give Him praise.

Stand in awe of Him always!

4/17

"Seek His presence continually!" (Psalm 105:4)

Greetigns!

Do you seek God's presence all the time? Like literally every second of every day?

No? Why not?

Don't quickly snap to, "That's impossible to seek His presence every second of every day!"

If that is your reply, then you're missing the point.

God desires for us to walk with Him and invite His presence to walk each step of the day with us.

Be Thou my Vision, O Lord of my heart
Naught be all else to me, save that Thou art
Thou my best Thought, by day or by night
Waking or sleeping, Thy presence my light

This old hymn sings of God's presence lighting our way!

Do you invite God's presence in all your decisions, relationships, games, work, family life, social life, and church life?

Please do!

Talk to Him throughout your day about anything and everything!
Read His letter to you, the Bible!

Walk with Him!

4/18

Hello and Greetings,

My happiness is God's utmost priority for my life.
Also, my glory is number one.
God saved me just for my eternal life security.

False!
Sorry for the harshness. Actually, not really.
I'm in the same boat as you and it's still false!

"Our fathers, when they were in Egypt, did not consider your wondrous works;
they did not remember the abundance of your steadfast love, but rebelled by the sea, at the Red Sea. Yet he saved them for his name's sake, that he might make known his mighty power." (Psalm 106:7-8)

God does love us and finds pleasure when we are happy, like a good parent feels for a happy child.

God saved us because He wants to give us heaven.

But take another look at the above verses.

They rebelled and God saved them "for his name's sake, that he might make known his mighty power." It was for Him! It was for Him! It was not for them.

We like to prioritize that we are the only reason God sent His Son to earth. He did come for us, but also for His namesake as it is more important than ours. God saved us in that He might receive glory and that others would know of His mighty and saving power!

Remember to prioritize Him and remember He does mighty acts for the credit, glory, and fame He deserves!

Don't dare seek to steal it for yourself!

Live for His name, not yours!

4/19

Good Greetings,

Care for some stew? Would you like it for breakfast, lunch, or dinner today? I made some last night and will be selling it online at the reasonable cost of $1,000,000,000,000.00 per cup.

I know, I know, I'm selling it at way too inexpensive of a price, but I guess it's just the generous spirit of Christmas still lingering. And I do realize it's almost May.

"Once when Jacob was cooking stew, Esau came in from the field, and he was exhausted. And Esau said to Jacob, 'Let me eat some of that red stew, for I am exhausted!' (Therefore, his name was called Edom. Jacob said, 'Sell me your birthright now.' Esau said, 'I am about to die; of what use is a birthright to me?' Jacob said, 'Swear to me now.' So, he swore to him and sold his birthright to Jacob. Then Jacob gave Esau bread and lentil stew, and he ate and drank and rose and went his way. Thus, Esau despised his birthright." (Genesis 25:29-34)

How hungry are you? Not physically, but how hungry is your carnal flesh? At what price are you willing to pay for material possession or fleshly pleasures? Possession and pleasures are not necessarily wrong, just as eating is not wrong but the product or outcome is not always worth the cost!

Esau would later realize that the stew he wanted to assuage his hunger was not worth the cost of selling his birthright.

Take some time to reflect upon the costs you are paying daily for the possessions, pleasures, or outcomes you desire. The money (you spend for possessions), time (you give to activities), words (you speak to others for a desired action or feeling), thoughts (you think that reflect your desires), and actions (you carry out for a desired result or the obtainment of an item) are all forms of payment.

Is the price worth it? If it honors God, then it is worth it, and you should continue. If it is not honoring God, then you must cease--please cease!

Christ is with you and will give you the wisdom and discernment you need and the ability to carry out the correct decision.

Don't dally, think up!

4/20

Good morning to you all,

Years ago, I saw a child in a jungle gym. He told his father he couldn't see him. His father though, replied that he could see him (the child).

In the midst of the madness of life, God always sees you. Always.

"And because you are sons, God has sent the Spirit of his Son into our hearts, crying, 'Abba! Father!' So you are no longer a slave, but a son, and if a son, then an heir through God." (Galatians 4:6-7)

You have become a son or daughter of the King of the Universe as soon as you accept Jesus Christ as your Lord and Savior! No matter what your experience shave been with your earthly father, God is your perfect Father.

In the midst of the madness of life, God always sees you. Always.

I remember when I was young and on the diving board, I was scared of the deep end of the pool. But when my dad was in the water below, I was able to jump. I knew my dad was there and he would protect me. I was secure in him.

The same picture is true for all believers in God the Father.

In the midst of the madness of life, God always sees you. Always.

Believe and rest in this truth!

4/21

Greetings,

Food is a good thing.
Witnessing is a great thing.
Jesus is the greatest thing.

The end. Have a great day!

Crimeny! Only kidding.

Johnny Tyler, a buddy of mine since the age of 4 years, showed me a powerful way to pray before a meal. He would ask God to bless the food to the nourishment, the strength to our bodies, our bodies to His service.

Powerful.

"Other boats from Tiberias came near the place where they had eaten the bread after the Lord had given thanks." (John 6:23)

Do you pray before each meal (both when you are out in public or at your home)? It's an opportunity to thank God for the food He has provided, and to ask Him to use it to fuel you physically in order to serve Him. It also serves as an opportunity to witness others around you and/or minister to your family.

I encourage you to make this a habit!

Now go grab ya some food!

4/22

Good night or Good morning
Or simply…
Greetings!

Have you ever been asked by someone, "What are you doing?"
To which you reply, "Nothing."

How does one do nothing? Does that mean you are simply relaxing?
Relaxing is a good way to spend some of your time, but it is still "something" and not "nothing."

Let us press onward!

Don't do "nothing" right now. Read this:

"Some sat in darkness and in the shadow of death, prisoners in affliction and iron, for they had rebelled against the words of God, and spurned the counsel of the Most High…He delivered them from their distress…Whoever is wise, let him attend to these things; let them consider the steadfast love of the Lord." (Psalm 107:10, 13a, 43)

How often do you consider the steadfast love of the Lord? Have you spent time truly reflecting deeply upon His love for you and how He demonstrated it?

Take some time and read all of chapter 107 to learn more about the Lord and His love for you.

Reflect and consider the unfathomable richness of His love!

So next time you want to do "nothing", consider doing "something", and read His Word to consider His steadfast love.

Here's to "nothing" becoming "something"!

4/23

Greetings on this snowy day,

Snow, snow, snow! "I'm dreaming of a white..."
My apologies...we are only a few months away from Christmas. Well, maybe more than a few.

There are stories about it, songs with it, and movies that depict scenes in it.
It can be dangerous, or the composition of a Christmas card.

It is the same way, in a sense, as your spiritual foundation. With God's character.

"Therefore, let us be grateful for receiving a kingdom that cannot be shaken, and thus let us offer to God acceptable worship, with reverence and awe, for our God is a consuming fire." (Hebrews 12:28-19)

God is a loving Father and He has placed you in His saving hands, a place where no person or thing can steal you away from. But look at the ending portion of this verse. A consuming fire is not a "safe" depiction. It is not a phrase that card companies would be apt to place on their Christmas cards!

But nonetheless, it is a depiction of the God we believe in and trust our souls unto.

Approach Him with the respect and honor when He is due. He is approachable, but dangerous. Approachable through the sacrifice of Jesus Christ. Dangerous in that His power is uncontainable, unquenchable, and able to strike us or any person or spiritual being down in a time faster than a millisecond! He is not to be trifled with!

Would you want a Navy Seal or a teddy bear with you in a fox hole during battle?
Exactly! The Navy Seal.

Come unto God your Father through, and in, His grace, mercy, and love.

But remember His power. Give Him the honor and respect He is due - all of it. He's not the "man upstairs."

Go Forth!

4/24

Hello and Greetings,

There is a date that has come to be labeled by some with the term "weed day."

Pause for station identification as to why a pastor would bring this up…

Now before outrage occurs (insert a laugh for comic relief), I am by no means advocating for the celebration or legalization of recreational marijuana use. I do not hold that using this would be honoring to Christ. I would by all means be open to further discussion of this. You can email me: nathankaspar@yahoo.com

But let us journey on…

Marijuana is used recreationally by many to calm one's nerves, escape from reality, ease stress, and relax. It also alters the mind. There are negative effects on the body as well.

"Or do you not know that your body is a temple of the Holy Spirit within you, whom you have from God? You are not your own, 20 for you were bought with a price. So, glorify God in your body." (1 Corinthians 6:19-20)

When anything alters our state of mind, it is not honoring God Almighty. There's no way around that for you or me, as Christians.

What have you allowed to control your body other than Christ Jesus? Is it caffeine, working out, alcohol, food? None are wrong nor sinful in and of themselves. But to the extreme, yes, they become sinful practices.

When we use these instead of Jesus to relax or to fill a void, they are no longer honoring to Him.

Please take some time today and do a self-check of the above. It's not easy, but a good thing to do spiritually!

Run to His arms always!

4/25

Greetings and Hello,

Power to create
Power to destroy
Who are we that He would make Himself known?

Creator of the tiniest and Creator of the mightiest
Destroyer of every stronghold and Destroyer of death itself
Who are we that He would make Himself known?

Who are we that He would make Himself known?
We are sinful, wretched, enemies of His wrath!
For we are the ones whose sin He died for!

Mercy to not punish
Grace to give freely
Who are we that He would make Himself known?

Merciful upon those who call upon His name
Merciful to not give us the penalty due our name
Who are we that He would make Himself known?

Graceful to bless us with gifts from above
Graceful to bestow upon our souls eternal life upon heaven's shores
Who are we that He would make Himself known?

Who are we that He would make Himself known?
We are nothing, Jesus Christ is everything!
He adopted us into His family and made our souls anew!

Please take a moment and open your Bible, or search the passage on
the internet, to Psalm 8 and dwell upon the words God has written. It's
not a long chapter, I pinky promise!

You are His because of His great love, mercy, and grace for you!

-169-

4/26

Howdy,

Remember the saying, "When it's cold outside and the pigs are flying, make sure to get your Thanksgiving turkey!"?

I don't either.
I made that up.
You may have guessed.
You may have not.

Sometimes strange things will happen in life that just straight up don't make any sense. You have the choice to turn to God, or turn away.

The enemy will attack you and seek to have you become angry, bitter, hateful towards and doubtful about, God.

Characters throughout the Bible went through hellacious times and were faced with the same decision we are. Will we succumb to these feelings or turn them over to God, who is big enough to handle them and strong gracious to aid us through the valleys and take away those feelings.

Please turn to Him!

4/27

Good Greetings,

Glorify and attack!

Whoa, whoa, whoa…what on earth! I ain't looking to fight today.

That's a good and bad thing. I'll explain…

First, for the glorify aspect:
"Be exalted, O God, above the heavens! Let your glory be over all the earth!" (Psalm 108:5)

Do you truly desire and seek to exalt God in all you do and above everything else? This includes work, exercise, family, friends, and we can't leave out self!

Dig deep, real deep, and ponder this question.

Do you put your quiet time on the back burner because of work or family?
Do you put work ahead of your family?
Do you do the same with exercise, family, friends, and self-time?
Do you put your spouse ahead of God?

Do you give God the credit when any success comes your way?
Do you blame Him when bad things happen?

Take a moment to search your soul.

Now for the attack aspect:
"Oh, grant us help against the foe, for vain is salvation of man! With God we shall do valiantly; it is He who will tread down our foes." (Psalm 108:12-13)

Don't sit back and be comfortable in your walk with God.

Attack the darkness! Take stands when you are out and about. Speak up with topics come up and share your beliefs from a biblical standpoint. Vote in such a way that reflects biblical values. Help serve and protect those through word and physical action to display the salvation of God that you have experienced.

Attack through prayer. Pray for others and against Satan.

Glorify and attack today and every day!

4/28

Hello,

Appearance is, I would dare say, the most important aspect for a Christian to be mindful of. Just think of it: the way we look, our height, weight, skin color, social-economic background, education, zip code, etc... it's all that matters!

False! Did I have you going?

Remember the Titans is a movie that traverses through the story of a football team battling with the reality of racial integration. As you watch the movie, you journey through the ups and downs of a team and community that will either be brought together, or torn apart by this reality.

Coach Yoast, one of the central characters, says the following: "Yeah. I hope you boys have learned as much from me this year as I've learned from you. You've taught this city how to trust the soul of a man rather than the look of him. And I guess it's about time I joined the club."

Get to know people.
Build and foster relationships.
Get to know people that you would rather not as they are vastly different than you or those that get on your nerves.
Cease and desist making judgments on people that prevent you from even speaking to them or speaking but not truly getting to know them. You don't have to condone what people do, but you are called to love them!

"Let brotherly love continue. Do not neglect to show hospitality to strangers, for thereby some have entertained angels unawares." (Hebrews 13:1-2)

Love and don't neglect!

4/29

Hello Everyone,

Do you pursue broken people?
Do you pursue needy people?
Do you pursue poor people?

OR

Do you pursue only those that can be of some sort of benefit to you and/or your family?

We come across a man in Psalm 109 that "did not remember to show kindness, but pursued the poor, needy, and the brokenhearted, to put them to death." (Verse 16)

Whoa, wow, yikes.

Do you want that to be said of you? Do I?

"I haven't put anyone to death!" you may be saying or thinking.

Have you put them to "death" with your thoughts or actions, albeit not physically?

I'm guilty…are you?

How can you serve the poor, needy, and brokenhearted? Some ways include:
- Delivering care packages that include non-perishable food items like water, a calling card, bus fare, church info, etc. in baggies to the poor and needy you come across.
- Giving to your church's benevolence fund. If you church doesn't have one, seek to begin one.
- Sharing God's love by giving a smile, a kind word, and sharing His Word with others.

Take time and don't rush!

Go forth today and be one that is described as giving kindness and pursuing the poor, needy, and brokenhearted with the love of Jesus!

Go on and get on out there in His love!

-175-

4/30

Good Howdy to Ya,

Ready, set...hut, hut!

I know it's not football season, but you know what they say…nope, me either.

Anyway, just a quick reminder today:

Love and serve
Serve in love
This is our commission from the Lord above

Deed and word
Word in deed
Our actions must reflect our faith's creed

Love and grace
Grace in love
These banners of Jesus must be ours as we run life's race

"By this all people will know that you are My disciples, if you have love for one another." (John 13:35)

Go in love!

4/31

Good Old New Day,

He's at it again! He's talking in a strange and peculiar fashion!

Have you ever thought or been told or heard that the Old Testament is just that -old? Or that the New Testament is really all we need to focus on? Or simply that Jesus is not really relevant until the New Testament?

Even if you would answer no to the above questions, stick with me.

"The LORD says to my Lord: 'Sit at my right hand, until I make your enemies your footstool.'" (Psalm 110:1)

LORD means 'YHWH', and Lord means 'Jesus'. This is a foretelling of God the Father telling Jesus to sit at His right hand until He (God the Father) subjects all who stand against Him (Jesus) and underneath Him (Jesus).

Always remember, though this may or may not seem like a simple reminder, that Jesus always has existed and is within the Old Testament. This is just one example.

Jesus was, is, and is to come!

All will one day bow to the Lion!

Follow the Lion through it all!

5/1

Greetings,

Did you know that in order to gain wisdom you have to be frightened!?
Like really frightened!

You know, like to the extent you're frightened when the gifts for Christmas are almost wrapped and you run out of tape! Or if you're making a peanut butter and jelly sandwich and all you have is cheese and Worcestershire sauce!

AHHHHHHHH!!!
What just happened?

Whelp, let's continue on…

"The fear of the LORD is the beginning of wisdom; all those who practice it have good understanding. His praise endures forever!" (Psalm 111:10)

This is not a fear to approach God, but a reverence. Having a reverence for Him means you admit you know nothing, and He knows everything. It's humbling yourself before Him.

When you are in that posture, God bestows upon you, wisdom (godly knowledge/information), and understanding (how to carry out and implement the wisdom).

Place your heart and mind in that posture and stand amazed at God's work in your life. Seek Him in prayer, the reading of His Word, and the fellowship amongst His people at church.

Don't live in an "afraid" posture, but in a "fearfulness of God" posture!

God's praise, glory, and honor never end!

Live in the reverence of God!

-179-

5/2

Good Day,

Does it ever seem that the news each and every day is anything but cheerful or hopeful, let alone good?

Does this seem to apply to the world, country, and/or your own personal life?

There's a funny quote *from Fiddler on the Roof* that says, "As the good book says, good news will stay, and bad news will refuse to leave."

First, let me say this quote is not from the Bible.

Second, you and I all enjoy good news and would like for that "feeling" or "moment" to stay. But sometimes it seems that bad news has the upper hand and has roots so deeply grounded that it will not be uprooted.

Psalm 112:7 says, "He is not afraid of bad news; his heart is firm, trusting in the Lord."

You don't know what the future holds, news or outcomes. But God does.

Don't dwell upon the unknown or bad news. Dwell upon your Savior in the trust rooted in the hope of Him.

Trust and be not afraid!

5/3

Greetings to You,

Let's talk politics, shall we? I feel…If only…Why would you…When will they…

Well, let's talk politics in a different manner.

We are prone to place hope into the hands of politicians, believing they can fight for our belief platform and turn our plight around into the correct direction.

But…

"The LORD is high above all nations, and His glory above the heavens!"

God is our hope, not any politician (left, right, middle, Democrat, Republican, Libertarian, Independent, etc.)!

God is not up for re-election at any time. He's not dependent upon earthly power. His plan will not falter, regardless of who is president.

God is God, no one else is.

God is above all nations--all!
His glory is higher than the heavens--the heavens!

Find your hope in that, in Him.

Be active in standing for biblical principles within the political spectrum, but don't misplace your hope!

Set your eyes on Him!

5/4

Gooooood Howdy,

"You're gonna need a bigger boat."

Name. That. Movie.

You are correct…it's "*Flipper*"!!

Kidding, it's "*Jaws*". The movie that sent a shockwave through those that enjoyed the ocean. This quote was in the movie to express the power behind the shark which the three men were hunting and seeking to destroy.

Powerful was the shark! Very powerful!

Now, let's turn to Psalm 114:8, which says that God "turns the rock into a pool of water, the flint into a spring of water."

Those are leaps and bounds more powerful! You may feel that there are challenges within your life that are insurmountable and on your own, they may be. But the God whom you believe is more powerful still.

Submit your challenges to Him and see what He would do, how He would handle them. The doesn't always end our challenges, but our hope can be in the One who is more powerful than the challenge.

Your challenge is a great white shark.
God is…well, He's God.
God will supremely dominate a great white shark any day.

Walk with the One who's bigger than your challenge!

5/5

Greetings Everyone,

What is the measure by which you measure your success? Think deeply. Take a pause and contemplate.

The mark of a man or woman is not measured by the temporal, but by the eternal in Jesus Christ.

Your worth is not a reflection of what you possessions you obtain, promotions you earn, places you travel to, relationships you have, or the ideas you gain recognition for.

A person's worth is found in Jesus, and only in Jesus.

"…I have more: circumcised on the eighth day, of the people of Israel, of the tribe of Benjamin, a Hebrew of Hebrews; as to the law, a Pharisee; as to zeal, a persecutor of the church; as to righteousness under the law, blameless. But whatever gain I had, I counted as loss for the sake of Christ. Indeed, I count everything as loss because of the surpassing worth of knowing Christ Jesus my Lord. For his sake I have suffered the loss of all things and count them as rubbish, in order that I may gain Christ and be found in him, not having a righteousness of my own that comes from the law, but that which comes through faith in Christ, the righteousness from God that depends on faith—that I may know him and the power of his resurrection, and may share his sufferings, becoming like him in his death…" (Philippians 3:4b-10)

Paul lists his top-notch earthly resume, and says it means nothing to him. Christ means everything to him!

This doesn't mean you should not work hard. God may give you promotions and earthly success. But it is all for His glory and to reflect Him to a dying world.

You must use all earthly success for Him. If you don't, it is for naught and sinful. Plain and simple. For me and you.

Your worth is in Christ. Go forth to do His work through the tasks He has given you.

Go forth!

-184-

5/6

Hello Everyone,

All children love to share right? Wrong. It's as though it's innate in a child to desire to take what is not his or to not share what he ought to.

It's because we are sinful creatures, even as a child, in need of Jesus' grace and forgiveness.

And we ought to share His forgiveness with others, but often times we don't. We use His gift as a "get out of hell free card" and then willingly choose to not share what has been given to us with others.

Grace received, woven with mercy and love
Jesus' sacrificial, eternal, gift from above

Far be it form us to withhold from sharing
And lo, thus guilty of Commission failing
[Our Savior's gift of home in arms ever caring]

"Freely you received, freely give." (Matthew 10:8b)

Be about His giving today!

5/7

Good Greetings,

What are you currently setting your gaze upon? Is it the next item you wish to purchase? Or simply you're next meal? Is it money, a relationship, or a certain hobby? Is it upon serving your needs or desires?

None of the above are bad things in and of themselves, but should our fixed gaze be upon them?

Set your gaze, above all else, upon Jesus.
Isaac Watts penned these lyrics many years again:

When I survey the wondrous cross
On which the Prince of glory died,
My richest gain I count but loss,
And pour contempt on all my pride.

Forbid it, Lord, that I should boast,
Save in the death of Christ my God!
All the vain things that charm me most,
I sacrifice them to His blood.

See from His head, His hands, His feet,
Sorrow and love flow mingled down!
Did e'er such love and sorrow meet,
Or thorns compose so rich a crown?

Were the whole realm of nature mine,
That were a present far too small;
Love so amazing, so divine,
Demands my soul, my life, my all

"Indeed, I count everything as loss because of the surpassing worth of knowing Christ Jesus my Lord. For his sake I have suffered the loss of all things and count them as rubbish, in order that I may gain Christ..." (Philippians 3:8)

Fix your gaze above all upon Christ!

5/8

Hello,

Let's take a journey through the book of *Snaitalag*!

What? You've never heard of that book? Take a good, hard look…

Still nothing?

You're right. Although it is Galatians spelled backwards.

Hehe.

"For am I now seeking the approval of man, or of God? Or am I trying to please man? If I were still trying to plea se man, I would not be a servant of Christ." (Galatians 1:10)

It's wearisome trying to please person after person. Christ has called you to something better! There is a difference in doing your work well and to the best of your ability, and doing it for the sake of man's approval instead of God's.

Pursuing the path of winning the constant approval of others is one that will never end, but continue in a circle for the remainder of your days.

Stand for Christ. Care only of what He thinks of you. By doing so, your soul will be at peace and you will live a life of love, which is honoring to Him.

The houses, clothes, body type, cars, abilities, education, job, words of affirmation…all these and more that we seek in the approval of others are a poison to our souls when we elevate their importance above Christ.

Seek Him.
Seek His approval.
Find Peace.

Seek and you shall find!

5/9

Hello and good morning,

Smile, wave, look at people in the eye.
Reciprocate a "how are you doing?"

Through these actions, you show the love of Jesus.

Simplicity is the avenue by which Jesus is reflected to a lost and dying world.

Do the simple things. Do them well. Remember them.

Today and every day, practice simplicity for the sake of Jesus Christ!

5/10

Greetings,

Have you ever pondered about who you were, are, and hope to become? It can sometimes be a mix of emotions when thinking about such things. But it's a necessary action for us to take…and it's not just a one-time action!

Do you like fig newtons? I know, random question…or is it? I do, but there is a quote I would like to share with you:

"I am not what I ought to be, I am not what I want to be, I am not what I hope to be in another world; but still I am not what I once used to be, and by the grace of God I am what I am" (John Newton).

Like the connection?!

Life is a journey of ups and downs. God desires to change you each and every day to become more and more like His son, Jesus.

Do people notice who you were and who you are now? Would they if they knew who you used to be? If not, do you desire that to be the case?

Look at this verse:

"They only were hearing it said, 'He who used to persecute us is now preaching the faith he once tried to destroy.' And they glorified God because of me." (Galatians 1:23-24)

I hope you desire to have same this same ideal mentioned about you and that you are not who you were, but are different because you know Christ, and you glorify God because of it!

Pursue Him!

5/11

Good morning and stop it!

What is he talking about? Stop what?!

Refrain from it!

What in the wide, winding, world of nacho making are you speaking of?

Please do not persist!

You keep saying the same thing, just using different verbiage.

I say, you're right. But take a look at the below verse:

"Yet we know that a person is not justified[b] by works of the law but through faith in Jesus Christ, so we also have believed in Christ Jesus, in order to be justified by faith in Christ and not by works of the law, because by works of the law no one will be justified." (Galatians 2:16)

Even if you believe that you are not saved by, or through works, you can sometimes fall into the trap of thinking that you can maybe gain more of God's favor or that you're a better person or Christian than another person based off of your good works.

Don't fall prey to this way of thinking!

You may even fall back into thinking that a person is saved by works.
Don't let the enemy sabotage you!

Jesus is, and will always be, enough. Do good works out of gratitude for His grace and to reflect Him to a lost and dying world, not for another reason of earning something!

He's enough!

5/12

Greetings Everyone,

How do you like pain? No…not like paper-cut pain. Like real pain.

Physical pain can be monumental.
Emotional pain can be monumental.
Spiritual pain can be monumental.

Pain can be easy…just kidding, well it can, but the point here is that pain can be monumental.

"I have been crucified with Christ. It is no longer I who live, but Christ who lives in me. And the life I now live in the flesh I live by faith in the Son of God, who loved me and gave himself for me." (Galatians 2:20)

Are you truly seeking to die each and every moment of your days? Paul is urging us to do so when we become a Christian.

Ask God to purge you of your desires and sow in you His desires that will reap a wonderful harvest!

When He does this, though, it may be painful as crucifying your old desires is not always pleasant.

It's worth it!
I promise.

Do you want your faltering self on the throne of your heart of the Creator and Sustainer of the Universe?

Choose wisely.

He was crucified for you. Crucify your desires for Him.
All for His glory!

Go forth in Him!

5/13

Hello Everyone,

Read the following verses please:

"And so, from the day we heard, we have not ceased to pray for you, asking that you may be filled with the knowledge of his will in all spiritual wisdom and understanding, so as to walk in a manner worthy of the Lord, fully pleasing to him: bearing fruit in every good work and increasing in the knowledge of God; being strengthened with all power, according to his glorious might, for all endurance and patience with joy; giving thanks to the Father, who has qualified you to share in the inheritance of the saints in light." (Colossians 1:9-12)

Who would you initially think I would mention this should be prayed for - yourself right? Well, this is a good prayer to pray for yourself, but have you ever prayed this prayer for fellow believers?

Take a moment and pray this specific prayer for fellow believers, as well as yourself.

Now go forth in that power, the power of Christ Jesus and keep that prayer going each day!

Go on, get out there, and live for Him!

5/14

Hi and Howdy,

Take a read about who Jesus is:

"He is the image of the invisible God, the firstborn of all creation. For by him all things were created, in heaven and on earth, visible and invisible, whether thrones or dominions or rulers or authorities—all things were created through him and for him. And he is before all things, and in him all things hold together. And he is the head of the body, the church. He is the beginning, the firstborn from the dead, that in everything he might be preeminent. For in him all the fullness of God was pleased to dwell, and through him to reconcile to himself all things, whether on earth or in heaven, making peace by the blood of his cross." (Colossians 1:15-20)

That's Who you believe in.
That's Who you serve.

There's a lot to unpack here for a daily devo, so take your time and read, seek good commentaries, and ask trusted, mature Christians.

Power to create.
Power to rule.
Power to hold together.
Power to be the head of the church.

Preeminent--way above all others!

Power to make peace for us.

Soak these verses in and dig into them.

That's Who you believe in.
That's Who you serve.

Go in Jesus!

5/15

Let's talk about suffering!

Oh… and Greetings!

Let's talk about suffering from a different standpoint.

"Now I rejoice in my sufferings for your sake, and in my flesh I am filling up what is lacking in Christ's afflictions for the sake of his body, that is, the church, of which I became a minister according to the stewardship from God that was given to me for you, to make the word of God fully known…" (Colossians 2:24-25)

Next time you are suffering, and I'm not saying this will be easy by any means, view it as an opportunity to encourage fellow believers and make Jesus known to those that do not know Him.

They have the opportunity to see how you handle suffering compared to others in the world.

It's not easy.
It's eternally worth it.

Seek Christ, that He may help you accomplish this for His sake and His glory!

Suffer well!

5/16

Greetings and Hello,

How about some Clive Staples Lewis today?! "Who is that?" you might be asking. Why C.S. Lewis of course!

"When He [God] talks of their losing their selves, He means only abandoning the clamour of self-will; once they have done that, He really gives them back all their personality, and boasts (I am afraid, sincerely) that when they are wholly His they will be more themselves than ever." (*The Screwtape Letters*)

You see, when you give your will to God through submission, He takes it, molds it to His, and gives it back to you. He uses the characteristics He has given you in accordance with His will to live out His mission that He has given you. You are more alive than you have ever been because you are truly who you were created to be when you are in submission to the Father!

"Teach me to do your will, for you are my God! Let your good Spirit lead me on level ground!" (Psalm 143:10)

Let this verse be your prayer today and every day. Watch God mold you to His Son.
Do you desire this?
He will not fail to answer this prayer if you desire it.

Go for it!

5/17

Greetings,

Remember when that happened?!
Yep, that sure was great!
What are you talking about?
Go Cowboys!

Remembrance is a topic that can bring both joy and sorrow. When you receive a card from someone you haven't heard from in a while. On your birthday, someone sends you a card. During a period of illness or period of tribulation, someone calls and remembers to check on you to see how you're doing.

You're reminded through remembrance that you're cared for and not forgotten.

"The LORD has remembered us; He will bless us…" (Psalm 115:12a)

God remembers you. In fact, He has never forgotten you in the first place.

The God of all things, through capabilities incomprehensible to the human mind, remembers each believer through their trials.

He remembers you.
Take heart.

Remember Him!

5/18

Greetings and Hello and Hi,

Hello?! Do you hear me?
I know, I know…the truth is you can't hear me because I'm writing this to you, not speaking to you.
Hehe.

"Because He has inclined His ear to me, therefore I will call on Him as long as I live." (Psalm 116:2)

Not only has God remembered you, but He turns His ear to hear you. It's not like He is acting like He is listening to you, but really paying attention (which we all are guilty of).

The God of all the universe turns His ear to listen to you.

Don't take that for granted and don't take it lightly. But, also realize the immense amazingness found in that truth!

Talk with Him now.

He has a listening ear!

5/19

Greetings,

Do you remember seeing Bible running down the street?
No, not Bill.
Although, come to think of it, I do remember Bill saying that he was going for a run today.
But I need to know if you saw Bible running down the street?!

What do I mean?
What do you mean when you ask me what I mean?

Anyway, I digress with fun…

"The Bible is alive, it speaks to me; it has feet, it runs after me; it has hands, it lays hold of me." (Martin Luther)

See, I told you!

On a lighter note. Just kidding. On a serious note, the Bible is alive because it is God's Word. His Word is sufficient for anything you are going through or will go through or are trying to heal from.

Because of this:

"Praise the Lord, all nations! Extol him, all peoples! For great is his steadfast love toward us, and the faithfulness of the Lord endures forever. Praise the Lord!" (Psalm 117)

Give Him praise!
Remember His love, which is shown through His love letter for you (the Bible)!
Remain faithful to Him as you remember His faithfulness to you!

Run always to Him!

5/20

Greetings,

Do you like scented candles? I do!
Even if you don't, stay with me.

In order to really have the candle do its job, which is for the scent to permeate the area, the wick has to be lit. Fire has to be applied.

The same is true of our lives. Fire must be applied in order for the aroma of Christ's salvation to permeate the souls around us.

Don't be afraid of the fire. Know Jesus walks with you through it. Know He sometimes brings the fire. But it's for your good and His glory if He does.
If He allows it, trust Him to bring good to you through it.

Pursue the flame!

5/21

Good Greetings,

"The tragedy of life is what dies inside a man while he lives." (Albert Schweitzer)

There is a way to be fully alive. There is a way to not be a walking dead-man or dead-woman. There is a Way.

"The thief comes only to steal and kill and destroy. I came that they may have life and have it abundantly." (John 10:10)

Jesus is the way! Life has a way of sucking life, energy, mental life, and purpose from us as we traverse through valleys and experience tribulations. But, God has given you a purpose and a mission. As you live these out, through the power of His Son, you will experience life as you have never before. No, it won't be easy. No, it won't guarantee earthly success, promotions, pleasures, and material gains.

Yes, it will be worth it. Yes, it will guarantee your soul to come alive, your heavenly Father to smile, your ears to hear Him say, "Well done good and faithful servant," when you reach heaven's shores.

Seek God and His path for your life. Pledge to give your life as service to your King...every part of your life. Pledge to live out and shar the Gospel! Plug in to and serve at your church, dig into His Word, dwell in prayer, give of your finances to your church and in other avenues God leads you, fellowship with believers, and share Jesus with unbelievers!

May your life be a Bible for others to read!

5/22

Greetings and Hello,

It's a good use of time to take a look at the lives of the great cloud of witnesses that have come before us, which the Hebrews have talked about in Hebrews 12:1-2a.

"Therefore, since we are surrounded by so great a cloud of witnesses, let us also lay aside every weight, and sin which clings so closely, and let us run with endurance the race that is set before us, looking to Jesus, the founder and perfecter of our faith, who for the joy that was set before him endured the cross..."

Below are the words from one such witness. Read them and reflect upon the verse above.

"But the proconsul urged him and said, 'Swear, and I will release thee; curse the Christ.' And Polycarp said, 'Eighty and six years have I served him, and he hath done me no wrong; how then can I blaspheme my king who saved me?'" (Polycarp, before he was martyred)

You may not verbally say, "I deny Christ," but you spit in His face each time you sin. You spit in the face of Jesus, who bled and died for you, each time you say something, think something, or physically do something that is not honoring to Him. We are all guilty.

Choose to speak, think, and live out the same words Polycarp uttered!

5/23

Hi and Hello,

"...let us run with endurance the race that is set before us, looking to Jesus, the founder and perfecter of our faith, who for the joy that was set before him endured the cross..." (Hebrews12:1b-2a)

Remember - Reflect - Prepare

Remember Jesus' love, mercy, and grace!
Reflect upon His sacrifice!
Prepare your heart each day, using this remembrance and reflection, as you journey through life with Christ and tell others about Him!

Remember - Reflect - Prepare!

5/24

Greetings Greetings,

I would like to invite you to speak with someone today. You may know him. There's also a good chance you don't.
Any guesses!?

No, it's not Santa Clause. Although I do know him…

Let me introduce you to Brother Lawrence, a man that lived in the 1600's.
You might be thinking, "What in the Sam-hill is going on?!"

Read it and see its weight.

"There's no greater lifestyle and no greater happiness than that of having a continual conversation with God."

Do you rejoice each and every day? Everyday? How about even those days you feel the chances of you getting out of bed and going through your day are 0.0000000000000000000001%?

Brother Lawrence is telling us that life's greatest joy is being in constant communication with Jesus through prayer, reading the Bible, and dwelling upon Him. Talk to Him throughout the day!

Now let me show you a quote from a man named David:
"This is the day that the Lord has made; let us rejoice and be glad in it."
(Psalm 118:24)

He was a man acquainted with days like that, yet, he wrote this. How does it apply to us?!

You don't have to wear a fake smile, for life is hard. But joy can still be in your soul.

God made this day. God made you. God is allowing you to be alive. Therefore, God has a purpose for you and He desires you to live that purpose to bring glory and others to His name.

That's worth rejoicing in!
Ask God to turn your heart, mind, and soul upon such a mindset!

Rejoice!

5/25

Good Short Greetings,

Are you ready for a quick read?

If you answered yes, why are you continuing to read this?
Just kidding…please keep reading!

Psalm 119 is the longest Psalm, but it is very much worth you taking the time to read in its entirety, even if it's not in one sitting.

One portion is the following (verses 9-16):
"How can a young man keep his way pure? By guarding it according to your word. With my whole heart I seek you; let me not wander from your commandments! I have stored up your word in my heart, that I might not sin against you. Blessed are you, O Lord; teach me your statutes! With my lips I declare all the rules of your mouth. In the way of your testimonies I delight as much as in all riches. I will meditate on your precepts and fix my eyes on your ways. I will delight in your statutes; I will not forget your word."

If you desire, truly desire, to live like and for Jesus, the above is your instructional manual, your "how-to," your game guide, your--it must be your game plan!

It's tough, but worth it. It's not popular, but it's worth it. Dying on a cross was excruciating…but you were worth it to Jesus!

Live in, with, and by Jesus!

5/26

Good Works Greetings,

Wait, I mean good faith greetings,

Or should I mean good faith works greetings?!

"So also faith by itself, if it does not have works, is dead." (James 2:17)

You aren't saved by works, not one iota! But if you don't have works as a result of your faith, you aren't saved.

That is harsh, I know. And you won't always do good works because you're imperfect. But truth and faith in Jesus will result in a lifestyle of living it out through works.

"Evangelism without social work is deficient; social work without evangelism is impotent." (John R. Mott)

We cannot simply meet the physical needs of others. We must couple meeting their physical needs with sharing the Gospel, which meets their spiritual needs.

I've heard it said before that if we simply meet a physical need and not a person's spiritual need (by sharing Jesus with them), we've made their path to hell a little smoother.

As the poignant and genuine Christian singer Rich Mullins sang:

It's about as useless as
A screen door on a submarine
Faith without works baby
It just ain't happenin'

Get to workin'!

5/27

Hello Everyone,

There used to be an advertising campaign put on by Under Armour that would show athletes answering the question, "Who will protect this house?!" and the athletes would yell out, "I will!"

Pop quiz: Did knights wear Under Armour?
Of course, they did! They wore something under their armor!

Ha
Ha
Ha

Now to the serious portion.

"China is not to be won for Christ by quiet, ease--loving men and women. The stamp of men and women we need is such as will put Jesus, China, souls, first and foremost in everything and at every time--even life itself must be secondary." (Hudson Taylor)

A line has been drawn in the sand. You can't stand on the line. Will you be in "ease" as a loving Christian? Or will you be a biblical Christian, one who is willing to give everything for the sake and call of Christ Jesus?

If you desire, truly desire, to follow Jesus, your life must be secondary to His cause and desires for your life!

The line has been drawn.

Step over it to live the life of a biblical Christian!

5/28

Good isolate greetings,

You may be thinking to yourself, "At this point I have no words for his lunacy."

I digress…

"By everything true, everything holy, you are your brother's keeper."
(Seventh Earl of Shaftesbury)

You are not responsible for what someone else chooses to do, but you are responsible as a Christian to share with them God's ways, love, grace, mercy, and wisdom.

"Two are better than one, because they have a good reward for their toil. For if they fall, one will lift up his fellow." (Ecclesiastes 4:9-10a)

We are not meant to walk this life alone. We are meant to band together as brothers and sisters in Christ and have each other's backs.

It's time for our hand to be used for a pat on the back, instead of a stab in the spine.

Live it.
Speak it.
For Jesus' glory and the good of others.

Go forth!

5/29

Good life greetings,

Some issues in life are give and take. There are issues that can go either way, and neither is wrong. Then there are other issues that are cut and dry. And sometimes, there are words that are point blank.

Here is one such occasion: abortion. I said it, but I urge you to keep reading.

"For you formed my inward parts; you knitted me together in my mother's womb. I praise you, for I am fearfully and wonderfully made. Wonderful are your works; my soul knows it very well. My frame was not hidden from you, when I was being made in secret, intricately woven in the depths of the earth. Your eyes saw my unformed substance; in your book were written, every one of them, the days that were formed for me, when as yet there was none of them." (Psalm 139:13-16)

According to God's Word, abortion is wrong and evil. If we want to do what our flesh desires, that is our decision. But, if we are going to live for Christ and do what he desires, we will stand against abortion.

This issue has to do with the murdering of a creation that was fearfully and wonderfully made by God. When a pregnant woman is murdered, it's considered a double homicide because there are two lives being lost.

It has nothing to do with the issue of it being a woman's body and her choice. Though she is fearfully and wonderfully made. Even if it is the result of a rape or incest, abortion is wrong. The cause of a pregnancy cannot justify truth, morality, or ethics. If it did, then that is saying truth, morality, and ethics are relative.

I could say I was wronged in order to justify my killing or harming someone.
Right and wrong must be grounded in a principle that is constant.

The constant and foundation of truth is God's Word.

As a Christian, you must speak up when injustice, on any front, takes place.
This is an injustice.

Stand up for the tough truth!

5/30

Good peaceful greetings,

No peace!
What is he talking about?!

You can have peace within your soul. In fact, that is what Jesus offers as it only comes through Him.

But our world is not at peace and will never be until all is made right one day through Jesus Christ.

But for now, we are called to war, a spiritual war.

"From the days of John the Baptist until now the kingdom of heaven has suffered violence, and the violent take it by force." (Matthew 11:12)

I'm not calling for violence. That's not what this verse means. It means we are men and women of action and that we fight against the darkness of Satan with the armor of God.

Take a look at a conversation from the movie, *Open Range*:

Mac: Shame what this town's come to.
Charley Waite: You could do something about it.
Mack: What? We're freighters. Ralph here's a shopkeeper.
Charley Waite: You're men, ain't you?
Mack: I didn't raise my boys just to see 'em killed.
Charley Waite: Well you may not know this, but there's things that gnaw at a man worse than dying.

You're Christians, ain't you?

Take a stand for God's truth in your conversations, in your thinking, in your voting, in your everything! Battle in prayer, through the reading of the Bible, and in gathering with fellow believers at church and out-side of church.

Hang out with unbelievers and love them sincerely, while standing for God's truth and telling them what it is.

You're Christians, ain't you?

Get in the fight!

5/31

Good Greetings,

Dad has told me before to keep looking up and keep moving forward.

I would say that same to you. Out of all the promises in the Bible, God never said life would be without devastating loss, horrendous challenges, or even monotonous tasks. He promised He would never leave you.

Move forward in His steps and keep looking up to Him.

Look up!

6/1

Greetings and Good Day!

That which you are willing to die for will reveal that which you are passionate about.

Are you passionate about Jesus? Are you really? What are you willing to do for Him? *Anything*? Are you sure about that?

At this point you may be thinking, "If he uses one more '?', I'm going to take down the Christmas tree! At this point, you're thinking, "Did he just say Christmas tree and what does that even mean?!"

Valid question.

Back to the business at hand--do you prefer colored or white lights on your Christmas tree? Ha, just kidding. I like both but prefer colored.

Now really back to business--really take time to think if you're in 'like' with Jesus or in love with Him (passionate about Him). If you're passionate about Him, step out of your comfort zone and do what He calls you to, as He leads. Invite at least one person to your church this week. Ask to pray for people. Go out of your way to serve others and let them know Jesus loves them.

Then these high officials and satraps came by agreement to the king and said to him, "O King Darius, live forever! All the high officials of the kingdom, the prefects and the satraps, the counselors and the governors are agreed that the king should establish an ordinance and enforce an injunction, that whoever makes petition to any god or man for thirty days, except to you, O king, shall be cast into the den of lions. Now, O king, establish the injunction and sign the document, so that it cannot be changed, according to the law of the Medes and the Persians, which cannot be revoked." Therefore, King Darius signed the document and injunction." When Daniel knew that the document had been signed, he went to his house where he had windows in his upper chamber open to-

ward Jerusalem. He got down on his knees three times a day and prayed and gave thanks before his God, as he had done previously. (Daniel 6:6-10)

That which you are willing to die for will reveal that which you are passionate about. If you're not willing to be ridiculed or take a step out of your comfort zone for Jesus, are you really willing to die for Him? Therefore, are you really passionate about Him? Are you in like with Jesus or in love with Him?

He'll give you the strength to step out for Him. Follow!

Step out and follow!

6/2

Greetings,

As I write this, I have a mango flavored candle lit on my desk. Yes, I said flavored. No, I haven't tasted it. Yes, I should have said scented.

But what if they made edible candles?!

Your life may feel like a candle at times--that you are on fire for God! Or you may feel that your purpose and joy has been extinguished, like when the light of a candle has been blown out.

The wick remains. Hope remains. Jesus remains.

The Lord is my light and my salvation; whom shall I fear?
The Lord is the stronghold of my life; of whom shall I be afraid? (Psalm 27:1)

He will again relight your wick.
Trust Him during the good and bad seasons of life.

He will remain your stronghold!

6/3

Candle Greetings,

One more candle devo!
But first, a candle joke: How do you get a candle to walk across a road?
Candles can't walk.

Anyway, there are many, many different types of scented candles. But, for the candle's scent to truly function properly, the wick must be lit on fire! Fire must be involved. Then the sweet aroma proliferates the air.

"But thanks be to God, who in Christ always leads us in triumphal procession, and through us spreads the fragrance of the knowledge of him everywhere. For we are the aroma of Christ to God among those who are being saved and among those who are perishing…" (2 Corinthians 2:14-15)

Our lives are to be lit on fire by the Holy Spirit in order to spread the sweet aroma of Jesus Christ to a dark world that smells of death's odor.

Is your life spreading the sweet aroma of Christ amongst all whom you come into contact with? Your words and thoughts and actions must be like a sweet-smelling candle!

God will help you. Call upon Him!

Be a candle!
6/4

Hello and Hi Everyone,

Compassion. It's a word that we all would agree with and would raise our hands in response to being asked if we desire to demonstrate this trait to others.

But do we understand the depth of the compassion that Jesus

showed us and the depth of the compassion we are called as Christians to show others?

"Put on then, as God's chosen ones, holy and beloved, compassionate hearts, kindness, humility, meekness, and patience." (Colossians 3:12)

We are called to wear clothing of compassion! When you wear clothing, it is visible to others as should be our compassion. But you may fall into the trap of thinking, as towards clothing, that it doesn't quite fit well. You need to give yourself sometime to lose weight and then the clothes will fit, and you can wear them. You do not need to allow more time to pass before you wear the clothing of compassion for all to see.

The time is now! Wear the clothing of compassion and when people ask who the brand of your clothing is, you have the opportunity to share Jesus! When you're compassionate to people, let them know, even before they ask, that Jesus is the great Savior!

"Give me…a compassionate heart, quickly moved to grieve for the woes of others and to active pity for them, even as our Lord Jesus Christ beheld our poverty and hasted to help us. Give me grace ever to alleviate the crosses and difficulties of those around me, and never to add to them; teach me to be a consoler in sorrow, to take thought for the stranger, the widow, and the orphan; let my charity show itself not in words only but indeed and truth." (Johann Arndt)

Wear compassion each day of your life!

6/5

Merry Christmas,

We are about 7 months away from Christmas! Have you put up your tree yet? How about the lights? Are your stockings hung and are your currently drinking hot chocolate?!

No?
Pray tell, why?

I know, I know. You're waiting until Christmas is only 5 months away. I understand and respect that.

I digress…

"Faith is believing something when common sense tells you not to."
(*Miracle On 34th Street*)

There are things within Christianity that do not make sense according to human logic, understanding, and common sense.

But, then again, if we could fully understand and explain God, He wouldn't be God. Why would we want to put our faith in Him if He was completely on our level? He wouldn't be big enough to create the universe or save us from hell.

God came near, and is near to those that call upon Him, but is also way above our understanding.

"Now faith is the assurance of things hoped for, the conviction of things not seen." (Hebrews 11:1)

You can have assurance in the things you hope for (like heaven) and a conviction that it exists and it's your destination, all through believing in Jesus Christ!

Believe in Jesus and the Bible, even when common sense tells you not to. You'll also find that having faith in Him is easier than having faith in something that came out of nothing.

Practice and live out your faith!

6/6

Greetings on this 6th of June,

It is the anniversary of D-Day. That day of days shall be remembered as a victorious day of tremendous sacrifice. Take a moment to reflect upon their sacrifice.

"This operation is not being planned with any alternatives. This operation is planned as a victory, and that's the way it's going to be. We're going down there, and we're throwing everything we have into it, and we're going to make it a success." (General Dwight D. Eisenhower)

Do you have this same mindset when it comes to the spiritual battle that is currently underway?

"But thanks be to God, who gives us the victory through our Lord Jesus Christ."
(1 Corinthians 15:57)

Live and fight each day knowing Jesus has won the victory; fight from the ground He has positioned you on.

There will be failures on your end, but don't lose heart. Awaken each day with your eyes fixed upon your Supreme Commander, Jesus Christ.

Prayer and the Bible are your weapons.
Seek not to relegate these to the back of your war chest.

Fight in the victory of Jesus Christ, your Lord and Savior!

6/7

Greetings and Good Greetings,

Remember the old Louis Armstrong song lyrics:

I see trees of green, red roses too
I see them bloom for me and you
And I think to myself what a wonderful world
I see skies of blue and clouds of white
The bright blessed day, the dark sacred night
And I think to myself what a wonderful world

We know that this world has many ugly parts and we are not home yet. But there is still beauty that God made for us and for His glory most importantly.

Psalm 19:1 says, "The heavens declare the glory of God, and the sky above proclaims his handiwork."

"The war made me poignantly aware of the beauty of the world." (J.R.R. Tolkien)

There is anti-beauty in the world, but those things can remind you of that beauty that you took for granted.

Don't take it for granted.
Be in awe each day of God's creation.
He created it for us, but most importantly to reflect Himself to the world that they might believe in Him, be in His presences, and bring Him honor and glory!

See it today and every day!

6/8

Greeeeetttttiiinnnngggssss!

The end of the world is today! Well (and that's a deep subject [like a well]), it could be tomorrow. It was probably was yesterday.

"Don't worry about the world coming to an end today. It's already tomorrow in Australia." (Charles Schultz)

Don't get caught up on when Jesus is coming back. Don't give ear to those that would claim they know when it's taking place. Just focus on knowing Jesus more and more each day and doing His work!

"But concerning that day or that hour, no one knows, not even the angels in heaven, nor the Son, but only the Father." (Mark 13:32)

"Have this mind among yourselves, which is yours in Christ Jesus, who, though he was in the form of God, did not count equality with God a thing to be grasped, but emptied Himself, by taking the form of a servant, being born in the likeness of men." (Philippians 2:5-7)

When Jesus was on earth, He voluntarily restricted Himself of some of His supernatural abilities, such as knowing all things. He was still 100% God and 100% man.

No man knows when Jesus is coming back so don't stress or seek to figure it out! Jesus, once He ascended back to heaven, unrestricted Himself and knew when His return would be.

Leave it in His hands! Be about His business, which is loving Him and telling others about Him!

He's coming!

6/9

Hello,

The Band of Brothers mini-series tells the true story of men who fought as members of the 101st Airborne Easy Company. One of the episodes focuses on the character, Sgt. Denver 'Bull' Randleman, after he made it back alive after being trapped behind enemy lines. Some of the men had gone after him on a rescue mission. He ended up making it out safely prior to them finding him, but their actions spoke volumes! Take a look at the following exchange:

Bill Guarnere: I don't know whether to slap you, kiss you, or salute you. I told these scallywags you was okay.
'Bull': And they didn't listen?
Bill Guarnere: Naw...they wanted to go on a suicide run to drag [you] back.
'Bull': Is that right?
Bill Guarnere: Yeah, I told 'em don't bother. [in jest]
'Bull': Never did like this company none. [in jest]

These men loved each other and risked their lives for each other. Love and devotion to each other compelled them onwards.

"And He said to them, 'Go into all the world and proclaim the gospel to the whole creation.'" (Mark 16:15)

Are you compelled to go out seeking for those that don't know Jesus? Are you compelled to seek out those that don't have a church home and invite them to yours?
Are you compelled by your love and devotion to Jesus Christ!?

"Declare His glory among the nations, His marvelous works among all the peoples!" (Psalm 96:3)

Are you compelled?

6/10

Greetings and Merry…greetings to you!

You thought I was gonna say it didn't you?! Ah ha!

Navy SEALs are an elite fighting force that protect our freedoms that God bestowed upon us which we so readily enjoy in the United States. We take these freedoms for granted; give thanks unto God and don't forget those that fight for our freedom's sake.

Here is a SEAL saying: "The only easy day was yesterday."
Their training is utterly intense, but here is a purpose behind it. It brings about the skills, both mentally and physically, that will equip them to accomplish their missions. They are truly a band of brothers.

So should the same mindset be with your walk with Christ.

"Share in suffering as a good soldier of Christ Jesus. No soldier gets entangled in civilian pursuits, since his aim is to please the one who enlisted him." (2 Timothy 2:3-4)

Look to accomplish the missions your Lord, your Commander, gives you each and every day! Embrace suffering, knowing that your fellow brothers and sisters in Christ are suffering as well. Suffering strengthens your relationship with Jesus, through and by the power of the Holy Spirit.

Don't flee suffering. Jesus will not flee from you.

Suffer and fight on in the strength of Jesus!

6/11

Good Greetings Everyone,

I hope you're doing well. But, even if you are not, remember Jesus' promise to never leave you nor forsake you. I came back yesterday from the Southern Baptist Convention and want to share the following with you that was brought up there: "When you belong to Jesus, you belong to love."

John 13:34-35 says, "A new commandment I give you, that you love one another: just as I have loved you, you also are to love one another. By this all people will know that you are my disciples, if you have love for one another." Wow, this is very easy to do! By no means. But we are called to nonetheless, by and with and through the power of the Holy Spirit. Loving like Jesus means being a servant, laying down our pride and desires, for the sake of others and for the glory of Jesus.

Romans 12:10 says, "Love one another with brotherly affection. Outdo one another in showing honor." This doesn't mean it's a competition and that we approach it in such a way that someone wins and another loses. The concept is that we strive to give and demonstrate through our words and actions all the love we possibly can towards others in the name of Jesus!

Approach today with these two verses at the forefront of your mind.

Approach tomorrow the same.

Approach each second of your life in such a way. Jesus did and He died and rose again that we might!

Go in His love!

6/12

Greetings on this day that God has made,

You can do and accomplish anything you set your mind to! Through hard work, sacrifice, and dedication, all of your dreams are attainable. Opportunities are around the bend and awaiting your passion to drive them to fruition.

Actually, that's a lie and unbiblical.
Don't stop reading. But do stop believing the above lies and stop perpetuating them to others, including children. We cannot, nor can or children, do and accomplish anything we set our minds to, only those things which God allows or gives us the abilities to accomplish.

A child may hope and dream about being a pro football player, a singer, a teacher, a mechanic, a doctor, a writer, etc., but God may have other plans through which He desires to use them for His glory.

And, if you were thinking towards one or some of the above, "Who dreams about being that?", reverse your thinking and never think that a certain job is below or above someone.

We must believe for ourselves, and communicate to others, including children, that we must pursue God and ask Him what He wants us to become! If He wants it, it will happen!

The word that came to Jeremiah from the Lord: "Arise, and go down to the potter's house, and there I will let you hear my words. So, I went down to the potter's house, and there he was working at his wheel. And the vessel he was making of clay was spoiled in the potter's hand, and he reworked it into another vessel, as it seemed good to the potter to do." (Jeremiah 18:1-4)

God will mold you into what He desires, both adults and children, and lead both into becoming who He has planned and doing what He has planned.

Seek Him and accomplish for Him!

-231-

6/13

Hello Everyone,

Captain Nixon said the following after a Nazi solider was killed in action: "That's Edelweiss. It grows in the mountains, above the tree line. Which means he climbed up there to get it. Supposed to be the mark of a true soldier." (*Band of Brothers*)

This soldier, though he had the mark of a true soldier, was fighting for the wrong side. He was fighting for a "kingdom" that was evil. He was not the example of a true solider.

What is the mark of a true Christian?

"He has told you, o man, what is good; and what does the Lord require of you but to do justice, and to love kindness, and to walk humbly with your God?" (Micah 6:8)

Be about doing the right thing and being a voice for those that don't.
Display friendliness to, and carry out consideration towards others in our speech and actions.
Be not prideful in all you do.

All for the sake, renouncement, and reflection of Jesus Christ.
Be one whose life displays the mark of a true Christian.

Be about Him!

6/14

Hi and Hello Everyone,

Do you ever feel distant from God? Do you question if He has left you?
Do you wonder if He even lives inside you anymore?

This is not some strange path your heart is on. But it's not one you should remain on. Get off when Christ is your guide!

Truth is the following from the Bible:

"Who shall separate us from the love of Christ? Shall tribulation, or distress, or persecution, or famine, or nakedness, or danger, or sword? For I am sure that neither death nor life, nor angels nor rulers, nor things present nor things to come, nor powers, nor height nor depth, nor anything else in all creation, will be able to separate us from the love of God in Christ Jesus our Lord." (Romans 8:25, 38-39)

Even when you don't feel Him, He's there with you. He has not abandoned you. Keep seeking Him, keep crying out to Him, keep Him above all other things in your life.

Keep Him for He keeps you!

6/15

Greetings,

Use this a quick reminder:

"It is the root of all religion that a man knows that he is nothing in order to thank God that he is something." (G.K. Chesterton)

Without Christ, each of us is nothing. We have nothing good in and of ourselves. This doesn't mean we treat people (regardless of religion) without love, respect, and kindness as if they are nothing.

We "were by nature children of wrath…" (Ephesians 2:3b)

But look at this:

"Therefore, if anyone is in Christ, he is a new creation. The old has passed away; behold, the new has come." (2 Corinthians 5:17)

We must remember who we are, who Jesus Christ is, and then who we are in Him.

Remember the order and its significance!

6/16

Greetings Everyone,

Are you ready?
For what?
Are you ready?!
I just asked for what?
You don't know?!

How could I know when I don't know?!
Good point.

Well, are you ready for a Disney quote?

"Life's not a spectator sport. If watchin' is all you're gonna do, then you're gonna watch your life go by without ya." (*The Hunchback of Notre Dame*)

So, as it is with the Christian life. You were not saved to be a Christian spectator. Neither was I. We were all saved to get into the battle, for that is what life is, a spiritual battle.

Will you watch, or will you participate?

"But be doers of the word, and not hearers only, deceiving yourselves." (James 1:22)

Find where God desires for you to serve and be active in your church! If you're unsure as to what area of ministry, ask someone at your church! Just don't stand by and watch.

You were saved not only to go to church, but to *be* the church!

Don't be a spectator!

6/17

Greetings,

Baseball season is upon us and spring training is taking place! Take a look see at this quote from one of the best to ever step foot on the diamond:

"My approach to every game was to try to erase the games that were before and try to focus on the game at hand." (Cal Ripken, Jr.)

A baseball player must have this approach in order to perform at his highest level. Cal's career is a testament to this mindset. He reaped the reward.

Paul said, "But one thing I do: forgetting what lies behind and straining forward to what lies ahead, I press on toward the goal for the prize of the upward call of God in Christ Jesus." (Philippians 3:13b-14)

The past is purposeful, but not all-powerful. Use it to learn from in order to live as Christ wants you to in the present. But don't dwell in the past! Press forward to the future prize of heaven! God has called you to such!

When you approach the plate of life today, you'll have a pitcher staring at you ready to throw his best pitch your way. As in baseball where you don't know what sort of pitch is coming your way, you don't know what sort of "pitch" you'll get thrown your way in life today. Remember this verse and stare down life today with God's Spirit dwelling in you:

"Just as I was with Moses, so I will be with you. I will not leave you or forsake you. Have I not commanded you? Be strong and courageous. Do not be frightened, and do not be dismayed, for the Lord your God is with you wherever you go." (Joshua 1:5b, 9)

Go forth today using the past to live more like Christ Jesus in the present, staring down the pitcher today in the power of Christ Jesus, who saved you from Hell's fire.

Step up to the plate!

6/18

Greetings,

Have you greeted someone with a graciousness and joyfulness that can only be described as godly? If not, why?

Don't let the world or your circumstances dictate your greeting. Don't walk around with a fake smile either. But even in trials, ask God to sweeten your speech and allow you to greet people with sincerity and love.

It matters. It really does!

It makes a difference!

It honors Jesus!

Greetings!

6/19

Hello Everyone,

I remember calling my mom and when she would answer, I would find out she had been spending time with the Lord. She wasn't bragging about it at all, it's just what she was doing.

She loves spending time with her Savior, in prayer and in the reading of His Word.

Do you love it? If someone were to call you and they found out you were having prayer time with God or were reading His Word, would they be shocked?

If not, today is the day that you can change that and make it a way of life, not for others, but for your walk with God and for His glory.

If yes, then don't become prideful, but press deeper and deeper into your relationship with God!

Ring ring!

6/20

Hi and Hello,

Take some time today to not use social media, email, TV, radio, or any other form of modern technology. Just be in Christ without any added feature.

Breathe and meditate on His goodness. That doesn't mean the world is good or events are good. God is God and God is good, regardless of our situations.

Reflect upon all He is and all He has done.

Sign off in order to sign back in refueled for life!

6/21

Greetings,

Have you seen *The Great Muppet Caper*? If not, I forgive you! (Just kidding of course)

But here is an exchange from the movie:

Beauregard: [driving a cab] You can call me Beauregard. Where are you guys going?

Kermit: The Happiness Hotel.

Beauregard: Oh good, that's where I'm going. How do you get there?

Fozzie Bear: Haven't you ever been there?

Beauregard: Of course! I live there. I just don't know how to get there.

Could this describe your faith, in a way? Your home is in heaven, but you aren't really comfortable in knowing how to explain to someone why they need Jesus and how to become a Christian?

If so, faint not! Take time, even if you have done it before and are comfortable, to practice sharing your faith with others and sharpening up in order to be prepared to discuss questions that come your way.

Don't worry, the Holy Spirit will guide you and if you don't know answers to questions, don't make up an answer.

Let the person know you don't know and that you'd like to take time to find out and talk with them again!

Know your faith!

6/22

Good Morning or Evening,

Why did you tie your shoes like that?
They're my shoes.
Why did you do it that way? I would have done it this way and it would have been better.

We can be so very critical at times. Why? Our eyes are horizontal instead of vertical.
God could critique out every little smidgeon of your life and reveal it to others. How would you feel then?

There is a balance of critiquing with the correct motive, but don't do it for your own ride.

Thank goodness Jesus didn't choose to abandon the cross out of the result of critiquing His Father and choosing another path that would not lead to the salvation of our souls!

Go forth in His grace!

6/23

Greetings,

Live on the doorstep of Hell.
What?!!!!!!!

Seek to tell anyone and everyone you can about Jesus. Don't live in your safe and comfortable world, unwilling to go where He calls and do what He tells you to do.

Seek those that no one else desires to seek because Jesus loves them. They are no different than you. Hell is real.

Live on this side of it, but on its doorstop in order to grab all you can from its flames (through the power of the Holy Spirit because you are a servant, not the Savior).

Live to tell!

6/24

"'Good Morning!' said Bilbo, and he meant it. The sun was shining, and the grass was very green. But Gandalf looked at him from under long bushy eyebrows that stuck out further than the brim of his shady hat.

'What do you mean?' he said. 'Do you wish me a good morning, or mean that it is a good morning whether I want it or not; or that you feel good this morning; or that it is a morning to be good on?'
'All of them at once,' said Bilbo."
(*The Hobbit*)

What do we really mean by the words we say? Communication is vital and the consequences are weighty therefore, be aware of how and what you always say!

"Let no corrupting talk come out of your mouths, but only such as is good for building up, as fits the occasion, that it may give grace to those who hear." (Ephesians 4:29)

Dwell on this verse.
Remember this verse.
Fall in love with this verse.

Live it as you let the Holy Spirit lead you with each thing you say.

Good morning!

6/25

Good Gut-Punch Greetings!

"I like your Christ, I do not like your Christians. Your Christians are so unlike your Christ." (Mahatma Gandhi)

You're not perfect, but you're held to a higher standard. Be mindful of this reality.

Don't walk on eggshells, but take up your cross and follow your Savior, knowing you're a target.

Embrace this reality and relish its opportunities to reflect Jesus.

Be a willing target!

6/26

Greetings,

You know something that I've never experienced?

True, I have never had fried-bologna or wrestled a human-sized ant, but what I was really talking about was night vision in the wilderness.

Those goggles utilize the moon's light in order to illuminate your sight. Don't spend today trying to self-illuminate your vision in a dark world. Use His light, His Word. Use prayer.

Jesus will give you clear vision to see the both what He wants you to do and the enemy's traps.

See in the light with His light!

6/27

Hello Everyone,

Provider and Giver.

Those are two of God's characteristics. Remember them in a world of take and exploit.

God gave unto you. Give unto Him. You are a steward, and a manager of the money and possessions He has given you.

Do they possess you? How willing are you to give before getting? Do you give faithfully to your church?

Check yourself and see.

Give unto the One who gave everything for you!

6/28

Good Greetings!

Do you feel a fire and passion? Do you have a relentless desire? If yes, for what? For sharing Jesus Christ with others?

"And he said to them, 'Go into all the world and proclaim the gospel to the whole creation.'" (Mark 16:15)
**Jesus said it and therefore we must obey it and give it our all!

"I would rather die now than live a life of oblivious ease in so sick a world."
(Nate Saint, who died for Christ in South America)
**Do you have this same mindset? Or are you content with living in your comfortable circle without taking risks for Christ in a lost and dying world?

"God uses men who are weak and feeble enough to lean on Him."
(Hudson Taylor, who served as a missionary in China)
**God uses people who don't think they have it all together. We must be humble and understand that we cannot do His work apart from His strength.

"All God's giants have been weak men who did great things for God because they reckoned on God being with them." (Hudson Taylor)
**Humility is key, knowing you can't do anything apart from Christ and having faith that He will walk with you through whatever He calls you to do.

"Every Christian is either a missionary or an imposter." (Charles Spurgeon)
(As Christians, we are commanded in the Great Commission to tell others about Jesus, which makes us missionaries.

These quotes can come across as harsh, but they are the truth used to wake us up and show us how we should be waking and walking in Jesus.

"And he said to them, 'Go into all the world and proclaim the gospel to the whole creation.'" (Mark 16:15)

Reflect on these quotes and memorize these Scriptures. Take action. Share Jesus with others. Invite others to church. Be a missionary wherever you are and wherever He calls you. He died for us. He commands us. He loves us. He saved us. Live for Him! Go forth in the power of the Holy Spirit!

6/29

Home Greetings,

Remember the movie, *Wizard of Oz*? Dorothy would tap her heels together and say, "There's no place like home. There's no place like home." Why? Because home was a place of love and peace.

Is your home like that, or is it a place of chaos and unrest?

Through Christ and in Him, your home can be a place of rest, love, and peace regardless of size or location. Seek to put Him first through the showing of grace to each other.

Seek to listen to each other and choose to have your home be a place of refuge.

Pray, read His Word.
Resolve to have moments where work is not discussed, and laughter is medicine.

Seek to have your home be His home!

6/30

Greetings and Hello,

Do you like Disney movies?
I like them, not all, but some. Here's a quote from the movie, *Cinderella*:

"No matter how your heart is grieving, if you keep on believing, the dream that you wish will come true." (Cinderella)

It's a good movie, but this quote is unbiblical. When we are grieving, sometimes we are apt to follow any sort of "feel good" message that says if you claim it, it will happen. The name is and claim it message of people like Joel Osteen is false.

God does not necessarily promise relief from pain. He promises eternal rest and to never leave you. He does not promise that all of your dreams will come true.

But, keep reading.

Give you dreams to God and ask Him to either take them away from you and replace them with His plans for your life or guide and direct your steps in obtaining the dreams if they are of Him. Ask Him to conform your dreams to His desires. His desires for your life are infinitely better than your own!

Desire His desires!

6/31

Good night,

Gotcha.

Remember the phrase that said, "Sticks and stones may break my bones, but words will never hurt me?" That's a lie from the pit of hell. Words either cut or give life.

A great philosopher once said, "If you can't say something nice, don't say nothin' at all." (Thumper from the movie *Bambi*)

Your words are important and the Bible is clear about this.

They can turn someone towards, or away from Jesus. You can rewind a movie at home, but not the words that come out of your mouth.

Be word-wise today and every day!

7/1

Greetings and Hello,

Katie Kaspar, my beautiful wife, is an example for me to follow. She's godly, diligent, hardworking, caring, loving, and creative amongst other qualities.

Have a good day!

But seriously, seek to tell how great someone else is today, not for a personal agenda, but because you want to praise someone (not in an idolatry sort of way) that you care about.

Doing this will reflect Jesus to a lost and dying world and be good medicine for the person you are speaking about.

By the way, God has a great plan for your life! He does, despite any circumstance or the arrows fired your way from the enemy!

7/2

Greetings,

I love Pooh Bear. I do. We have a Christmas Pooh Bear currently out in our home.

But I also like to share things that can be different in thinking.
Do I have your curiosity peeked?

"You're braver than you believe, and stronger than you seem, and smarter than you think." (Christopher Robin to Winnie the Pooh)

As much as I love Pooh Bear, this quote is humanistic and promotes self-empowerment over Christ-empowerment.

Seek Christ to give you courage, strength, and wisdom.

Don't look unto yourself, look to God in His Word and through prayer.

Long live Pooh Bear, just not the above quote!

7/3

Greetings,

"God won't give you more than you can handle."
Have you heard this before?

It's untrue!
You will encounter multitudes more than you can handle.

God is God and He can handle it!
Release it into His hands!

"Come to me, all who labor and are heavy laden, and I will give you rest. Take my yoke upon you, and learn from me, for I am gently and lowly in heart, and you will find rest for your souls. For my yoke is easy, and my burden is light." (Matthew 11:28-30)

Release!

7/4

Good freedom greetings,

What in the wide round world do I mean by that?! Freedom is a gift for you this morning and is present with you. How so?
There are two different types of freedom I want to briefly talk about.

Today Independence Day. It has been said, "land of the free because of the brave." This week think of ways you can thank veterans for their service. When you see someone that has served, shake their hand. Give them a warm smile accompanied with thoughtful words of thanks.

We must not forget our veterans and present service members, but most importantly, we must not forget God who is the ultimate source of the freedom we experience in America. He is most gracious to give and sustain the freedom we have.

Yet, there is an even greater freedom that some experiencing the freedom in America do not experience. This is the freedom of Jesus Christ!

"For freedom Christ has set us free; stand firm therefore, and do not submit again to a yoke of slavery." (Galatians 5:1)

Jesus Christ offers freedom from sin, addictions, your past, and any shackles that are holding you down and keeping you from experience life abundantly in Him. Someone can experience this freedom when they accept Jesus! If you haven't, I plead with you to not let this moment pass you by. Take time to pray, confessing and repenting of your sin, professing to Jesus that you believe in Him, and asking Him to come into your live as your Savior and Lord!

But...
For those that have already accepted Jesus, they can still become shackled by the flesh through the desires that can slowly and deceitfully gain footing within their soul.

Are you shackled right now? Don't quickly say 'no'!
Are you?
You may not be, but you may.

If you are, come to Christ right now and humbly confess your sin, shackles, and cry out for freedom.
He will answer.
If you're not, gives thanks for Christ and continue this prayer each moment of each day.

For each follower of Christ, stand firm through the Holy Spirit by praying, reading the Bible, and having fellowship with believers.

Thank veterans and the active service members you come in contact with. Pray for them and thank God for them.

Remember the freedom we have in America.
Vote, especially for those who hold closest to the values of the Bible.

But remember most the freedom offered in Jesus. Thank Him for the freedom in America, but most importantly for the freedom of your soul through Jesus Christ.

Let freedom ring!

7/5

Hello Everyone,

"Let us run with endurance the race that is set before us, 2 looking to Jesus, the founder and perfecter of our faith, who for the joy that was set before him endured the cross…" (Hebrews 12:1b-2a)

Remember Jesus' love, mercy, and grace!
Reflect upon His sacrifice!
Prepare your heart for the journey ahead, wherever He may lead (no matter if it doesn't involve a physical move).

Each day should be a spiritual journey with Jesus!

Remember - Reflect - Prepare

Go in Him!

7/7

Greetings and Hello,

It seems that each thought we have and discussion that takes place is always upright and firm yet loving.

You may be wondering if I'm asleep and dreaming as I write this! There are many heated discussions or rants taking place nowadays.

Here is a tidbit for the day as you go forward in Christ, clinging to Him, and standing for Him as you plant your flag on heaven's shores:

Conviction must not be confused with emotion. Conviction leads to unyielding resolve while emotion leads to faltering regression.

The first is founded on truth, while the second is founded on sentimentalism.

Be one of conviction!

7/8

Good Greetings,

God is still on His throne.

He was not, and shall never be, up for election or re-election. Rest in that truth.

Rest in Him. Music--like the old CD players where you would shuffle to a song of your choosing. Or when you're driving through town with your sweetheart, or on the highway after a long and stressful day at work, or across the open plains as you seek to clear your head, you shuffle songs searching for music to listen to that plays to the emotions of your heart and soul.

Death. The mere word conjures a variety of emotions for the brain to shuffle through. How do you find the right emotion to settle on? Sorrow for loss.

Joy for the remembrance of fond times. Questioning for wanting to understand the reason of their passing.

The shuffle will continue. There will be times for the remainder of your days when you experience one or all of these emotions.

Over the past short period of time, people within my circle have been suffering the loss of someone. Maybe your circle has as well. I have lost a friend recently myself. Maybe you have as well.

I do not understand why. I do not understand God's timing. I do not understand.

But He is still sovereign. He is still loving. He is still good. He is still faithful. He is, He is, He forever will be.

I remember reading a quote from Rich Mullins in which he said how God never gave Job an answer as to why he went through that multitude of suffering. God simply gave Job Himself and that was enough.

For anyone that has or is suffering the loss of someone, remember God is loving, faithful, good, and sovereign over every single rain drop that falls and every event that transpires.

"Even to your old age I am He, and to gray hairs I will carry you. I have made, and I will bear; I will carry and will save." (Isaiah 46:4)

"'For my thoughts are not your thoughts, neither are your ways My ways,' declares the Lord. 'For as the heavens are higher than the earth, so are My ways higher than your ways and My thoughts than your thoughts.'" (Isaiah 55:8-9)

My grandfather used to say, "This is not my home, I'm just a-passin' through."

Indeed, our home is in heaven with Jesus. Jesus loves and knows us, this we know.

From one who's just a-passin' through to another, have a solid day in Jesus!

7/9

Greetings,

God made men and woman equal in value, but different in roles. Both are to bring God glory through Jesus Christ.

These differences in roles are vital and important. They do not diminish either man or woman in value.

The human error takes place when we switch the roles in the name of elevating value for it is then that we stray away from Jesus' plan and purpose for our lives and forfeit the glorious bi-products that result from living out our God-given roles in equality of value.

Be of His business today and every day!

7/10

Helllllllooooooo and how are we this morning?!

Remember God loves you and desires to make you more like His son. He will never give up on you no matter what--*never*.

Christianity is more than Facebook posts, songs we listen to, doctrines we hold to, and creeds we confess.

Christianity is a personal and authentic walk with the creator of the universe, who is Jesus Christ which leads to holy speaking, thinking, and living.

To live in a holy manner means living set apart in Jesus radically different from the world, yet always loving (but never compromising or condoning) the world with the love of Jesus.

Seek to live a holy life that reflects Jesus to a lost and dying world!

7/11

Greetings,

Picture a candle burning brightly.
Picture a large bonfire aglow.

Now…

The fierceness of God's all-encompassing character burns eternally, despite the ashes of sin that exude from our broken humanity.

He desires to refine our lives by His holy fire.

Ask Him to burn away the old twigs of your fleshly desires, blow away the ashes, and cultivate His roots deep within your soul!

Second…

Ask someone if you can pray for him or her today.

It's a witness for Christ to those that don't know Him.
It gives you another opportunity to talk with your Creator, Lord, and Savior.
It encourages fellow Christians.

Pray and ask to pray!

7/12

Greetings on this morning!

Do you ever feel that life is just one battle after another? That old saying, "when it rains, it pours," seems to be very true sometimes. But God (aren't those two powerful words which are seen in the Bible?!) will walk through life's battles with His people.

The spiritual battle is a real one and must not be taken lightly. Paul writes in Ephesians 6:12:
"For we do not wrestle against flesh and blood, but against the rulers, against the authorities, against the cosmic powers over this present darkness, against the spiritual forces of evil in the heavenly places."

We can only battle through the power of Jesus Christ.
See this portion of a prayer that I invite you to pray and meditate on, possibly written by St. Patrick:

Christ shield me today
Against wounding
Christ with me, Christ before me, Christ behind me,
Christ in me, Christ beneath me, Christ above me,
Christ on my right, Christ on my left,
Christ when I lie down, Christ when I sit down,
Christ in the heart of everyone who thinks of me,
Christ in the mouth of everyone who speaks of me,
Christ in the eye that sees me,
Christ in the ear that hears me.

I arise today
Through the mighty strength
Of the Lord of creation.

Battle on as a Christ follower with the Holy Spirit indwelling you.

Battle and hold to Him!

7/13

Greetings Everyone,

Remember the sacrifices of saints before
Remember the calling of which they bore

Remember the joy with which they served
Remember the prize which for them was reserved

Remember the doctrine that each one held
Remember the mercy by which they were compelled

Remember Jesus and His gift of pure grace
Remover the promise by which one day we shall see His face

Remember...

Please remember!

7/14

Greetings,

That which you are willing to die for will reveal that which you are choosing to live for.

Please take time and ponder. Then fill in the blanks:

I am willing to die for ______________________ (include as many things as you desire). Therefore, I'm choosing to live for ______________________ (include the same things).

Are they all God-honoring? If not, follow God's leading to ensure they are.

Be willing!

7/15

Greetings and Hi,

As Christians, we cannot base our beliefs and our interpretations upon our feelings. We must base them solely upon the Bible, God's Word.

God built the foundation for our beliefs.
God gives us wisdom to interpret.
Believers before us have suffered and died for the sake of God's Word.

Let us not fail in holding the line!

7/16

Merry Morning Everyone!

Wait...it's not Christmas and how can a person be merry on a Thursday morning? We can be merry every morning of the year knowing that we belong to Jesus and that whatever comes to pass, He is in control. He still speaks. The Lion of Judah still roars.

Are we listening?

Have you ever been at a concert where the music, or a restaurant where the noise, was deafening loud and you could not hear what the person next to you was saying? Or have you been on the phone with someone and the reception was not clear and you could not fully understand the other person? Maybe someone has even been calling your name, but you did not hear their voice...or heard it and chose to ignore it.

1 Samuel 3:10 says,
"And the LORD came and stood, calling as at other times, 'Samuel! Samuel!' And Samuel said, 'Speak, for your servant hears.'"

Samuel heard the voice of God and responded. He submitted himself before God and chose to listen to whatever God would tell him.

God spoke. Samuel listened.

There are many voices that cry out to us during the course of the day. Many. But there is only one voice that we should, and must, listen to. The voice of Jesus Christ.

That voice is spoken to us through the Bible, prayer and a variety of venues that God so chooses. Always rely upon the Holy Spirit to decipher the voices that shout out and you will know which are of God and which are of this world.

The Lion of Judah still roars.
The Lion's voice is still more powerful than the world's.

Listen and find joy is your Master's voice.

Have a great day as you listen!

7/17

Good Greetings,

Our mere mortal words fall into an inadequacy chasm
For how can we express thanks for a love we cannot fathom

Our souls were sentenced to eternal damnation
For we were enemies of God's heavenly nation

Our Christ, He came and dwelt among men
For to pay our penalty for our sin He left heaven

Our hearts He calls to and desires to live in
For thus let us forever give thanks for our salvation He did win!

7/18

From one wretch saved by grace to another, good morning!

Have you ever driven through the kind of rain that is falling so powerfully upon your windshield, that your vision is obstructed to the point where you become fearful, anxious, or worried? It's a serious moment and one that the individual feels a sense of relief when it passes and clear vision has once again been gained.

What does the forecast upon your own life look like? Have you or do you currently feel as though the rains of day to day life are falling so powerfully upon the windshield of your soul, that you no longer have clarity about the future or a particular situation?

Solomon says in Proverbs 25:2,
"It is the glory of God to conceal a matter, but the glory of kings is to search things out."

God will conceal answers and direction from us until He sees fit in His infinite wisdom to reveal them to us. God desires to us to seek Him in prayer and the reading of His Word for direction and clarity for every aspect and course of our lives. When we become frustrated, worried, or anxious...we must approach the throne of love and grace...asking the Father to help us in our weakness. We must ask Him to help us continue to seek after Him, trusting and obeying through it all.

In fact, sometimes He will never give us an answer as to why something happened. Why? Because He is God and we are not...and He desires for us to trust that though we may never know the answer, we know the One who does know the answer...and that is more than enough.

And it is really and incomparably more than enough...just to know Jesus.

Seek Jesus and make Him known today and for the remainder of your days!

7/19

Hello and Hi,

Suggestions, not commandments, our hearts do prefer
Many teach "it's about you" and our feelings concur

Yet Jesus did not leave a list of suggestions
His way, not our feelings, must fill our confessions

Jesus loves and He saves, for He showed us the way
To obey His commandments, waiting for that glorious day

Follow His commands and not your heart's suggestions!

7/20

Good Greetings,

How often do we let those we love, those we lead, those who are our friends and family...know that we have confidence in them? Not in a way that we are placing our trust and confidence in them over Jesus. But in a way that encourages them and affirms that we trust them and have confidence in them that they can get the job done with and through Jesus Christ.

Paul said, "I rejoice, because I have complete confidence in you." (2 Corinthians 7:16)

Let those you love, those you lead, your friends and family...know that you rejoice because you have confidence in them to accomplish what God has given them and through the power of Jesus Christ!

Hold onto Jesus,

7/21

Greetings and Hi,

Time.
?
Time.
What do you mean?

Be a reflection of Jesus with your time. Don't be lazy with it. When no one is watching, what are you doing with your time? Even if it's not "bad," is it honoring to Him. If not, take some time to pray on how to change your game plan.

When you mention a time to someone, honor it…either by beginning on time, or showing up on time. Actually, the old saying is that if you're on time, you're late. Be early!

Strive to honor God with your time!

7/22

Greetings!

How do you live? Do you live with a desire to eat an Aunty Ann Pretzel right now?
They are good and even better with a nice cold lemonade!

Pretzels for everyone. In fact, if you turn the page, you'll find a coupon for a free one.

But in all seriousness…

Live for eternity by living in the present!

GOD calls you to impact HIS kingdom by giving you a grip on reality with heavenly vision!

Ask Him to give you wisdom and His eyes!

7/23

Greetings!

Quick thought for today…

In a world full of knives and spoons, be a fork!

Knives seek to cut people down, criticize, communicate disrespectfully, and not take stands in and through love.

Spoons are passive, fearful of being criticized for standing up for truth, desire for everyone to get along at the expense of lovingly holding the live for truth.

Forks stand in and for the truth of God, passionately and in love. They are respectful, but not passive. Encountering a fork is encountering Jesus, for Jesus is so apparent in their life.

When someone comes into contact with them, they see Jesus and are brought to a decision point: Do I follow Jesus or turn away from Him?

In a world full of knives and spoons, be a fork!

7/24

Good Afternoon Everyone,

There are many imitations out there right? But you know when you come across the real deal. The imitations may appear to be legitimate at first, but sooner or later something happens that awakens you to the fact that there is a falsity present.

Have you ever seen imitation fruit that's for display purposes? It could never satisfy someone's hunger.

What about some of the posts that go around on Facebook that state certain "facts"? Then they turn out to actually be false posts.

Paul says in 1 Thessalonians 5:21,
"but test everything; hold fast what is good."

You see, there are many different imitations of truth out in the world. There are pleasures, places, activities, etc. that reflect a false sense of what is good...what is godly. There are many people that speak, claiming to communicate truth, when in fact, they are verbalizing evil and beliefs that contradict God's Word.

We must test everything using God's Word as our truth source... everything. Movies, places we eat at, music we listen to, magazines we browse at the store, topics we discuss, jokes we laugh at or tell. For even the slightest imitation of good can lead us down a perilous path to destruction.

Is an imitation worth hurting our relationship with God, family or friends? Though the answer is "no," are we implementing a process in our lives to test everything in order to see what is good and godly? Are we then choosing to hold fast and not be moved from the truth?

We must choose for ourselves today what our answers and actions will thus be.

Press into Jesus and He shall not fail you.

Have a wonderful day testing and holding fast!

-279-

From One Beggar to Another
Nathan Kaspar

7/25

Greetings,

Don't live in the past, but look back at it to a healthy extent. Why would I want to look back at my past…it's the past for a reason!

There's a difference between dwelling in your past and looking back at it. Dwelling is unhealthy because it prevents you from living in the present.

Looking back allows you to remind yourself from whence God brought you and motivate you to live better in the present, for the renown of Jesus Christ's name!

Maybe you never healed from wounds in the past. You may have put a band aide on a wound instead of going through the necessary surgery. It's time to revisit the past in order to fully heal the right way in Christ Jesus.

Revisit, but don't dwell in the past in order to fully live for Jesus in the present.

Past for the present!

7/26

Greetings,

Quick devo today…

"You have made us for yourself, and our heart is restless until it rests in you."
(Augustine, Confessions)

No relationship, job, hobby, amount of money, vacation, talent, dream come true…can truly give you rest.

Stop fighting it. Stop pursuing others means.
Rest in Jesus and pursue Him above everything else.
Everything else will be ordered by His providence.

Rest and pursue!

7/27

Greetings,

Do you attend church for yourself or for God? The point of attending church is not that you would feel better, but that God would be glorified.

We obey God when we attend church and we glorify Him in doing so with a sincere heart.

As you worship through song and the hearing of the Word and through fellowship, your soul will be strengthened, but that is a bi-product of glorifying God.

Keep the correct order, for His glory!

Second…

Observation or no observation?
What does thou mean?

Should you go through observation or should you not?

What in the name of all that is candy canes, multi-colored lights and tinsel are you talking about!?

You mentioned Christmas, I didn't. Let the record show.

Ok, now that we covered that.

A member of our church fell last night and is still at the hospital for observation. The medical staff wants to make sure she does not have a concussion in order for her to go back home in the proper health state.

Don't be too quick to respond once you have suffered a tough day, heartache, disagreement, etc. Take pause to make sure your heart and mind are right, according to God's Word and His will. Sometimes this will mean keeping your mouth shut. Sometimes it will mean not pursuing another relationship. Sometimes it will mean agreeing to disagree, say I love you, and going to sleep, not in anger, but with the agreement that you'll both address the issue at hand tomorrow.

Instead of counting to ten, count on God's Spirit to guide you into action!

Be quick to count, slow to act!

7/28

Good modest day to you,

Modesty is a way of reflecting Jesus to a lost and dying world. You may be thinking to yourself, "Oh no. He's going to say that all women have to wear bonnets and ankle length dresses!"

Honestly, those are not wrong to wear. And if you think so or make fun of those that do, then quit it.

But the trend of clothing, for both men and women is not one of modesty. Take time today to think if they way you dress reflects modesty? The stores you shop at…do they reflect modesty?

If not, what are you prepared to do?

Extremely tight and form fitting clothing for women, both tops and bottoms, are not godly and do not reflect Jesus.

Extremely right and form fitting clothing for men, both tops and bottoms, are not godly as well and do not reflect Jesus.

I know it can come across as harsh and point blank, but it's the biblical truth.

What is your motive for wearing them? Even if you don't feel you have a bad motive, you must stop.

The truth is that it does not encapsulate modesty. It does not encourage pure thinking from others.

Yes, people have their own responsibility with how they think, but you are responsible for setting a good example and not being a stumbling block.

You are responsible for reflecting Jesus.

This is a hard, harsh day of statements. But harshness resides in truth sometimes. Please know we are all in this together.

Embrace harsh truth to reflect Jesus to a harsh, lost and dying world!

-285-

7/29

Hello and Hi,

You are going to die. No, no, no…that's not a threat or any sort of a call to violence against you or anyone else.

It's a fact. You and I are going to die one day. Although, that day is unknown to us.

Are you prepared? Not just are you a Christian and prepared for where you will go, but are you prepared in the sense that how you are living now is how you want to go out?

If not, change! Ask God to help you! Get plugged into His Word, Prayer and His Church!

Be ready!

7/30

Other forms of a salutation insert here,

Some of today's message may seem obvious, or it may seem foreign, or it may seem controversial. Here we go on some points that are important for your Christian walk.

Horoscopes have no room in a Christian's life! The crux of the matter is that they are of Satan. God is the only that knows the future. Trust it in His hands.

Strippers are never ok, no matter what the occasion! Neither are strip clubs. Also, don't fall into the trap of "one last night of freedom" before your wedding. Don't get married if that's your mindset.

Movies such as 50 Shades of Grey are evil! They don't promote godly sexuality or godly relationships. It's not honoring to God or your spouse or your future spouse.

Pursue Jesus, not these! What may seem harmless is very harmful. Pursue Him, not these! It's not being legalistic, but biblical!

Pursue Jesus passionately!

7/31

Hello and Greetings,

Do you exercise? No, sitting up to get out of bed and laying back down does not count as a crunch or sit-up!

I average running 26.2 miles each day. Well, maybe not.

But, I do average 26.2 miles in the morning.

Bottom line is that we as Christians, and I'm completely guilty, do not honor God with our bodies as we are called to. That doesn't mean we become addicted to working out or obsessed with it (as some indeed have become).

But it does mean we are called to take care of our bodies, which are the temple of the Holy Spirit, through the food we eat the through the exercise we partake in (as we are physically capable of).

Get fit spiritually and physically!

Now get after it!

8/1

Greet to the ings,

Time for a good military movie! If you don't like them, that's completely fine. But, I encourage you to still take some time to watch a good one that depicts the history of what our armed forces have gone through to protect this country.

Here is a quote from the movie *Patton*.

"For over a thousand years Roman conquerors returning from the wars enjoyed the honor of triumph, a tumultuous parade. In the procession came trumpeters, musicians and strange animals from conquered territories, together with carts laden with treasure and captured armaments. The conquerors rode in a triumphal chariot, the dazed prisoners walking in chains before him. Sometimes his children robed in white stood with him in the chariot or rode the trace horses. A slave stood behind the conqueror holding a golden crown and whispering in his ear a warning: that all glory is fleeting."

The point here is not slavery. Slavery is horrendous and unbiblical. The point here is the last portion of the last sentence.

Remember it and don't waste your days. Seek not your fame, but the fame of Jesus.
His glory is not fleeting. Yours is.

Pursue Him!

8/2

Good Day!

Can we all agree that a balanced dosage of self-esteem is healthy for one's personal life?

Wait...but is it really?

The definition of esteem is: "to regard highly or favorably; regard with respect or admiration."

If we take an honest look at this definition and reflect upon God's Word, should we desire any sort of self-esteem?

Let's take a look...

"Christ in you, the hope of glory." (Colossians 1:27)
**Christ is the hope in a person, not the person himself or herself. There is nothing hopeful within a person on their own.

"I have been crucified with Christ. It is no longer I who live, but Christ who lives in me. And the life I now live in the flesh I live by faith in the Son of God, who loved me and gave himself for me." (Galatians 2:20)
**When a person becomes a Christian, they surrender their life over to Christ. He is their new commander instead of their selfish-flesh. A believer now lives no longer by faith in their own ability, but by faith in Jesus and His sovereignty.

Both of these verses speak nothing of self-esteem or self-empowerment. Why? Because the truth is we have nothing redeeming or self-saving in and of ourselves. It is only in and of Jesus.

Jesus, not ourselves. Christ-esteem, not self-esteem. We have a devo earlier in the year about this, but we all need a reminder!

Rest in the truth you don't have to be your personal savior. Rest in the truth that you don't have to find the strength or hope in and of yourself. Jesus, Jesus, Jesus. Nothing more and nothing less.

Ask Jesus to build up your Christ-esteem today and always!

8/3

Greetings,

Are you a Christian on any day that ends in "y"? Yes, once a Christian, always a Christian. But, are you truly living out your faith each and every day. Or do you reserve that for Sunday or other times your up at church?

The Navy SEALs have a motto: All In, All The Time.

That must be every Christian's motto. Christ didn't suffer and die so we could be casual, comfortable, part-time Christians.

Be all in!

8/4

Greetings and Hi,

Don't be envious. It's tough because we like things we see and think, "How does he or she deserve them?"

"As a moth gnaws a garment, so doth envy consume a man." (St. John Chrysostom)

Pray for a grateful heart, not matter what, and for all and at all times. Truth is that there is not one single good thing which God has given us that we did not deserve.

Jesus is gracious. Be not envious.

Be thankful instead (of all He has given and done)!

8/5

As I write this, I'm waiting to pick up Katie after she gets off work. This is a place of much pain, sickness, despair, anger, fatigue, and questions.

Children and adults, all going through suffering…as a patient or the caregiver.

The world, from a spiritual sense is full of the same. We as the church are called to direct them to the Great Physician. He alone can heal hearts and save souls.

Medical staff must tell patients hard to swallow truths. This news is not desirable to hear, nor is it what seems fair to hear.

But it's the truth. Then the medical staff can take the proper steps and the patient can as well.

The same is true of Christians. We must tell the world hard truths in order to tell them of the One who is their only hope…Jesus Christ.

Go forth today and be His follower. Be one that tells others hard truths, in order to tell them about the Great Physician of their soul!

Hard truth in a hard world with a solid hope!

8/6

Hi Everyone,

Hang with me through what I'm initially going to mention!

Truly He taught us to love one another;
His law is Love and His gospel is Peace;
Chains shall he break, for the slave is our brother,
And in his name all oppression shall cease,
Sweet hymns of joy in grateful Chorus raise we;
Let all within us praise his Holy name!

Chorus
Christ is the Lord, then ever! ever praise we!
His pow'r and glory, evermore proclaim!
His pow'r and glory, evermore proclaim!

Yes, it is a Christmas song, but look beyond that. Look at the rich meaning and the depth of the Christian faith of which it proclaims. There are various Christmas songs that are praise and worship songs!

Songs with this kind message are for all seasons. Dwell on the above lyrics and sing them out to your Savior, even now!

Seek another such Christmas song today!

8/7

Greetings,

Make a prayer plan today!
What?
You know a prayer plan!
No, I don't know. Which is why I asked.

My bad!

Each day, write down the following on a piece of paper and store them all together: something you're thankful for, person you're thankful for, characteristic of God you're thankful for, person you desire to come to know Jesus, the prayer need of another, a prayer need for yourself, a prayer want.

Prayer them through, but always end with thanking God again for what He has given you and who He is. Ask that His will be done.

Do this for a month and revisit it. Try to do it each month!

8/8

Greetings!

"So neither I nor my brothers nor my servants nor the men of the guard who followed me, none of us took off our clothes; each kept his weapon at his right hand." (Nehemiah 4:23)

We live in a very comfortable country, compared to many other countries in this world. Very comfortable. This comfortability can very easily lead to our letting down our guard. We don't feel we have to be on alert as much.

But..."Be sober-minded; be watchful. Your adversary the devil prowls around like a roaring lion, seeking someone to devour. Resist him, firm in your faith, knowing that the same kinds of suffering are being experienced by your brotherhood throughout the world. And after you have suffered a little while, the God of all grace, who has called you to His eternal glory in Christ, will Himself restore, confirm, strengthen, and establish you." (1 Peter 5:8-10)

Don't let your guard down. Always seek Jesus through prayer and the reading of His Word. Know that the devil is pursuing you, seeking to bring you down and cause you to fall as he knows your weaknesses. But, also know that one day all will be made right when you get to heaven. This life is but a milli-milli-milli-second compared to eternity. Be encouraged that others Christians are going through trials and tribulations as well.

Jesus will always walk with His people!
Walk with Him through it all!

8/9

Greetings,

Knock, knock!
Who's there?
I don't know.
I don't know who?
Exactly.

What in the name of all that is peanut butter and chocolate does that mean?
Yep, exactly.

Confusing right? So are the ways and tactics of the enemy. Don't go forth without seeking God for His wisdom and discernment today that you may combat the enemy's confusion and deception with the might of the Holy Spirit!

Don't be confused!

8/10

Greetings and Hi,

As I sit here, I just took a drink of water. Two thoughts for today…
First, don't take for granted clean water to drink. Thank God for it!

Second, it's tough to drink enough water, the amount you should, when you're not thirsty. You want to drink it after your parched from activity or simply due to length of your last fluid intake. Drink water and don't wait until your dehydrated.

Don't wait to read your Bible or pray until storms come! Make these a practice as they are good for your heart and soul, and are desires of Jesus for you.

Don't wait!

8/11

Greetings,

I love how when you hit a homerun in baseball, you get awarded 6 points. Then you have to sing, "Take Me Out To The Ballgame" in order to be awarded 1 point.

Yes, I am being serious. What baseball have you been watching?

I jest…

"My dad was part of the Oriole way. I think he was there 14 years in the minor leagues; I think seven of those years, they had the same people in place. So it was about continuity. It was about stability." (Cal Ripken Jr.)

Has your church, team, family, company, etc. ever gone through trying times? Times with moments of various degrees of tribulation?

Truth is, we all have. If a person says they haven't, they are lying. Plain and simple.

But what is a Christian response? A Christian doesn't quit. Jesus didn't quit on us.
Stay the course and seek continuity. That reaps success in all walks of life. Continuity comes with sacrifice, dedication, love, forgiveness, humility, godly discernment and wisdom.

Pursue these things!

8/12

Greetings,

I'm at Panera writing this and have just purchased an ice cream Sunday!
Wait just a Maryland second…

Kidding. They don't sell those. They do have good food though. I ate a bagel with cream cheese.

There are a variety of food items that you can purchase at various costs.

Life is the same way. So is the Christian life.

There are various choices each and every day that come at different costs, some long term and some short term.

Choose wisely. Choose those that will honor God in the short and long term!

Those decisions will taste good to the soul!

8/13

Good Disney Greetings,

Are you ready for a quote from a Disney movie?
I present to you a quote from Braveheart:

"Listen with your heart, you will understand."

Gotcha! That's from the movie *Pocahontas*.

What I'm about to say does not mean I don't like the movie.

The Bible says that heart is not to be trusted because it is wicket. Don't let your emotions, your fairy tale thoughts, of your desires fuel your decisions.

Pursue God and His wisdom. Ask Him what He wants.
Listen to His Spirit over all else!

God over heart!

8/14

Hello and Hello,

Movie time! I would suggest getting popcorn, pop, candy, a nice pillow, recliner, and blanket before proceeding further!

Ready?!
Here we go.

"Your identity is your most valuable possession. Protect it." (The Incredibles)

But, where is your identity? Is it in your looks, job, family, abilities, hobbies, car, other possessions, money, etc?

Did deep for a moment or take longer if you need, please!

Check your heart to make sure your identity is in Christ alone, His Word and how He sees you…nothing else!

Your identity is protected in Christ Jesus!

8/15

Greetings,

Do you like rabbits and watches?
What in tarnation?!

Sorry.
Do you like watches?
And rabbits?

"If you don't think, then you shouldn't talk." (Alice in Wonderland)

This is biblical. Do not be quick to speak, fuels by the emotion of the moment. Ask God to guide your mind and speech.

Be wise with your words. Speak with wisdom. Know when you need to stop speaking. Take time to listen, truly listen.

Speak and stop. Continuing on and one causes you to look foolish.

Be wise in all things and be controlled by Jesus!

8/16

Greetings Everyone,

Wisdom from a lion in a movie for a world where passivity has grown in strength.

"I'm only brave when I have to be. Being brave doesn't mean you go looking for trouble." (The Lion King)

My dad told me years ago to not go looking for a fight, but never back down from one.

This mindset is the same for each person today that would claim Jesus as their Lord and Savior.

Don't go around seeking to puff out your chest and ego in order to "prove" yourself. But when trouble comes knocking, take a stand. I don't mean it has to be physical.

Stand up for biblical values.
Stand up for those that are being bullied.
If necessary, take physical action to protect others.

Being a Christian is not about being passive. But take stands in love and with the right motive.

Stand!

8/17

Unpredictable Greetings,

You may be thinking to yourself, "What is he saying now?!"

"The only thing predictable about life is its unpredictability." (Ratatouille)

God is not caught off guard by anything that happens, but we are. Trust Him with the unpredictability of life, having faith that He has a plan through everything.

Also, don't be so stringent that you forget to be flexible when things don't go as you had planned. Be willing and able to change things up. Or, as in football, call an audible.

Hut, hut!

8/18

How's your mission field going?
Yep, you're a missionary!
You may be thinking, "No, I'm not!"

If you're a Christian, you are.

"If a man cannot be a Christian in the place he is, he cannot be a Christian anywhere."
(Henry Ward Beecher)

Wherever God calls you…whatever city, state, job, church, country…if it's in a hospital, school, airport…wherever you are is your mission field for that moment in time!

Do well there!

Ask God each day you arise to give you the thoughts and words that will honor Him and lead to missional action!

Go forth to your mission field!

8/19

Greetings,

The Creator of everything loves you. Remind others!

No matter what you've done.
No less.

No more because of how "good" you think you are.

Remind yourself this.
Ask God to remind you.

"God loves each of us as if there were only one of us." (Augustine)

Take this promise with you into a day that the enemy will try to sabotage with thoughts to the contrary.

The Almighty, All-Powerful GOD loves you!
Tell others too!

Go in Jesus' name!

8/20

Reflection Morning!
Mirror Morning!

Yeppers.
What?
Yeppers.

This is where I will say that I need Whataburger!

Anyway, check this out:

"A Christian is a keyhole through which other folk see God." (Robert E. Gibson)

Pause and think if your actions are a direct reflection of Christ? If they are not, why? The way you speak, look at others, drive, conduct your body language, the stores you go to, the restaurants you eat at.

Are they currently reflecting Jesus?
What you have planned today…does it?

If not, ask God to change your course! Seek Him through prayer and His Word!
Seek godly friends that you all can spur one another on closer to Chris!

That others may see Jesus!

8/21

Good greetings on this day God has made,

Do you have a highlighter, or a pen, or a pencil?
You may be asking yourself why or you may not.
If you are or aren't, you'll see what I mean...

"A Bible that's falling apart usually belongs to someone who isn't."
(Charles Spurgeon)

This does not in the slightest mean that life's surroundings are not hellacious at times, but that a person can still have peace, hope, faith, joy, and strength because they are leaning upon the promises and sure foundation of God's Word!

So, take out that highlighter, pen, or pencil and begin your journey through the Bible. Read, write, and mark.
The Bible is holy, but that does not mean you cannot make notes. God's Books is meant for the ups and downs of life.

Therefore, when He's speaking, take notes! Your mind will forget, so notes are important!
Pray before you begin and let the Holy Spirit lead!

Pray, read, write, and mark!

8/22

Good Greetings,

"Gracious words are like a honeycomb, sweetness to the soul and health to the body." (Proverbs 16:24)

Picture right now your favorite tasty dishes that you enjoy eating. If you're trying to be strict with your diet, hold strong! But take a moment to remember how good those items taste and cause you to feel.

It's a good feeling.

Now think about the worst thing you have ever tasted. Cue brown bag if necessary.
How did those foods make you feel?

It's not a good feeling.

Now think about eating spoiled meat, mixed with spoiled eggs, combined with spoiled milk and spoiled fish.

The effect that this has on your mind right now and if you were to eat that, your body, is the picture of the negative effect our words have upon people when we don't speak graciously.

Our words are powerful and we must be wise and thoughtful with them. We must remember that when we speak, text, email, or any other way we communicate...we must speak as if we are the recipient of those words. Do we want a tasty dish or spoiled food?

Serve tasty dishes!

8/23

Good Defense Greetings,

Let's examine a controversial subject from a biblical perspective. Controversy raises eyebrows, but eyebrows have the ability to be raised. Controversial topics need to be discussed and not shied away from a Christian conversation.

Guns.

I said it, guns.
Oh boy, here we go.

It's quite simple, really. Stay with me.

"A gun is a tool, Marian; no better or no worse than any other tool: an ax, a shovel or anything. A gun is as good or as bad as the man using it. Remember that." (from the movie *Shane*)

The Bible does not say a person cannot defend their family. It does not say killing is wrong (self-defense, police, military in the proper context, protection of another), but it does say murder is wrong.

Let's not ever utilized the Bible to justify something when that justification is not implicitly in the text. If you desire to not have a gun, that is your choice and one that others should respect.

The character of the person holding the gun is vital. Focus on that aspect.
Know that David was a king and a warrior after God's heart.

His sword is our gun.

Use biblical wisdom in all things.

Go forward in truth!

8/24

Hello and Greetings,

How much does your life mean to you? Really take some time to think about this.

As Christians, we tend to value self-preservation above self-sacrifice. At what length are you willing to go for the sake of another?

This quote is from Lord of the Rings: "If by my life or death I can protect you, I will." (J.R.R. Tolkien)

Have you resolved today that you are willing to protect others like this? Are you willing to sacrifice your own comfort and even life for the sake of another…even someone you don't know.

The world will long forget our successes, but our sacrifices will point them towards our Savior.

Sacrifice well.
Sacrifice for the sake of reflecting Jesus to a lost and dying world.
Resolve before you take another step this day that you will be willing.

Sacrifice with Christ as your example!

For the sake of another and for His glory!

8/25

Friend greetings to you,

What kind of a friend are you and what kind of friend do you desire? There are many people we meet and spend time with during the course of our lives, but what separates acquaintances from friends?

"Faithless is he that says farewell when the road darkens." (J.R.R. Tolkien)

A true friend doesn't leave you in that fox-hole. He or she hunkers down with you as the bombs of the enemy explode around you. He or she fights side by side with you as you wage war against life's attacks.

Seek that kind of friend.
Be that kind of friend.
Point each other to Christ.
Say that things that need to be said, but in love.
Be rooted in the truth of Jesus.

Friendships like that reflect Jesus to a lost and dying world. Friendships like that are rare. Friendships like that are blessings from God.

Seek and be!

8/26

Greetings,

Let's begin this by singing! Ready? And a 1, and a 2, and a…what?
I don't hear you!

Why, pray tell, are you not singing?
What do you mean?
Don't' believe it for one second!
I think you have a completely average voice!

Just kidding.

I hear the Savior say, "Thy strength indeed is small
Child of weakness, watch and pray Find in Me thine all in all"
Jesus paid it all, All to Him I owe
Sin had left a crimson stain, He washed it white as snow.

Have you come to the realization that your strength is small and on top of that, it's ok? This hymn if powerful and completely full of biblical truth.

You are not strong enough!
The world would preach that you are.
God says you're not.
With Him and by Him, you have the strength.

You couldn't earn your salvation, so why do you think you have enough strength to live the life He wants you to?

Found in Him.
Rely upon Him.

Always!

8/27

Greet,

What? You may be thinking, "Must be a typo. How could they not have noticed that during the writing and editing process? Wow. Utterly preposterous!"

Now, now, now. Hold your horses…or opinion, or judgment, or dogs, or cats, or reindeer.

I shortened the word on purpose.

"Short cuts make long delays." (J.R.R. Tolkien)

We think we are saving time, but often, short cuts are not the right way for us to go! Yes, they can be ok and save time. But we must use wisdom and discernment to know when a short cut is necessary and the right decision at the right time.

Don't allow impatience to lead you to a place worse off than before. The illusion of quickened success that lead to frustration, remorse, and problems.

Stay the course that God sets. Don't seek a quick fix. Quick fixes often to lead to completely cracked lives.

Seek His path, not the path of quickness and of least resistance.

Jesus took no short cuts to the cross. Follow His example.

Stay the course!

8/28

I'll get around to it!

What?

It.

What's it?

You know.

No, that's why I asked.

Greetings.

What?

I got around to it.

Come again?

I got around to saying, "greetings."

Oh…

"It's the job that's never started as takes longest to finish." (J.R.R. Tolkien)

God is a God that calls and sends. He will tarry at times, but we must trust His timing. When He does say go, you need to go!

Take time to pray, search His Word, and talk with other godly people. Then follow Him in making a decision and beginning the task He has called you do.

Don't be a person of procrastination. That is one of my faults and I'll work on it, but…you know that they say.

But seriously, we must seek to not be people of procrastination! What is He calling you to do?

Get up and go!

-318-

8/29

Fence greetings to you,

"The wide world is all about you: you can fence yourselves in, but you cannot forever fence it out." (J.R.R. Tolkien)

Do. Not. Live. In. A. Christian. Bubble.

"And as Jesus reclined at table in the house, behold, many tax collectors and sinners came and were reclining with Jesus and his disciples. And when the Pharisees saw this, they said to his disciples, 'Why does your teacher eat with tax collectors and sinners?' But when he heard it, he said, 'Those who are well have no need of a physician, but those who are sick. Go and learn what this means: *I desire mercy, and not sacrifice. For I came not to call the righteous, but sinners.'"* (Matthew 9:10-13)

Hold to His truth and don't compromise. But, that doesn't mean you can't be friends with non-Christians. That must never mean you are better than another.

Understand that the world is not cheery and nice.
Understand what issues are warring.
Understand that not everyone has heard of the name of Jesus.
Understand that everyone is not like you.

Understand and go forth to share Jesus with a lost and dying world!

Go!
Seek!
Share!
Love!
Forgive!

All for Jesus Christ because of all He has done for you!

8/30

Hello and Hi,

"Never laugh at live dragons." (J.R.R. Tolkien)

You may be thinking to yourself, "And how does this apply to me?" Wait just a jolly second…you didn't realize there are fire breathing dragons in the world?

I hate to burst your bubble, but I'm not kidding.
Yes, I am.

Ok, good. I'm glad we go that out of the way.

But in all seriousness, don't laugh that the fact that spiritual battles are real. Demons are real. The darkness is real.

But don't take your enemy for granted. Don't be fearful because of him, but also realize he is real, his attacks are real, and his power is real.

At the same time, remember and believe that Jesus is more powerful still!

"For the weapons of our warfare are not of the flesh but have divine power to destroy strongholds." (1 Corinthians 10:4)

Fight the dragons with the sword of the Spirit, God's Word!

Know…the full scope of your enemy.
Believe…that Jesus is more powerful than the devil!
Fight…in and through the power of the Holy Spirit!

KBF, remember it!

KBF

8/31

Ready?!
Here we go…

Oh, to grace how great a debtor
Daily I'm constrained to be
Let that goodness like a fetter
Bind my wandering heart to Thee
Prone to wander, Lord, I feel it
Prone to leave the God I love
Here's my heart, oh, take and seal it
Seal it for Thy courts above
(Robert Robinson)

Dwell upon this hymn. Dwell upon it and soak it in.

Now soak this Scripture in: "Let your hand be ready to help me, for I have chosen your precepts. I long for your salvation, O Lord, and your law is my delight. Let my soul live and praise you, and let your rules help me. I have gone astray like a lost sheep; seek your servant, for I do not forget your commandments."
(Psalm 119:173-176)

Realize and be aware that your sinful nature is prone to walk, and even sprint, away from the God you love and believe in.

Know your flesh is weak.
Know that Jesus is greater.
Know He is able to guide and keep you on His path.

He won't force you to obey Him, but He will keep you on His path as you seek Him.

You're weak, very week!
Jesus is all-powerful!!

Give God your heart and mind each and every day to guide!

9/1

Good greetings everyone,

How can we show respect to others, wherein we reflect Jesus to a lost and dying world? Should we even still look at the small things?

Let me preface by saying that I'm the chief of sinners and have fallen many times. I have never been a person to get it right all the time.

I'm sitting at a small table by myself as I write this. There is a young man currently speaking with someone from this restaurant, seeking to obtain employment. He did not stand to shake his employers hand at the beginning.

You may think this is no big deal and I'm harping on insignificant details. You may even think I'm being legalistic.

You may fall on the other side and be screaming that this sort of behavior is ridiculous.

Either way, I will continue by saying that it is disrespectful, as well as a reminder to myself and you that the little things are important.

Don't forget them.
Don't cast them aside.

How you greet someone, the manner in which you do it (tone, title, firm handshake, eye contact, clear speech), are all forms of respect that reflect Jesus!

Take them seriously. I should and you should. We all must.

Do the little things!

9/2

Hi and greetings,

How does a Christian react when wrong is done to them? Should we be content with being a doormat or should we sock the person in the gut?

Sock them in the gut if they are attempting to harm someone. I have no qualms about that and the Bible doesn't either. Christians are not called to be passive in protection.

Did you think I was going to say that or have we been accustomed to not hearing that?

Either way, it's truth.

On the other hand, if someone does you wrong, aside from the above scenario, how are we called to handle it?

"It is useless to meet revenge with revenge; it will heal nothing." (J.R.R. Tolkien)

Seek reconciliation if at all possible. If at all possible!

Revenge comes from unrighteous anger, which is the wrong motivator. It comes from the wrong heart posture.

Seek communication. Seek peace. Seek forgiveness. Seek Jesus through it all.

Reconcile!

9/3

Psalm greetings to you,

One of the most famous chapters in the Bible is Psalm 22. Just kidding. Keeping you sharp. Psalm 22 is solid, but Psalm 23 is one of the most well-known.

The first part of verse 1 says, "The LORD is my shepherd…"

Is He? If you're a Christian, He is. Are you desiring, every day, to be His sheep?

Do you want to be shepherded, or would you rather fend for yourself? He laid down His life for you. Are you appreciative and thankful for that?

The shepherd is the boss. The sheep are not. Do you prefer to be the boss? We enjoy wondering off to our own fields, only to come back to God when the wolf shows his ugly head and begins to growl.

Will you run to Him no only when times are scary and uncertain, but each day? Will you seek His pastures over your own.

Be a sheep, knowing you have the Great Shepherd!

9/4

Verse 2 Greetings,

Psalm 23:2 says, "He makes me lie down in green pastures. He leads me besides still waters."

Have you experienced or are you experiencing this same God-given soul blessing? God desires for you to, but He must be your shepherd. You must dwell in Him.

This verse depicts peace, calmness and tranquility in the midst of a world that is anything but. The soul of a Christian is in the hands of the God of all Peace.

Will you remain there?

Water is often running, gushing, crashing, bubbling…moving of some sort. But the waters here are still. They are quiet.

When you see still waters, it creates a mirror of reflection. God reveals to you who you are and what He desires to do in your life. It also reflects the sky and His creation.

It reflects Him.

Rest beside those still waters and green pastures, where life is evident instead of famine. Green indicates growth. It reveals that water has fallen from the sky to negate the dying off of the pasture.

Choose to reside in the life giving pastures of His Word.

Reside in His pasture and by His waters!

9/5

Greetings and hello,

David said that God "restores my soul. He leads me in paths of righteousness for His name's sake." (Psalm 23:3)

God saves and God restores. Once saved, always saved. But you'll need restoration along the way. This is rejuvenation of what has grown weary and strengthening of what has grown weak.

Seek God in prayer for restoration!

God will lead you down paths that are honoring to Him. That are right in His eyes, instead of right in the world's eyes. Be willing to be led!

It's all for His glory, none of your own! All that He does that is for our good is for His glory. He does not share His glory…never has and never will. It is for the sake of spreading His renown!

Only He deserves it! Only the Creator and not the creation!

Go forth in and with His truth!

9/6

Hello Everyone,

When you become a Christian all bad things stop happening to you. Jesus promised it. In fact, we are immune and deserve better because we are Christians.

Wrong! David, who was a man after God's own heart, when through a plethora of just dang blasted, no way around it, tough times. Times where his life was on the line.

"Even though I walk through the valley of the shadow of death, I will fear no evil,
for you are with me; your rod and your staff, they comfort me." (Psalm 23:6)

You will walk this path. When you do, fear nothing. God has your soul. He is in command. God walks right beside you and will give you comfort that knows no end. Comfort that the world cannot quench.

No amount of uncertainty can overwhelm God. Don't hesitate to run to Him, that you may not fear uncertainty either. The same God that helped David kill Goliath, parted the Red Sea through Moses and sent His Son to take your place…is the same God that stands to quite your fears.

Forever He will.
Forever He is able.
Forever.

9/7

Greetings and hello!

"I try to create sympathy for my characters, then turn the monsters loose." (Stephen King)

Reminder for you that God is not sympathetic towards you in order to set you up for a frightening, shocking surprise. He's not waiting to strike you down.

 He's not waiting to jump out from the closet or from underneath the bed when you're almost asleep…or to prevent you from obtaining sleep.

Just know his compassion in sincere. You can trust Him.

Go forth!

9/8

Hello and Hi,

A reminder to you this day of a truth that is under attack in our world. I want to use this quote to illustrate, though it is dealing with a different subject, it conveys the point.

"It's none of their business that you have to learn to write. Let them think you were born that way." (Ernest Hemingway)

We cannot use the reasoning, or agree to it, that we are born homosexual. We are no more born a homosexual than we are born an alcoholic. We are born in the image of God.

That image, on earth and through us, has been tarnished with sin, but the root is still in God's image.

We may be born with a leaning towards a particular sin struggle, such as homosexuality or alcoholism, but it is still our choice on whether or not we want to follow that path.

This is not according to the world's understanding, but according to God's Word.

Stick to His Word. Hold to His Word. Engage the world in and through His love.

For His renown!

9/10

Hello,

"To produce a mighty book, you must choose a mighty theme." (Herman Melville)

I would call the Bible mighty and what is at the corps of its theme? Redemption!

Never forget that. Never forget that you were redeemed!

God is weaving this element through His story of both the Old and New Testaments. It's His desire throughout. He planned redemption before He created creation!

His mighty book is produced upon the mighty theme of redemption.

Live out this theme that the theme of the Bible would be clear to them!
Don't live in such a way that it's confusing!

Long live redemption!

9/11

Greetings,

This is a day that will live in solemn memory forever. Many Americans lost their lives on this day back in 2001. May we never forget those that died and those that sacrificed their lives for the sake of rescuing others.

Never, never forget.

Pray for those that survived and for their families and friends.
Ready for this…?

Pray also for all the terrorists that died that day and all the terrorists in the world and their families and friends.

It doesn't mean justice is not due to them.
It does mean we are called to pray for their salvation.

You can stand against while also loving. How? Through prayer.

It's a hard, difficult task to undertake. One that can only be done in and through the power of Jesus.

He did the same.

Go and do likewise.

9/12

Greetings and Hello,

Don't be afraid to be judged by the world today…and every day.

"I went for years not finishing anything. Because, of course, when you finish something you can be judged." (Erica Jong)

Don't pause and not fully stand for Christ. Stand all the way, they there would be no doubt upon whose foundation you stand. Don't be afraid about the opinion of others.

You have an audience of one: Jesus Christ!

Only focus and care about what He thinks of you. Stand upon that knowledge.

Stand and stand without being self-conscious!

Jesus is standing right with you.

Stand!

9/13

What should I say? What if they don't like what I have to say? What if I stumble through saying it?

"Don't try to figure out what other people want to hear from you; figure out what you have to say. It's the one and only thing you have to offer."
(Barbara Kingsolver)

God's Word says what they need: Him.
God's Word states what truth is and it's not your or anyone else's opinion. It's not up for debate.
It's up to whether or not we will follow and obey.

Stand upon that conviction and convey His truth in love and with passion.

Make up your mind where you stand.
Make up your mind that you will be His mouthpiece, no matter what opposition you face.

Speak, even if no one else is.
For, He is speaking through you. He is guiding you. He is with you.

Speak!

9/14

Greetings and Hi,

He made me do it!
She started it!
But, but, but…
I had no choice.
If the government hadn't…
If the government would only…
If they would only…

Do you know where all of that began? The same blame game that children and adults play today began in the garden.

"The man said, 'The woman you gave to be with me, she gave me fruit of the tree, and I age.' Then the LORD God said to the woman, 'What is this that you have done?' The woman said, 'The serpent deceived me, and I ate.'"
(Genesis 3:12-13)

You see, accountability was already showing itself to be in conflict with sin. Sin tries to destroy accountability and deflect responsibility upon another.

We must be people that take responsibility for our own actions and not live playing the constant game of blame!

The past is the past. You cannot control others. Bad things happen. Good things happen. A teacher I once had said to us that fair is what comes to the fair ground. Mrs. Jefries (Brinkman) was so, so, so correct!

We as Christians must not blame others, but focus upon what God would have us focus upon and move forward upon His path!

Don't play the game of blame.

Do play the game of aim…aim your eyes upon Jesus!

9/15

Quick reminder:

Your happiness is not God's highest aim. His glory is.
Remember your positioning in regards to God's position.

He seeks your good, but not above His glory.

You serve a gracious, merciful and loving God.
You serve a holy, righteous and jealous God.
Jealous for the praise and affection that alone is due to Him.

He loves you.
Show Him your love by remembering His position!

He likes for you to be happy, but this world's circumstances will not always lead to happiness.

Through it all, He will be with you. His desire is to grow you more into His likeness, reveal Himself through you to others, and lead others to Himself…all for His fame and glory!

Remember and in this remembering, find joy!

9/16

Greetings,

What makes you come alive? What brings your passion forward in such a way that you can do nothing, but focus on that particular thing?

Take time to do two particular thought endeavors.

First, pinpoint a handful of "My Come Alives". Don't rush and don't box yourself in. What really makes you come alive?! Have you suppressed it for years? Are you embarrassed to reveal it? Do you feel there's no way you could possibly accomplish it? Do you feel…

Don't base it upon your feelings.

Second, take the "My Come Alives" before God and lay them at His feet. Are they honoring to Him and do they bring Him glory? Ask Him to reveal the answer to this question. If the answer is yes, ask Him if this desire is of Him and if He wants you to pursue it.

If He does, He will give you all you need for the journey!

For too long have Christians lived in the gray twilight of passion-less lives. Resolve that this will be a past description of your life, not a present description.

Spur others on to be passionate as well…about the things of God. Passionate about the desires that He has given them, that are truly of Him.

Ask God to make you come alive!

"The thief comes only to steal and kill and destroy. I came that they may have life and have it abundantly." (John 10:10)

Pursue His passions for your life!

9/17

Greetings and hello,

Let's be honest, real honest, rawly honest. It's irritating sometimes when God doesn't explain things to us. When things happen and the reasoning is not revealed to us.

It flat out angers us at times.

Who is God that He would treat us this way? Doesn't He care about and love us?

"Who is this that darkens counsel by words without knowledge? Dress for action like a man; I will question you, and you make it known to me. Where were you when I laid the foundation of the earth? Tell me, if you have understanding. Who determined its measurements—surely you know! Or who stretched the line upon it? On what were its bases sunk, or who laid its cornerstone, when the morning stars sang together and all the sons of God shouted for joy?" (Job 38:1-7)

This is God. Wow.
And yet He still loves us!

Rich Mullins said:

"And then he [Job] went to God and wanted to know why the righteous suffer. And Beuchner points out, God never gave him an answer. That God merely gave him Himself. And when Job had encountered the Almighty, the questions lost their power over him. And I think that a lot of us are real interested in some easy answers, and some 'Wow, if I can, if we can come up with some kind of an easy answer to make life comfortable...' We're much more interested in answers than we are in the Truth. And the Truth is always going to be a mystery. It will always be a paradox. It will always be a little beyond our grasp. And if we're uncomfortable with that, that's okay, because a little bit of discomfort will keep us moving."

We must acknowledge our feelings, but not be content to remain that way. We must mature in our relationship with Christ for the next time these feelings arise. How will we deal with them. Will we succumb to them or bring them to Jesus?

Realize, through the power of the Holy Spirit, that Jesus is more than enough for you. You need Him more than an answer. Let Him be sufficient.

He is.

9/18

Greetings and Good Day,

Are you a safe Christian? Don't be.

Are you a reckless Christian? Don't be.

Be a content, uncomfortable, dangerous Christian.

"Christianity is not about building an absolutely secure little niche in the world where you can live with your perfect little wife and your perfect little children in your beautiful little house where you have no gays or minority groups anywhere near you. Christianity is about learning to love like Jesus loved and Jesus loved the poor and Jesus loved the broken." (Rich Mullins)

Be content with what God has blessed you with. Don't be selfish in your desires or covet the possessions or positions of others. Rest your soul's desires in the hands of the Father.

Be uncomfortable with your faith. By this I mean to not be afraid to step out of your box of comfort, out of your zone of familiarity, and out of your socially and culturally acceptable mode of thinking and speaking. Just follow Jesus wherever He would lead, to whomever He would lead, and think to speak whatever He would fashion and inspire.

Be dangerous on your journey with Jesus. Don't be afraid to risk your reputation, your livelihood, or your very life itself. Jesus died for you. Be fearless, with and in and through the power of the Holy Spirit, in order to be ready to die and suffer for Jesus Christ, your Lord and Savior.

CUD:
Content
Uncomfortable
Dangerous

Be a CUD Christian!

9/19

Greetings and Hello Everyone,

Facebook, Twitter, Instagram… They are all of the devil!

Back the Christmas sleigh up, but watch out for the elves!

Don't jump all the way to one side of the emotional pendulum. These social media platforms have good uses and purposes and can prove to be very beneficial!

At the same time, yes, they can be conduits of very harmful and exceedingly wicked actions and results.

How will you choose to use them?

If you are using them to vent, speak indirectly about someone in a negative manner, berate a certain social issue or political stance, then stop it! That is not a God-honoring way to use Facebook.

Use it to encourage, educate, and lift up the name of Jesus Christ. There can be certain posts you make that are not popular according to the world's standards, and that's alright.

Just make sure they are not fueled by unrighteous anger. Make sure they are not fueled by hate. Make sure they are not fueled by revenge. Make sure your emotions are not the motivating factor instead of the wisdom of the Lord.

Use social media, but use it wisely!
Be set apart in every aspect of your life, including this mode of communication.

Now get back on the sleight and ride for Christ!

9/20

Hello,

Be a doer of insignificance.

Well, that's really uplifting. Just what I wanted to read from this so-called devotional book! I want a refund! I want a refund!

You can actually write me at this address for a complete refund:

Jolly Old Saint Nathan
5758 Christmas Ave
North Pole, North Pole 122585

:)
Gotta have a little fun!

Be a doer of insignificance. What I mean is be someone that finds joy in doing things that, according the world's standards, would be insignificant. But, according to God's standards, bring a smile to His face and glory to His name!

Push the chair in. Pick up that piece of trash. Give the pen back to someone clicked back in. Be as prompt as you can in texting or emailing someone back. Smile. Allow someone to go ahead of you in line or give them the parking spot. When you're walking to your car, and someone is waiting in the parking lot, direct them to where your car is so they can obtain your spot. Have a good attitude to the cashier.

And do things that no one may ever notice…But Jesus.

Insignificant actions done for the significance of God bring significant praise to His name and reflect the significance of Jesus Christ to a significantly lost and dying world.

Be a doer of insignificance for a significant God!

9/21

Greetings, Hi and Hello,

Picture the theme music from the movie, Chariots of Fire, if you've seen the movie of course! If not, do not fret and do not go and eat a bag of jelly beans. Although, jelly beans are scrumptious.

I digress...

It's a movie about the true story of Eric Liddell. He was a missionary, Olympic runner, and a man of solid Christian faith. There is a powerful line from the movie where he says to his sister...

"I believe God made me for a purpose...He also made me fast. And when I run, I feel His pleasure. To give it up would be to hold Him in contempt."

God had given him a gift and he knew he must use it for God's glory! When he used the gift God gave him, he was in communion with God, and therefore felt His pleasure. Eric could, in sense, see God smiling.

"For we are his workmanship, created in Christ Jesus for good works, which God prepared beforehand, that we should walk in them." (Ephesians 2:10)

God has clothed you with the righteousness of Jesus as soon as you accept Him as your Lord and Savior. He prepared godly works for you to complete through the power of Jesus Christ that now dwells in you!
He has given you specific gifts and abilities in order to accomplish these works!

When you don't use them, you hold God in contempt! Meriam-Webster defines contempt as, "open dislike for someone or something considered unworthy of one's concern or respect." There is always grace and forgiveness when we drop the ball. But get on up and get back in the game! Christ goes with and before you!

Begin using these gifts in your home, at church, at your workplace... everywhere. But use them you must!

Feel His pleasure and see Him smiling as you run the race He has called you to!

9/22

Football greetings to you,

Not soccer, but football. Both sports require skill, conditioning and sacrifice. Here is a quote from a football coach of many years ago… Vince Lombardi.

"It's not whether you get knocked down; it's whether you get up."

No athlete experiences success all the time. It's impossible. There will be times when an athlete feels like they've been sucker-punched… or they actually were!

The same happens in the Christian life.

God says, "for the righteous falls seven times and rises again, but the wicked stumble in times of calamity." (Proverbs 24:16)

As you're walking with God through this adventure called life, you'll fall and fall flat on your face at times. But what does He say above? You will rise again!

This is through the power of His Spirit living in and through you!

Don't become discouraged when you fall. Ask God what He wants to teach you and how He wants to grow you. Ask Him for His strength, hope and peace.

Get up and go in His strength!

9/23

Good hello to you,

Time comes and remains, then ever it leaves
Cherished moments and memories through ones heart it weaves

Resolve not to squander this invisible gift
Thus in and through it Jesus name to uplift

Don't let a tragedy awaken you to this truth. Make a concerted, conscious, intentional effort each day to make each moment count.

Contact those you love. Reach out to those you need to seek or offer forgiveness. Live and create those cherished memories! God smiles when you do.

Seek Him and let Him guide you in the creation of them. Look back at the sweet times and thank Him.

The cliché is to not squander the present. Sometimes we can get tired of clichés but they are true.

Live. Live well.
Take chances. Be daring. All in and through Jesus. Don't step out in pursuit of the flesh. Be in pursuit of creating memories that are honoring to Him both presently and in the future.

Live! Live well!

All for Him and for His renown!

9/24

Greetings!

I shall begin with offering you a snow cone. Would you like one?
Now how on the planet Saturn am I supposed to give you a snow cone?!

Just kidding. There's one for you on your right. No, your other right.

Whelp…let us continue on.

"A champion is someone who gets up when he can't." (Jack Dempsey)

A quick punch for today: don't sit around and complain. Ask God for the wisdom to know what He wants you to do and the strength to do it.

Make no excuses. Don't think of others when you read this. Think of how you can do a better job…only for the sake of Jesus Christ.

Get up. Even if you do not have the ability to physically get up and stand. Get up mentally. Get up! By and in the power of Jesus Christ!

If you're alive, He still has work for you to do!

Get up and go!

9/25

Hello All,

Have you ever been a fan of a sports team that just can't find the side of the scoreboard that contains the most points at the end of games? Have you ever joked that at least they are consistent in that manner?

Laugh out loud.
Well, maybe you have or maybe you haven't.

Either way, there is something to be said about consistency.

"Winning is not a sometime thing, it is an all the time thing. You don't do things right once in a while. You do them right all the time." (Vince Lombardi)

What are areas of your life that you are showing good and bad consistency?

Take time for a self-evaluation. It's not the most fun way in the world to spend your time, but it's important. I encourage you to take time to do it!

Now, ask God for His help to not be consistent in the bad avenues and to be consistent in the good avenues. He will answer you!

Surround yourself with Christ-minded people, dig into His Word, and get or remain involved in church (beyond Sunday).

Be inconsistent in the worldly things and consistent in God's things!

9/26

Greetings Greetings,

There is a time for everything. Have you heard that before? It's true, even if it's annoying or hard to hear sometimes.

Ecclesiastes speaks upon this and gives us truth to stand upon. "For everything there is a season, and a time for every matter under heaven." (Ecclesiastes 3:1) There is that song from *The Lion King*, "Circle of Life," that also conveys this message.

There is a cycle of events in this world and we must accept this fact. Until we reach heaven's shores, we will have this cycle because we live in a fallen world.

There truly is a time for everything. That does not mean that each period of time is enjoyable. Not one bit. Some moments are wonderful and some are hellacious.

So, Nathan, what's your point. My point is that when we understand that there is a circle of life and a time for everything under the sun, then two truths can be grasped.

One, this is the reality of life. There's no getting around it. It levels the playing ground. Everyone goes through seasons of life. No one just goes through one season and no others.

Second, when we understand that good and bad times come, we can be prepared and have the proper viewpoint. We should enjoy the good times, knowing that they don't last forever…we must not take them for granted.

Soak them up. Also, realize that bad seasons of life will pass. They will end…whether it's this side of heaven or when you reach heaven's shores. Because bad seasons will come to everyone, don't cry, "unfair!" when they do arrive.

Ask God for the ability to traverse through all seasons of life. This season, called life on earth, will one day end. Live knowing your heavenly season will be the only one that will last forever and what a truth that is!

He's with you through this and every season!

9/27

Greetings,

As I write some of this, I'm waiting to pick up Katie from work. Dedication...this word describes her. She is dedicated to her job, being willing to stay later than she has to, while also having a balance to not make work her life.

This same mindset and character profile is one that you and I must strive to have. We must strive to be dedicated to the tasks and responsibilities we have been given, while also not being consumed by them.

Balance is vital. Balance is what Jesus desires for you to have. He desires and commands that you work hard, not for anyone else's glory but His...but He also desires for you to not make work or volunteering your god.

This can be as easy as not eating more than one Oreo when you're sitting down and watching TV with a whole pack in hand!

But ask the God of your salvation to help you take steps to set up a healthy balance. He will come to your aid and it will be worth it.

Don't live in order to work and find out you were working your God, family, and friends right out of your life.

Live His way...it's for your good and His glory!

9/28

Greetings and hello,

Na na na na na na na na na na na na na na na na…Batman! Is that how the old tune used to go?! I was trying to figure out how many "na's" to put!

Batman has long been a fictional hero (yes, he's not real) that I and many others have enjoyed…from action figures, to dressing up, to movies, to books, etc.

"The night is darkest just before the dawn. And I promise you, the dawn is coming." (The Dark Knight)

There are many dark areas of our world, many. It seems at times as if it has become cloaked with an ever present rain cloud, complete with rolling thunder and fierce lightning strikes. Will it or when will it ever end? How could the sun ever regain superiority?

First, remember that God has never lost His superiority, even if the world does not acknowledge Him. He has not, nor will ever, relinquish His throne.

Second, the dawn will come. The day is marching closer and closer. Jesus is coming back and will right all wrongs. Let us cling to this hope and tell anyone that will listen about it as well.

The struggles you go through…I don't know when they will end. The physical pain…I don't know when it will subside. The hurts…I don't know then they will be finished.

All I know is our Redeemer lives. His grace will and strength will sustain you through all of life's embattlements.
And He is coming again. When you reach heaven's shores, all will be right. All will be right.

"All shall be well, and all shall be well, and all manner of thing shall be well." (Julian of Norwich)

    All.

9/29

Greetings,

Have you ever been thinking to yourself, "Gosh is this a waste of my time or what" when speaking with someone or attending a certain meeting or when you find yourself in an sort of situation?

There are those moments when I feel, "I just want to get out of here!"

"I have never met a man so ignorant that I couldn't learn something from him." (Galileo Galilei)

There is always something to learn or sharpen yourself by. Always, when Jesus is at your center. Remember too that Jesus came to you. You are no better than someone else…take the time to talk and listen to others, even when you don't feel like it.

The simple, yet hard to do truth is: ask God to help you learn something from each person you speak with and each situation you find yourself in, that you would in turn grow closer to Christ!

It ain't easy, but it's the God-honoring way!

Seek God and ask Him to prepare your heart and mind to be in such a posture as to learn from each interaction you have and each situation you find yourself in.

He'll use all things to grow you in Him, no matter how aggravating or "a waste of your time" things seem to be.

Go forth in Him!

9/30

Greetings and Hello,

We live in a culture of isolation. We live in a culture where a person can have 2,000 Facebook friends and 3,000 Instagram followers, yet feel as lonely as ever.

We were not born for isolation.

This doesn't mean you have to be the most outgoing person…not by any means. We all have different personalities and that's healthy! But we were still created to have community.

"When I go home people will ask me, 'Hey Hoot, why do you do it man?...They won't understand why we do it. They won't understand that it's about the men next to you, and that's it. That's all it is." (Black Hawk Down)

This bond. This brotherhood. This camaraderie. This is a depiction of what the Christian life is supposed to be like. We are supposed to be there for one another, for the sake and honor and glory of Jesus Christ.

If you aren't, become involved in a men's group, a women's group, a youth group, a college group…a group where you can come alongside one another and battle together.

Couples groups are awesome and couples should pursue them, but alongside a group that is just men and one that is just women.

We were made for community. We were made to be there for the person next to us.

God made you for this. Now go pursue it!

Battle on!

10/1

Uncomfortable greetings to you,

Was that weird or what?!

What makes you uncomfortable? What situations, people, discussions, places seem to bring you out of the parameters that you'd prefer to reside in?

Here is a Navy SEAL saying: "Get comfortable being uncomfortable"

Now, I'm not saying to not use godly discernment when assessing situations that you are uncomfortable in. What I am saying that is that we must not remain in our bubbles of comfortability at the expense of the Gospel and the name of Jesus Christ.

Be uncomfortable!

10/2

Greetings,

Do you want to live a life that matters? No, that really matters?
If you live a life that simply impacts this world, you have failed.

Wait just a New York minute, that's mean of you to say! It's the truth for you and me.

"Unless the LORD builds the house, those who build labor in vain. Unless the LORD watches over the city, the watchman stays awake in vain." (Psalm 127:1)

Unless God is in the midst of your work, it's in vain!

If you want to live a life that really matters and impacts in an eternal manner, seek if what you are involved with right now…relationships, work, hobbies, home shopping, car shopping, school searching, etc…is it what God wants and is He in the midst of it?

If not, stop, turn around and pursue paths that are of Him and that He directs you on.

That is how to live impactfully for Christ.

You matter to Christ and He desire to be in the midst and guide what you do…for His glory and to reflect Him to a lost and dying world!

Go forth!

10/3

Greetings

It's time for Christmas, so get out the Christmas tree and begin decorating!

Not yet?
Ok, ok.

But at least let me share this:

"We are better throughout the year for having, in spirit, become a child again at Christmastime." (Laura Ingalls Wilder)

Jesus was very clear that the children were to be allowed to come to Him. He was also very clear that a person must have faith like a child.

Children have an awe and wonder about them at Christmas that we as adults often lost somewhere along the way…about Christmas, about life, and about our Savior.

That same wonder and awe that a child has about Christmas are characteristics we should pray to our God that He would keep ever present within our hearts and souls in regards to our view of our Savior, Jesus Christ, His Son!

Come before Him today and every day, asking for this awe and wonder to be renewed and kindles throughout the day, that others would see Jesus through you.

Christmas as a child reflects awe and wonder.
Christians always must reflect our awesome and wonderful Savior!

Long live such awe and wonder!

10/4

Greetings,

"One of the most glorious messes in the world is the mess created in the living room on Christmas Day. Don't clean it up too quickly." (Andy Rooney)

God is a God of order, but He's also a God of the big things. What I mean is that God desires for us to pursue order and cleaning up our messes, of course. But He also wants us to focus on what really, really matters.

Don't get caught up on "cleaning up the mess" that you forget to enjoy those that "made" the mess.

People!

Leave the bed unmade.
Leave the dishes in the sink.
Leave the wrapping on the floor.
Leave the leaves unraked.

There's a time and place for everything.
Remember and keep each in their proper place in your life.

God gives you moments like these to enjoy and savor!

Take some to just relax and enjoy the little moments, enjoy the people you're around, and soak up the moments…they will not be there to enjoy forever.

Smell the roses.
Smell the daisies.
Smell the grass.
Smell the tulips.
Smell the Christmas tree.
Smell and have fun at it.

Take time to smell!

10/5

Greetings to give,

"Christmas is a season for kindling the fire for hospitality in the hall, the genial flame of charity in the heart." (Washington Irving)

Don't let Christmas be the only season you choose to be a giving person. Give during every season of life!

And don't let the amount you have to give dictate whether or not you give at all!

Give a generous tip!
Pay for the person behind you in live!
Give to your church, which is biblical!
Give random gifts to people!

Give, but give in the name of Jesus that you would reflect Him to a lost and dying world!

Give because He gave!

See what happens!

10/6

Greetings and Hello,

Wait, wait, wait. That's a word we love to hear, right?!

The golly-rabbit microwave won't heat this hot pocket fast enough!!!!

AHHHHHHHHHHHHHHHHHHH!

Yes, I'm a very patient person. Why do you ask?

"I wait for the LORD, my soul waits, and in His word I hope…" (Psalm 130:5)

Wait on Him and in His patience. Read the Bible and dwell in prayer. His Spirit will guide your spirit on the path He wants you to take.

Don't grow impatient and yell at God because you don't feel He's going at your speed.

He won't over cook or under cook the meal.

Wait.

10/7

Greetings,

Rest in not knowing.

What in the name of all that is snow do you mean?!

"O Lord, my heart is not lifted up; my eyes are not raised too high; I do not occupy myself with things too great and too marvelous for me. But I have calmed and quieted my soul, like a weaned child with its mother; like a weaned child is my soul within me. O Israel, hope in the Lord from this time forth and forevermore." (Psalm 131)

Don't be concerned or worried about things you can't understand or don't know.

Rest in the fact you know the One who does know the answers and does understand.

Give it all to Him. Lay it in His hands.

Trying to understand things that are not meant for you to understand will lead to unrest, frustration and anger. It may lead to hate.

Seek to know Jesus better instead. He's better. This will lead to rest, peace and joy. It will lead to love.

Turn your eyes upon Jesus,
Look full in His wonderful face,
And the things of earth will grow strangely dim,
In the light of His glory and grace.
(Helen H. Lemmel)

Turn your eyes!

10/8

Good Afternoon!

Monday, for many people, is not a day that has been anticipated with joy. Why is this? Is it because we desire another day of rest? Is it because we fear the unknown that the week holds?

True, we may desire and even need an extra day of rest. Also true, we don't know what will unfold this week.
BUT...
We do know the ONE who will give us the strength and rest we need.
We do know that ONE who already knows exactly what will happen this week.

God speaks to us in Isaiah 40:28-31 saying,
"Have you not known? Have you not heard? The LORD is the everlasting God, the Creator of the ends of the earth. He does not faint or grow weary; His understanding is unsearchable. He gives power to the faint, and to him who has no might he increases strength. Even youths shall faint and be weary, and young men shall fall exhausted; but they who wait for the LORD shall renew their strength; they shall mount up with wings like eagles; they shall run and not be weary; they shall walk and not be faint."

God is all powerful and will never grow tired. He will provide for you according to His will and understanding. He will be your strength in order for you to live for Him!

Rest in God's words to you. Seek God's face today through prayer and the Bible. He never promised a life without valleys and struggles. But, take heart! He promised He would never leave you!

Have a good and godly day!

10/9

Good Morning!

God is still on His throne. Nothing can dethrone God Almighty. Therefore, take heart that God's grace can never be dethroned as well.

Paul writes in 2 Corinthians 12:7-10...
"So to keep me from becoming conceited because of the surpassing greatness of the revelations, a thorn was given me in the flesh, a messenger of Satan to harass me, to keep me from becoming conceited. Three times I pleaded with the Lord about this, that it should leave me. But He said to me, 'My grace is sufficient for you, for my power is made perfect in weakness.' Therefore I will boast all the more gladly of my weaknesses, so that the power of Christ may rest upon me. For the sake of Christ, then, I am content with weaknesses, insults, hardships, persecutions, and calamities. For when I am weak, then I am strong.'"

Paul tells us that God gave him a thorn (something painful) that served to keep him humble in light of all the revelations God had given to him. We are not told specifically what this thorn is, but it was great in its persecution upon him. Paul asked God to take it away, but in His infinite wisdom and sovereignty, God chose to have the thorn remain.
WHY?!
God had a greater purpose, as He does for you. God's purpose was to display to Paul the grace and strength that only He can give. God's purpose was for Paul to rely completely upon Christ and nothing else. One commentary describes God's power being made perfect in weakness as having "its most perfect manifestation" when Paul was weak and not trying to rely upon his own human ability.

When Paul fully relied upon Christ for strength, Christ's power was upon him. Tribulations didn't have the same effect upon him for he was content in knowing that God's grace would be sufficient through it all. Paul knew that the best place to be in was the place of human weakness. For then, it was upon Jesus Christ that he must fully submit to and rely upon.

Today and everyday, remember Jesus' grace and rely upon Jesus' strength.

From one sinner saved by grace to another, have a solid day in Jesus!

10/10

Hello,

Our days are passing, twill soon be time
To enter eternity as death's bell doth chime

Hope we have in the name of Christ Jesus
He defeated death and shall never leave us

Thus, while on this side of heaven's splendor
Seize the day, serve Jesus, in joyous candor

Don't waste today! Follow Jesus and live for Him!

10/11

Greetings,

The fear and anxieties of the world cave in
No light of hope seems to shine from within

Cease searching for joy in a world of unbelief
For that will never assuage your heartache and grief

Call to mind the message the shepherds received
In that field, long ago, the angel spoke and they believed

Go forth today in the strength of the Lord
Jesus has come and joy to you, He will restore

Go forth in Christ!

10/12

Jesus loves you. More than you can possibly fathom. Did you know that?

Jesus loves you. He also knows every single thing about you...every single thing.

And you know what?

Jesus loves you. He died for you. He fights for you. Jesus loves you.

"Why the repetition? I know He loves me!" But do you really know the depth with which He loves you? Has it radically changed your life?

The famous verse (resist with the power of the Holy Spirit the urge to relegate this verse to thoughts of "I've heard this a thousand times", "I know what it says and there is nothing really for me to grasp from it," etc.), John 3:16, states:

"For God so loved the world, that he gave his only Son, that whoever believes in him should not perish but have eternal life."

Truth be told, we will never fully understand or comprehend the depth of Jesus' love because its vastness is incomprehensible for our human minds. The magnitude of His sacrifice and the immensity of His grace are too much for mere mortals to measure. How could we? How could we possibly fully understand the love of a God, who became man, yet retained His divine nature, who, though sinless Himself, took on the sins of the world (past, present and future), while dying a horrific death upon a cross?

We can't. Thank God we can't. This exemplifies His Godhead and our humanity. This assures us that He is all-powerful, all-knowing and all-sufficient. We can put our trust and hope upon His mighty and unfaltering foundation.

See and know Jesus' love anew today.
Jesus loves you...more than you'll ever know.

From one who is loved and forgiven to another, go in Jesus!

10/13

Good Greetings Everyone,

"Therefore encourage one another and build one another up, just as you are doing." This verse if found in 1 Thessalonians 5:11 and is always the easiest command for us as Christians to carry out...not really!

It's not always easy to encourage one another. It's not always easy to go out our way to say a kind word. But the easy way is not the path our Savior took.

We are not called to keep to ourselves, although alone time is important.
We are called to encourage one another.

Ask God how you can encourage those around you for His glory. He'll show you.
Remember how it felt to receive a kind word. Remember and do the same.
A simple things to do, yet it can be so tough to carry out.

But...

Jesus will help you to. Jesus loves you. Jesus will encourage you. Be the hands and feet of Jesus as you encourage one another.

My grandfather used to say, "This is not my home, I'm just ah-passing through."

Encourage others in Jesus' name as you pass through.

10/14

Good Greetings!

Today is...yes, it is Monday, but it is another day that God has given us, therefore He still has purpose for our lives! You may not see fully yet what His plan is for you today, but you can be sure of this: He has purposed for you to enjoy Him and light your world for Him.

Jesus said,
"You are the light of the world. A city set on a hill cannot be hidden. Nor do people light a lamp and put it under a basket, but on a stand, and it gives light to all in the house. In the same way, let your light shine before others, so that they may see your good works and give glory to your Father who is in heaven." -Matthew 5:14-16

As Christians, we must not remain in a bubble of comfort and safety. We must choose to step out into the world around us, while remaining clothed in the purity and love of Jesus Christ.

In The Hobbit, Gandalf (the wise old sage) says to Bilbo (younger character),
"The world is not in your books and maps. It's out there."
Then, on another occasion as Bilbo decided to join on the adventure,
"You will have to do without pocket handkerchiefs, and a great many other things, before we reach our journey's end, Bilbo Baggins. You were born to the rolling hills and little rivers of the Shire, but home is now behind you. The world is ahead."

You see, we must step out into the adventure God has placed before us. We are not meant to live any other fashion. God's adventure for us is designed by and for Him. Comforts of life? We will need to give certain ones up in order to be this light upon the hill for His glory.

We must not stand back in the shadows of life. We must step out to light up the darkness by the light of Jesus Christ!

Go forth and shine for Him!

10/15

Greetings,

I saw a description of a conference and it mentioned that you are bigger than your problem.

That's not biblical. Remember, your problem is bigger than you.

But…

Your God is bigger than your problem and by Him, and Him alone, can you deal with the problem.

For Jesus and for His glory! Run and rely upon Him!

Run and rely!

10/16

Good Morning!

Please bear with me on a longer devotional for this morning.

One night this week I was going through some old things, keeping some and throwing away others. I came across a birthday card my grandfather (dad's dad) had given me back in 2015. He passed away January of 2017. He wrote about me and my own dad and expressed his live towards us. How do you describe a life well lived? How do you carry on the legacy?

You let the person's life speak for itself...

There are men that walk this earth and never obtain worldly treasures or renown. Yet, they leave a legacy that is far more important and lasting. A legacy that will transcend generations. Our grandfather is one of those men. He lived a simple life, yet his impact was the antithesis of that six letter word. His life was lived for others and his love was deep.

He did not live to work, but worked to live and provide for his family. He was married once, to our grandma, and only death separated them. He was wholeheartedly devoted and faithful to her. He upheld his vows with the utmost honor and served her through his words and actions. I asked him what made him and grandma work for so many years. He gave a simple answer: She agreed with what I did. I agreed with what she did. We didn't have money, but we knew we were going to make it.
Simply...he loved her. Yet, his love was anything but simple. His love for her was deep and profound.

He provided for, protected, and guided his son, our dad. He was never able to provide the most monetary items, yet he provided our dad with priceless items: time, presence, wisdom, and love. He paved the foundation for his son to one day be a tremendous dad to his grandchildren, me and Jonathan, and husband to his daughter-in-law (whom he loved), our mom.

Simply...he loved him. Yet, his love was anything but simple. His love for him was deep and profound.

He supported and provided for his grandsons, Jonathan and I. He enjoyed hearing the events which were transpiring in our lives and found delight in the grandsons that his son and daughter-in-law raised.
Simply...he loved us. Yet, his love was anything but simple. His love for us was deep and profound.

Simply...Papa Dan left a legacy that will be carried forth beyond his earthly days. Yet, this legacy is anything but simple. His legacy is deep and profound.

He left an example for me to follow and hold to.

Paul says in 1 Corinthians 11:1, "Be imitators of me, as I am of Christ."

Paul was a mature follow of Christ. He had walked with Jesus and his faith had been tested and strengthened over the years. Paul was not saying that he was God or on the same level. But he was giving the Christians in Corinth an earthly example to follow.

We should do the same.

Find someone that can be your "Paul." Seek it out. It is worth it. Ask God to show you who.
Men, find another Christian brother. Women, find another Christian sister.

Stand in Jesus! Love Jesus! Love each other!

10/17

Hello and Howdy!

Are we saved when we accept Christ? Yes
Are we better than others because we accept Christ? No
We are prideful creatures and can become puffed up sometimes due to self-righteousness.

And it's so incredibly easy for us to never be prideful! Completely kidding...not at all.

It is a rich blessing to live in America and this country is a special place. But, we can have the mindset that we need to pick ourselves up by our own bootstraps and our success is ours alone, due to our ingenuity and hard work.

Now, hard work and ingenuity are very important and respectable character traits. Yet, may we never forget that it is by God's grace alone. May we never forget that it is God who has given us everything that is good. Who are we to try to steal glory from God and think we are "something special" in and of ourselves?

In the Old Testament, it is said of David...
"Then King David went in and sat before the LORD and said, 'Who am I, LORD God, and what is my house, that you have brought me thus far?'" -1 Chronicles 17:16

Humility, awe and reverence. These describe the heart of David towards God Almighty as he reflected on what God had done for him.

"Christianity is one beggar telling another beggar where he found bread." -D.T. Niles

Let us never forget that we are beggars and that Jesus Christ is the Bread of Life. He gave Himself for us. He pursued us. He pursues us still. He satisfies us and nourishes our souls when we eat of His Word. We are special not in and of ourselves, but because God made us and loves us deeply.

May we always ask, as David did... "Who am I, LORD God, and what is my house, that you have brought me thus far?"

-378-

10/18

Hello Everyone,

Are you ready for a friendly neighborhood Facebook reminder? Whelp, ready or not, here it is…

Facebook and other multimedia sites should never be used to share one's disgust for a family member, friend, or other individual on a personal level.

Multimedia has positive uses, but has also become a substitute for personal interaction...which is a transgression against interpersonal relationships.

This may seem like an unspiritual topic for the day, but it's something everyone should keep in mind, for we must be about reflecting Christ at all times.

Our social media behavior gives either a biblical representation of Christ or a false representation of Him.

Face Jesus always!

10/19

Good Greetings,

How are you doing? No, how are you really doing? Don't think to yourself the answer you would like for others to hear or how you would want others to think about you. How are you really doing?

You may be doing really well and that is truly a good thing. But, you may be traveling through a deep valley. Either way...

Always the enemy will seek to fill you with worry to steal life from you. For you see, one can be breathing, yet not truly living.

Death is a very real tragedy and one that brings deep sorrow. But a living death is what many people experience on a daily basis.
Alfred Lord Tennyson wrote: "As tho' to breathe were life!"
We may be alive physically, but inside we are dying. Worry, anxiety and cares of this world kill our hearts and wreck warfare upon our minds.

That is why Jesus said:

"Therefore I tell you, do not be anxious about your life, what you will eat or what you will drink, nor about your body, what you will put on. Is not life more than food, and the body more than clothing? Look at the birds of the air: they neither sow nor reap nor gather into barns, and yet your heavenly Father feeds them. Are you not of more value than they?" -Matthew 6:25-26

God values you more than the birds of the air. He will meet your needs according to His will. God never promised to give you everything you want, but as Paul says, "And my God will supply every need of yours according to his riches in glory in Christ Jesus." (Philippians 4:19)

Trust it. Believe it. Live it...for it will give you life. His Word is life. Give your worries to God. Rest in Him!

10/20

Top of the Day to You,

Delight...what does that mean to you? What do you delight in? You will find that word throughout today's brief devotional, but dwell on it as it relates to your relationship with Jesus.

Delight: a high degree of gratification or pleasure: JOY
also: extreme satisfaction
something that gives great pleasure
great pleasure, satisfaction, or happiness, or something or someone that gives this

What or who do you find joy in? Do you find extreme satisfaction in Christ?
We were made to find great pleasure in walking day by day with Jesus.

Ask the Holy Spirit, and He will help you take delight in walking with Christ. He will help you to keep Jesus as your supreme delight as well.

Psalm 37:4 says,
"Delight yourself in the Lord, and he will give you the desires of your heart."

When we are delighting in the Lord, He is our highest priority and most special desire. When we are walking with Him like this, He conforms our desires to His. Therefore, He will grant us the desires of our heart because they are in alignment with His as well.

There is no better pleasure than fully delighting in Christ. There is no better walk than walking with Him.

Walk and Delight today and always in Christ!

10/21

Good Greetings Everyone,

"Cheer up! You're a worse sinner than you ever dared imagine, and you're more loved than you ever dared hope." (Jack Miller)

You may be thinking to yourself, "Ha! Now there's a crazy thought to begin the morning!"

Do we actually take time to contemplate how wretched we actually are the great sinner we are?
While...
We take time to contemplate just how magnificent a Savior Jesus is and how much He loves us?

There are those out there that will not mention "sin" in their messages. But we must.
Sin is great. Our sin and sinful nature is great.
The more we remember just how great sin and our sin nature is, we will remember how much greater our Savior is!

We must remember.

"And you were dead in the trespasses and sins in which you once walked, following the course of this world, following the prince of the power of the air, the spirit that is now at work in the sons of disobedience - among whom we all once lived in the passions of our flesh, carrying out the desires of the body and the mind, and were by nature children of wrath, like the rest of mankind. But God, being rich in mercy, because of the great love with which He loved us, even when we were dead in our trespasses, made us alive with Christ - by grace you have been saved..." (Ephesians 2:1-5)

"He does not deal with us according to our sins, nor repay us according to our iniquities." (Psalm 103:10)

Spend the rest of your day and the rest of your life remembering how great a sinner you are, while at the same time remembering how much greater a Savior Jesus Christ is!

10/22

Hello and Hi!

Let's jump into some Scripture...

"Let your speech always be gracious, seasoned with salt, so that you may know how you ought to answer each person." Colossians 4:6

How is my speech seasoned? How is yours? Salt has been used to years to preserve food. The words we use to one another can preserve or destroy a relationship. They can bring life or death. They can build up or tear down.

You and I have a choice today in how we speak to one another. We also have a choice to try and reconcile a relationship if we have used poison in our speech previously in conversation with another person.

Picture your favorite meal and how it tasted. Let that be the way we seek to speak to any person we come across. Our words may sometimes be hard for another person to swallow, but we can still say them in a godly manner. The words may be spicy, but not poisonous. Jesus had hard words to say, but He never sinned in saying them.

May we strive to do the same.

Eat from the Bread of Life, that you may feed others His words.

Let's eat together and enjoy every morsel.

Have a full day as you savor Christ's every word!

10/23

Good Night!

Well...I hope you had a good night or will have a good night! And now I wish you a good greeting! Even if you didn't...God is with you and is still good and faithful.

The weather has changed and become cooler. Change...it's not a word that is always easy or pleasant to deal with. Some changes are ones we desire to happen, while others are ones we wish would never transpire.

Ecclesiastes 3:1 says,
"For everything there is a season, and a time for every matter under heaven"
This verse does not mean that every time will be fun. But, it does show us that life consists of change and we must be aware of this fact. This side of heaven will contain times that are enjoyable and times that are trying upon the soul.

We must not be unprepared to face these times of change without knowing Jesus as our personal Lord, Savior and friend.

Seasons will change, as they have today. Our lives will change. Events will change. But...

"Jesus Christ is the same yesterday and today and forever." (Hebrews 13:8)

Jesus will be your constant stronghold in the midst of an ever-changing world.
Be aware of changes and rejoice that Jesus walks with you through them.

Enjoy the day with Jesus as your best friend!

10/24

Good Helo!

"Behold, the virgin shall conceive and bear a son, and they shall call his name Immanuel" (which means, God with us)."
-Matthew 1:23

You may be thinking to yourself, "Why did he just share a verse from the Christmas story?" Valid question.

But, at the same time, let's not relegate the Christmas story to one month out of the year. For it bears eternal and everyday significance! Just think...the God of the universe chose to be with you. He chose to leave heaven and come down to earth for you.

He chose...for His glory and our redemption.
Will we choose to remember this not just during the Christmas season, but each and every day of our lives?

Let the remembering that Jesus is Immanuel, God with us, cause us to...
Thank Him
Rest in Him
Walk with Him
Love Him with our whole beings

Merry early Christmas!

10/25

Hello and Good Day,

If you were lost, where would someone go to look for you? Where would someone be led based upon the clues that your life would give through your actions, thoughts and words?

Philippians 3:7-9
"But whatever gain I had, I counted as loss for the sake of Christ. Indeed, I count everything as loss because of the surpassing worth of knowing Christ Jesus my Lord. For his sake I have suffered the loss of all things and count them as rubbish, in order that I may gain Christ and be found in him, not having a righteousness of my own that comes from the law, but that which comes through faith in Christ, the righteousness from God that depends on faith..."

Everything else that Paul had accomplished was worth nothing to him. He wanted to be found in Christ, in a right relationship with Christ, counted righteous because of Christ...for he knew he had no righteousness apart from Christ.

Do you have that passion to be found in Jesus? Does your heart beat for the sake of Christ? Is He your number one passion? Is He worth more...truly more...than anything else?

If Christianity is one day outlawed in the U.S., will you and I, if arrested, have enough evidence against us, that we would be found guilty without question of living for Christ?

Live in such a way that you compile an incredible case against yourself if you are one day arrested for following Jesus!

That is something worth being guilty of.

Be guilty today and every day!

10/26

Good Greetings to Each and Every One of You,

I hope you had a good Monday. Today marks an anniversary of an event that I wish never would have. It was the passing away of one of my grandfathers. There has been loss within our own church, Towne Baptist, over the past few weeks. Take solace in remembering that Jesus has conquered death.

In fact, Jesus experienced the pain we feel, as He says in Luke 11:33-36:
"When Jesus saw her weeping, and the Jews who had come with her also weeping, he was deeply moved in his spirit and greatly troubled. And he said, "Where have you laid him?" They said to him, "Lord, come and see." Jesus wept. So the Jews said, "See how he loved him!"

Rest in the loving arms of Christ. Jesus experienced the death of a friend and knows what your loss is like. He knows the hurt and pain you are going or will go through. He wept...He felt the searing pain of loss as you do.

J.R.R. Tolkien wrote in Lord of the Rings:
PIPPIN: I didn't think it would end this way.
GANDALF: End? No, the journey doesn't end here. Death is just another path, one that we all must take. The grey rain-curtain of this world rolls back, and all turns to silver glass, and then you see it. PIPPIN: What? Gandalf? See what?
 GANDALF: White shores, and beyond, a far green country under a swift sunrise.
PIPPIN: Well, that isn't so bad.
GANDALF: No. No, it isn't.

Find rest in Christ. Find rest. Death for a Christian is "white shores." We must share the saving grace of Jesus with others. For those that died not knowing Him, "a far green country" is not their destination. But we must find our comfort in knowing Jesus will never leave us and has promised us heaven for believing in Him.

Jesus wept as you weep.
Jesus felt loss as you feel it.
Jesus is comfort and peace.

Reach out to Him during times of loss. He loves you deeply.
Till one day we reach those white shores…

10/27

Greetings to you on this day God has made,

Being a Christian is a piece of cake right? I mean, when you accept Jesus into your life, then you never have to deal with heartache, stress, pain (physical and emotional), tough decisions, temptations, etc...right?! When we accept Jesus, we are promised all the material possessions we desire and a life of ease!

Not. At. All.

Being a Christian means accepting and following the Creator of the universe through this journey called life, knowing that He loves us and cares for us...while realizing that we are not immune to the struggles of a fallen world and sinful flesh.

Jesus said, "I have said these things to you, that in me you may have peace. In the world you will have tribulation. But take heart; I have overcome the world." (John 16:33)

Jesus is up front and does not sugar coat things. He says you will have very tough times, but He lets you know He is more powerful than those times. He has won the war, even though you feel defeated at times. Your soul is rescued in Him. He can be trusted and relied upon during every season of life.

Thomas a Kempis wrote:
"We will do better in dealing with temptations if we keep an eye on them in the very beginning. Temptations are more easily overcome if they are never allowed to enter our minds. Meet them at the door as soon as they knock, and do not let them in. One simple thought can enter the mind and start the process."

We are not responsible for a thought approaching us, but we are responsible for choosing to think the thought instead of dismissing it through the power of the Holy Spirit.

"No temptation has overtaken you that is not common to man. God is faithful, and he will not let you be tempted beyond your ability, but with the temptation he will also provide the way of escape, that you may be able to endure it."
(1 Corinthians 10:13)

Overcoming temptation is all about God...through and by His power. He will provide a way out, but you must choose to take that path.

"Submit yourselves therefore to God. Resist the devil, and he will flee from you." (James 4:7)

We can only resist the devil through the power of God. We have the power of God through Jesus Christ as we yield our lives to Him.

Temptation and trials are great. Jesus is greater!
Submit to Christ today and everyday and He will not fail you!

10/28

Hello Everyone,

Car, plane, boat, horse, helicopter, rollerblades, hover board, feet, bike, wheelchair.
What do these have in common?

Wrong! They all are composed of letters of the alphabet!

I jest. You were right (maybe or maybe not, I'm not there with you and I don't know what your mind thinks) in saying that they are all modes of transportation.

Reflect Jesus in whatever mode of transportation you use. Wave at people that let you over, say excuse me, use your blinker, don't cut someone else off, obey the rules of the road, say thank you, say please, etc.

He can be honored or dishonored through our actions during the modes of transportation we use.

Choose to honor Him in what seem like the small things.

Honor Him!

10/29

Greetings everyone on this day that the Lord has made and ordained,

Just think...this day does not catch God by surprise, nor will anything that happens today. The world and her events change daily. Constant and consistent are not words to describe our world, except to say that our world is constant in not being constant and consistent in inconsistency.

But God...
"The steadfast love of the Lord never ceases; his mercies never come to an end; they are new every morning; great is your faithfulness. 'The Lord is my portion,' says my soul, 'therefore I will hope in him.' The Lord is good to those who wait for him, to the soul who seeks him." (Lamentations 3:22-25)

Find consistency in the mercy and love of God. The hope He offers is constant. Wait for Him and don't rush to create your own plans. Pray and wait...believing He is constant and consistent and cannot fail to be faithful.

His love, mercy and hope are not dependent upon you, your past, or your future. They are dependent upon Him...therefore, they are never-changing.
What a relief!

God is good, all the time. All the time, God is good.
No matter the circumstances.
The circumstances may be terrible, but God will show...
Himself faithful, His love to never cease, and His mercies to never end.

We may not understand, but as was depicted in a scene from The Little Drummer Boy, our understanding is not what is of importance, but our reliance upon Jesus in the midst of not understanding.

The young drummer boy speaks to one of the three kings about healing his lamb that has been hurt. The king says that there is nothing he can do.

Drummer boy: "But you are a king!"
King: "A mortal king only. But, there is a king among kings..."
Drummer boy: "But, I do not understand."
King: "It is not necessary that you understand. Go to Him."
Drummer boy: "But...I...I have no gift to bring."
King: "Go...look upon the newborn king."

God will give you Himself when you don't understand. Rest your eyes upon Him. Great is His faithfulness. Never-ceasing is His love. Never-ending is His love.

As the hymn sings...
Turn your eyes upon Jesus,
Look full in His wonderful face,
And the things of earth will grow strangely dim,
In the light of His glory and grace.

10/30

Hello and howdy to everyone,

It's Saturday, which means tomorrow is Sunday. Now, that may seem obvious and it is. But that means we have one more day of work until a day of rest.

Exodus 20:8
"Remember the Sabbath day, to keep it holy."
Genesis 2:2-3
"And on the seventh day God finished his work that he had done, and he rested on the seventh day from all his work that he had done. So God blessed the seventh day and made it holy, because on it God rested from all his work that he had done in creation."

Does God need to rest because He grows tired. No. But, He is giving us an example to abide by. Both of these verses reveal God's plan and command for us to live by. Rest, Worship, Renew.

Your Sabbath may be tomorrow, Sunday. Or, your work schedule may be such that you work on Sunday. Therefore, your Sabbath needs to be another day of the week...where you rest.
"Certainly work is not always required of a man. There is such a thing as a sacred idleness, the cultivation of which is now fearfully neglected." (George Mac Donald)

I would encourage you still, if at all possible, to come to church, even if you work on Sunday, to be a part of God's family and worship corporately as the body of Christ.

Honor this commandment of God...it's good for your body and soul.

From one heaven-bound, saved by grace alone soul to another, go forth in Him!

10/31

Good Day Everyone,

I hope you all had an enjoyable weekend. Our church has an annual Trunk or Treat and it is truly a wonderful time! This month, October, is famous for the holiday called Halloween.

There are mixed emotions regarding Halloween from the Christian perspective. Although I respect both sides, I believe that Halloween can be used and participated in such a way that reflects Jesus Christ to a dark world.

"Therefore, if anyone is in Christ, he is a new creation. The old has passed away; behold, the new has come." (2 Corinthians 5:17)
*Jesus creates a new heart within the believer and discards the "pulp" in our lives and replaces it with a shining light for a dark world to see.

"In the same way, let your light shine before others, so that they may see your good works and give glory to your Father who is in heaven." (Matthew 5:16)
*As the light shines in a carved pumpkin, so the light from the Holy Spirit shines through the heart of a Christian whose heart has been carved by the hand of the Savior. This light is a witness to others of the saving grace and powerful love of Jesus.

Allow God to carve out the "pulp" in your life, whatever the "pulp" may be. Beseech Him to shine His light through you to everyone you come into contact with!

From one wretch whose heart was carved and by God to another, go in Christ!

11/1

He is Risen! He is Risen Indeed!

Wait...it's not Easter. The pastor has fallen off his rocker.

True, it's not Easter. As to the last above statement...I'll plead the 5th.

In all seriousness though, we all should guard against forgetting the fact that Jesus is risen! This is foundational to our faith. This reminds us that Jesus is more powerful than death, the devil, and any power on earth or under the earth.

"He is not here, for he has risen, as he said. Come, see the place where he lay."
(Matthew 28:6)

Jesus is Risen! Jesus is Alive! Jesus is Sovereign and All-Powerful!

If we believe this, then we must believe that He is more powerful than any political party or country. He is on His throne no matter who is elected. No political party can save our country. Only Jesus can save our country. Only Jesus.

The upcoming election day is very important. But not more important than unity within the worldwide Christian church. Not more important than your church. Not more important than our church. Not more important than Jesus.

Don't resort to bashing political parties or ideologies. Stand for biblical truth, but season your stance with graciousness.

Below are some Scriptures to guide you during this election season and always:

"If any of you lacks wisdom, let him ask God, who gives generously to all without reproach, and it will be given him." (James 1:5)

"But the Helper, the Holy Spirit, whom the Father will send in my name, he will teach you all things and bring to your remembrance all that I have said to you." (John 14:26)

"Your word is a lamp to my feet and a light to my path." (Psalm 119:105)

Remember...
Jesus is Risen! Jesus is on His throne! Jesus was, is, and is to come!
Let Jesus and His resurrection be in and on your mind always.
From one whom Jesus went to the cross for to another, go in Him!

11/2

Good Greetings,

If you are reading this, then you are still on this side of heaven's eternal gates. And if you are on this side of heaven's eternal gates, God still has a plan for your life on earth. He still has work for you to do. He wants to continue to work through you for His glory. He wants you. The GOD of the Universe wants you. That. Is. Amazing. Soak that truth in for a moment.

"for it is God who works in you, both to will and to work for His good pleasure." (Philippians 2:13)

Now, if it is God who is working through you, what must we be doing?
Working!

Not with a mindset to earn your salvation, but to serve the One who died for you. He purchased your soul to be part of His family.

"For just as the body is one and has many members, and all the members of the body, though many, are one body, so it is with Christ." (1 Corinthians 12:12)

Each person in God's family has been given gifts by Him to be used in His church for His glory. Are you serving in the church? If you have not taken that step, what is holding you back? If you are serving, are you serving with a pure heart for His renown and not your own?

These are not easy questions, but necessary ones for each one of us.

God loves you and more than desires, but commands, for you to serve within the church. Why? It is a lifestyle of giving to the Giver the talents He has given to you. It is a heart-style of living out your gratitude and love for the One that displayed His grace and love for you on that old rugged cross. It is the living out of the Great Commission to tell others about Jesus Christ!

Will you take time to contemplate the above questions and ask God to speak to you and guide you moving forward?

Find pleasure in serving the One who takes pleasure in working through you to a broken world to display His love!

11/3

Top of the day to you,

I have been listening to Christmas music this week. Yes, I know, it's not Christmas But, Christmas songs (albeit, not all Christmas songs) have sincere depth in their meaning and are rich in soul-discipling. Take the plunge this week, if you haven't already, and give it a go...listen to one or many good, solid Christmas songs!

One that I was listening to was "O Come, O Come, Emmanuel," sung by Steven Curtis Chapman. Take a look at the lyrics:

O come, O come Emmanuel
And ransom captive Israel
That mourns in lonely exile here
Until the Son of God appear

Rejoice, rejoice, Emmanuel
Shall come to Thee, O Israel
Rejoice, rejoice, Emmanuel
Shall come to Thee, O Israel

Emmanuel means "God with us" in Hebrew.
"'Behold, the virgin shall conceive and bear a son, and they shall call His name Immanuel' (which means, God with us)."
Immanuel and Emmanuel mean the same

Ransom, according to the dictionary, means "a sum of money or other payment demanded or paid for the release of a prisoner."
"For even the Son of Man came not to be served but to serve, and to give His life as a ransom for many." (Mark 10:45)

Exile, according to the dictionary, means "the state or a period of forced absence from one's country or home; the state or a period of voluntary absence from one's country or home."
"And if I go and prepare a place for you, I will come again and will take you to myself, that where I am you may be also." (John 14:3)

Those words describe the plight of every person apart of Jesus Christ. But they are words that we must not forget once we accept Jesus into our lives. We tend to associate preaching solely with the action that is carried out by the pastor of a church or an evangelist. But, we must preach to ourselves each and every day the truth of God's Word, lest we forget. In the beginning of the movie The Fellowship of the Ring, you hear the following: "And some things that should not have been forgotten were lost."

So, preach those three words above to yourself each and every moment of your life. Remember that God is with you, always. Remember that Jesus paid your ransom to release you from being a prisoner of sin and the devil. Remember that though we are in exile now, we will be home and in the presence of our Savior one day.

Remember. Remember. Remember. Never forget!

Relish in the fact that God is with you. Rejoice in knowing Jesus has ransomed you. Radiate with the anticipation of journeying to your eternal with Jesus one day.

From one exiled soul who was ransomed by Emmanuel to another, have a solid day in Jesus!

11/4

Hello and Good Greetings!

Truth has become relative to many people these days...based upon feelings and emotions, instead of something concrete. As Christians, truth can never be relative because God is truth and God does not change. Neither does His Word, the Bible.

Now, to the verse that will be the foundation to this morning's topic:
"So God created man in His own image, in the image of God He created him; male and female He created them."
(Genesis 2:27)

We live in a culture that loves to have choices. God has graciously allowed us to live in a country where we have freedom of choice. But... the gender of which we are born is not a choice we are given by our Creator. He has chosen that for us and created us in His image that we would bring Him honor with our lives. Our gender is based upon the sovereign decision of God Almighty, not our emotions or feelings.

But wait, there's more...

"But now the righteousness of God has been manifested apart from the law, although the Law and the Prophets bear witness to it - the righteous of God through faith in Jesus Christ for all who believe. For there is no distinction: for all have sinned and fall short of the glory of God, and are justified by His grace as a gift, through the redemption that is in Christ Jesus." (Romans 3:21-24)

As Christians, our sin is no different than someone who is a male and says he identifies as a female, a female who says she identifies as a male, or any other sexual identify situation. We must stand for biblical truth, but always in God's love. God is the only sinless being, not us! We are forgiven because of the grace, love and sacrifice of Jesus Christ.

While we are on this subject...and what I'm about to say may come across as extreme, but the grace of God is extreme in the sense that a holy God suffered, died and rose again for each one of our sins...a child molester, rapist, murderer, terrorist, or any other person that we sometimes characterize as having committed a more heinous sin than us, is no greater of a sinner than you or me.

God is the only one without sin and all of us humans are on equal ground regarding our sin. There is no hierarchy of sin. God is holy, blameless, perfect and all-powerful. There is grace from His hand for all our sins.

Us humans are all in the same sinfully doomed and sinking boat apart from the redemption offered by Jesus. The only unforgivable sin is blasphemy against the Holy Spirit...which is denying Jesus Christ and not accepting Him as Lord and Savior before our death.

Let us, as God's Church, stand for biblical truth and remain steadfast. But let us also do so in love. Let us remember that no one's sin is greater than another's.

"Jesus stood up and said to her, 'Woman, where are they? Has no one condemned you?' She said, 'No one, Lord.' And Jesus said, 'Neither do I condemn you; go, and form now on sin no more.'"

Follow Jesus' example...
We must not condone any sin, but not condemn anyone either. Stand in love!

11/5

Greetings on this day,

"Father, make of me a crisis man. Bring those I contact to a decision. Let me be a milepost on a single road; make me a fork that men must turn one way or another on facing Christ in me." (Jim Elliot)

Does this prayer run through our DNA as Christians? This man was a missionary who was martyred for the sake of the call of Christ.

His desire was for anyone that he came into contact with to see Jesus through him...both in how he lived and how he spoke. He wanted each person to know who Jesus was and the grace, love and redemption He offered. Because of such an encounter, each person would know they have the choice to either follow Jesus or turn from Him. Jim Elliot desired to not waste one single encounter with an individual.

We must understand and believe that Jesus is coming back.
We must understand that we are commanded by our Lord and Savior to share Him with others.
We must...

Never take for granted an encounter with someone!
This may be your last time to share with them the life-changing and life-saving love of Jesus Christ!

"Father, make of me a crisis man. Bring those I contact to a decision. Let me be a milepost on a single road; make me a fork that men must turn one way or another on facing Christ in me." (Jim Elliot)

Let's be crisis men and women!

Please, if you can, look up and listen to: "Here I Go Again" by Casting Crowns.

11/6

Good Hello,

Within a short frame of time, there have been a number of passing aways from within our church family. There was also, just recently, the horrific shooting and murdering at the synagogue in Pittsburgh. There are, every day, battles with which the enemy would seek to destroy you.

How do we deal with loss and grief? How do we no sink under the pressures of life? Isn't the Christian life supposed to be easy? When you follow Jesus, that means the struggles you face now will all vanish. All pain and suffering will subside. Whatever makes you feel good will transpire into reality.

This is not the truth. Pain and suffering, death and loss. uncertainty and stress, are all emotions and events that we experience this side of heaven.

So, how do we traverse this journey if these and all other sorts of emotions can so easily cloud our lives? Take a look at this passage from Matthew 14:22-33

Immediately he made the disciples get into the boat and go before him to the other side, while he dismissed the crowds. And after he had dismissed the crowds, he went up on the mountain by himself to pray. When evening came, he was there alone, but the boat by this time was a long way from the land, beaten by the waves, for the wind was against them. And in the fourth watch of the night he came to them, walking on the sea. But when the disciples saw him walking on the sea, they were terrified, and said, "It is a ghost!" and they cried out in fear. But immediately Jesus spoke to them, saying, "Take heart; it is I. Do not be afraid."

And Peter answered him, "Lord, if it is you, command me to come to you on the water." He said, "Come." So Peter got out of the boat and walked on the water and came to Jesus. But when he saw the wind, he was afraid, and beginning to sink he cried out, "Lord, save me." Jesus immediately reached out his hand and took hold of him, saying to him, "O you of little faith, why did you doubt?" And when they got into the boat, the wind ceased. And those in the boat worshiped him, saying, "Truly you are the Son of God."

Keep your eyes on your Savior. Believe His words of truth found in the Bible in the midst of a world that will seek to deceive you with its ever-fluctuating notion of truth. Follow Jesus into the waves of life, wherever He may lead you. Listen to His leading as He tells you how to handle each situation you encounter, how to speak to each person you engage with, and how to think and react every moment of every day.

Keep your eyes on Him. Always.

"If you look at the world, you'll be distressed. If you look within, you'll be depressed. If you look at God you'll be at rest." (Corrie ten Boom)

Rest your eyes on Jesus.

11/7

Good Greetings,

"So teach us to number our days that we may get a heart of wisdom." (Psalm 90:12)

Forget not that each day is a gift from God...no matter the circumstances we find ourselves in. God still has a plan. God is still sovereign. God still loves you. God still is on His throne.

Forget not that we are only on this earth for the mere blink of an eye. We must understand our mortality. We must then, after realizing that our time upon this earth is but a breath, seek God for His wisdom on how to live accordingly...with our actions, thoughts, and words. He will help us to not squander our time, but instead to make the days count for His glory.

Are you living in such a way that if you were to die this morning, you would feel as though you had lived your life to the full for God's glory?

I encourage you to meditate on the brevity of life. Then, seek God to reveal how you can begin or grow in living for Christ. Beseech Him to give you His wisdom.

Carpe diem!

11/8

Good Thanks-living!

"Oh give thanks to the Lord, for He is good, for His steadfast love endures forever!" (Psalm 107:1)

We have now entered into the Thanksgiving season. Although the many stores would have you possibly believe Christmas has already begun! Let us not forget this season that is upon us...and one that we should actually keep each day of the year.

Give thanks
Praise God and sincerely thank Him for SPECIFIC things...
What He has done for you, given you, and been to you.
Who He is
Etc.
God is good
Circumstances surrounding you may not be good, but God's goodness is not determined by circumstances. If it was, God would be dictated by circumstances and God would not be all-powerful.
God is good and His love, grace and mercy proves this to us.
Jesus knows what suffering is and thus, is a God who we can trust and knows what we are going through.
God's steadfast love endures forever
His love for you does not fluctuate according to your actions or the actions of the world.
Nothing can conquer or overthrow His love for you.
The love of God has not expiration date!

November Thanksgiving Challenge! Each day...Thank God for at least 1 different thing you are thankful for and keep a record of each one. Ask God to use you, guide you, and reveal His will to you.

Read your Bible. If you're having trouble figuring out where to begin, try one of the following: read one chapter from Proverbs or one chapter from Psalm, or begin reading through the book of John.

The God to which we owe all of our thanks will be with you today and always.

Happy Thanks-living!

11/9

From one wretch forgiven by Christ to another, good greetings!

I would like to share a story with you about Corrie ten Boom. She, along with her family, were Christians who helped Jews during the Nazi occupation. She and her sister were eventually sent to a concentration camp where her sister would perish, but she would be released.

"After the war ended, Corrie started a life of traveling and telling her story to encourage other Christians. Going back into Germany to minister was the most difficult of all for her, but she felt that she must go wherever God sent her.

In 1947, at a church in Munich, a man walked up to her who looked strangely familiar. As he shook her hand she realized where she knew him from: He had been one of the crueler guards at Ravensbruck [concentration camp]! As he realized that she recognized him, he looked at her with water eyes. 'Miss ten Boom, I have become a Christian since the war. I know now in my heart that God has forgiven me, but I must also ask for your forgiveness. Can you forgive me for all of the evil I did to you, your sister, and the others?'

It took some time for Corrie to respond. As she struggled over what she would say, she found that she had many more things than she had realized to release to God about what had happened to her during the war. In the end, though, her response was simple and straightforward: 'I forgive you, brother, with all my heart.'" (taken from the book Jesus Freaks: Revolutionaries)

Take pause and, through prayer, ask God to reveal to you anyone that you need to forgive...truly forgive...through the love of Jesus. This may not be easy and may birth pain. But the forgiveness of our sins was bought through pain. Jesus has forgiven you. With His help and by His power, forgive others. Call, text, write, meet up with...whomever it is that God is placing on your heart to forgive.

"Be kind to one another, tenderhearted, forgiving one another, as God in Christ forgave you." (Ephesians 4:32)

From one who is forgiven by Christ to another, have a solid day in Jesus!

11/10

Greetings and Greetings,

A quick thought for the day, at whatever point of the day you read this. It's not easy, pleasant, or desirable! But it's being like Christ Jesus and He did the same!

Love and respect
Respect through love

Through the love of Christ
Who reigns above

Go forth through His power alone!

11/11

Good Greetings Ya'll,

We live freely. Freely! Take a moment right now and let your freedom sink in.

There are many countries that its citizens cannot say this. They are not able to meet corporately as a church body either. Christianity in some countries is simply banned.

Freedom is a word and concept that many, many, many people do not understand or truly comprehend.

Today is Veterans Day...a day where we as Americans should honor and thank our men and women who have served in our armed forces. We should honor them. Take another moment and read the following quotes...

"The brave men, living and dead, who struggled here, have consecrated it, far above our poor power to add or detract. The world will little note, nor long remember what we say here, but it can never forget what they did here." (Abraham Lincoln)

"Poor is the nation that has no heroes, but poorer still is the nation that having heroes, fails to remember and honor them." (Marcus Tullius)

We should and must remember this day and our veterans!

At the same time, we must, this day and every day, remember the freedom, the ultimate freedom, that Jesus Christ offers us through Himself!

"So if the Son sets you free, you will be free indeed." (John 8:36)

This is the freedom from sin, our past failures, eternal damnation in hell apart from Christ's presence. This freedom is eternal life in heaven if we place our faith in Jesus Christ!

We should and must remember our Lord and Savior Jesus Christ! We must honor Him with our very lives. We must be prepared to give our very last breath for Him. We must!

I texted a buddy of my dad's today who served in the army over in Vietnam. He was a decorated combat veteran and served for many years. His rely back to me was: "you guys were worth it."

Let those words resonate within your very soul. That's the heart of a true veteran. On an even deeper level, that's the heart of Jesus Christ towards each person on the planet...you guys were worth it."

Oh, the love of Jesus Christ and oh, what amazing grace.

Celebrate and thank our veterans.
Celebrate and thank Jesus Christ more.

Remember the freedom our veterans have served for.
Remember the freedom our Lord and Savior died and rose again for more.

Let freedom ring!

11/12

Hi and Hello,

The leaves have changed in our neck of the woods and they are simply beautiful...part of the handiwork of God's creation. Now, this is the time of the year in which the leaves have changed, but will eventually fall when colder weather from winter arrives. Leaves change... circumstances change...sometimes for times of ease and sometimes for times that simply wears on a person's soul.

During the beginning portion of an old Christmas movie, It's A Wonderful Life, there is a dialogue that transpires:

Franklin: "A man down on Earth needs our help."
Clarence: "Splendid! Is he sick?"
Franklin: "No, worse. He's discouraged."

For you see, times of physical distress, though serious in nature and ones that test our faith, are not the only sorts of
soul-trying moments. Mental anguish, whether from... the passing of a loved one, family disagreements, employment or job searching, remembrances of the past or anxiety about the future, etc...has the capability to inflict serious discouragement, hopelessness, restlessness, worry, etc. upon the very soul of a man or woman.

Run...actually, sprint to the Word of God and find encouragement and be renewed!!!

"Be strong, and let your heart take courage, all you who wait for the Lord!" (Psalm 31:24)
Wait for God's timing. Take courage and be strong in God's Word with what it says and remember that God has your back. Stand firm on His promises against the enemy.

"See what kind of love the Father has given to us, that we should be called children of God; and so we are." (1 John 3:1)
God Almighty loves you! You, once you accept Jesus into your life,

are His child! Wow! No matter what is going on, remember that you are His and He loves you!

"The LORD will fight for you, and you have only to be silent." (Exodus 14:14)

Give whatever it is to God. Put your faith in Him. Pray asking that He would guide you in how to act and that He would help you give it over to Him. He will fight for you for His glory.

Stop trying to figure it out and fight it on your own. Pray and be silent as He fights for you and you listen to His voice. Dwell on Christ!

I shall leave you with the lyrics to an old song by MercyMe. "The Promise"

I love you
And I will never leave you
Nor forsake you
And I love you
And i will never leave you

You are my child
You are my child
When you're down
When your heart is broken
When no one seems to care
PLease know that I love you

Cuz you are my child
You are my child
And i want to wrap my arms around you
And i want to wrap my arms around you
And say everything, everything will be alright

You are my child
You are my child
Let me wipe those tears from your eyes
Let me wipe those tears from your eyes

Come to me
Come to me
Come to Jesus
Come to him
Come to Jesus
Come to him
11/13

Hello and greetings to you all. Remember that God loves you and is still in control! Let us now dive into today's food for thought...

There are many role models out there today, but few who actually live out their Christian faith. We must, must, must be a role model throughout our daily lives.

"Show yourself in all respects to be a model of good works, and in your teaching show integrity, dignity, and sound speech that cannot be condemned, so that an opponent may be put to shame, having nothing evil to say about us." (Titus 2:7-8)

We are commanded to model good deeds and show the above characteristics in our teaching of others about Christ. This means...

We gotta live like we profess to believe. We must live out our faith. Fully. Completely. Resolutely.

When you teach and explain the things of the Bible to others, make sure you're:
Teaching correctly about Scripture.
Taking you're responsibility seriously and being composed.
Teaching the Bible, letting God's Spirit guide you in such a way, that what you teach is not able to be overtaken by an unbeliever.

"Be imitators of me, as I am of Christ."
(1 Corinthians 11:1)

Imitate Christ. Period, end of the report. Then, when people see how you are living, they will know Jesus is the difference in your life or will ask how are you different.

Let me share this quote from the movie, The Last Samauri:
Emperor Meiji: "Tell me how he died."
Algren: "I will tell you how he lived."

Live in such a way, through Christ, that when you die, Christians will desire to tell others how you lived...not in such a way as to point to yourself, but to point others to Christ by the way your life reflected His ways.

Live to tell others about Jesus!

11/14

Hello on this day that God created,

Church is always fun. It's full of people without issues. In fact, everyone there always treats each other as Christ would desire!

False!
But you know what, that cannot be a reason we abandon it and aren't active.
Jesus doesn't abandon us!

Church is like a gas station. A car is like a Christian. A gas station doesn't make a car a car, but a car can't run properly without going to one.

Now get to church!

11/15

Good Greetings Everyone,

Jesus loves and knows you, this believe!

The year was 1793.
The date was November 8th.
The location was Paris, France.
The Louvre opened to the public.
According to britannica.com: "Louvre Museum, French Musée du Louvre, official name Great Louvre, French Grand Louvre, national museum and art gallery of France, housed in part of a large palace in Paris that was built on the right-bank site of the 12th-century fortress of Philip Augustus. It is the world's most-visited art museum, with a collection that spans work from ancient civilizations to the mid-19th century."

"That's great Nathan. Wow. Thank you for sharing. What on the circular earth does that have to do with my personal life?"

Well, since you asked...I'm personally financing trips overseas for people to enjoy this museum! You must say amen to this email first in order for this to happen.

Early April Fools...

I digress to two thoughts I would like to share in hopes that you will contemplate them.

Thought one: Please do not believe any Facebook posting that would seek to deceive people into thinking that blessings, wealth, health, etc. are coming their way if they type amen and share or anything to that effect. These are lies...absolute lies.

God does not work in such ways. He will bless according to His will, grace, mercy, faithfulness...as you walk with Him day by day. Not according to sharing a Facebook posting saying amen.

Christ loves you and longs for you to look to Him and He loves you deeply.

Thought two: Can you imagine the amazing treasures of art that are contained in this museum?! The many artists that were given gifts by God! Wow, wow, wow!

11/16

How much more God's Word?! The very words of God to you! God spoke through and inspired many authors to write down exactly what He wanted to say to you!

"Oh, the depth of the riches and wisdom and knowledge of God! How unsearchable are His judgments and how inscrutable His ways!" (Romans 11:33)

**This verse describes the sheer awesomeness of God! We will never be able to fully understand His riches, knowledge, judgments or ways. But, what He wants us to know, He has placed in the Bible. And it's available for us to read! It's a treasure!

"Your word is a lamp to my feet and a light to my path." (Psalm 119:105)

**His Treasure guides and instructs us! It's a treasure!

"The grass withers, the flower fades, but the word of our God will stand forever." (Isaiah 40:8)

**Truth is though, that museum (although hopefully not) could be completely destroyed and all the wonderful pieces of art destroyed. But God's Word will last forever, no matter what actions the devil may try to carry out! It's a treasure!

Dig into His treasure, which is the Bible. And you don't have to travel overseas to experience such rich and wonderful treasures!

Enjoy His treasure today and always!

11/17

Greetings to You,

Call me Reverend Kaspar.

Just kidding! Call me Nathan

We all like to receive respect, correct?
But, we must not want it out of a prideful mindset!

We should also be sure to respect others, even if we disagree with them.

"I speak to everyone in the same way, whether he is the garbage man or the president of the university." (Albert Einstein)

This is a way that will demonstrate Christ to a world that is disrespectful in disagreement.

Strive to show respect, even when disrespected!

11/18

Good Hello Everyone,

I encourage you to dwell upon the following verses:
"Thy word is a lamp unto my feet, and a light unto my path." (Psalm 119:105)
    *Look to the Bible, God's Word, to guide your every thought, word and action today.

"Thy word have I hid in mine heart, that I might not sin against thee." (Psalm 119:111)
    **By dwelling upon and memorizing Scripture, through the power of the Holy Spirit, you will know what God desires you to do instead of your flesh.

"But now thus says the LORD, he who created you, O Jacob, he who formed you, O Israel: 'Fear not, for I have redeemed you; I have called you by name, you are mine.'" (Isaiah 43:1)
    **God has redeemed you and made you His...nothing can steal you from His hand.

"If any of you lacks wisdom, let him ask God, who gives generously to all without reproach, and it will be given him." (James 1:5)
    **Ask, Ask, Ask.

"Peace I leave with you; my peace I give to you. Not as the world gives do I give to you. Let not your hearts be troubled, neither let them be afraid." (John 14:27)
    **Peace and no fear...all because of Jesus.

His words are the only ones of eternal value. Dwell upon them. Memorize them. Hold onto them. They are life, for they come from the Giver of Life...God Almighty!

11/19

Good Howdy,

Anticipation (according to Merriam-Webster):
"a prior action that takes into account or forestalls a later action"
"the act of looking forward," "especially: pleasurable expectation"
Katie and I were at the opening night of the BCMD Convention. The hosting church had their Christmas decorations up. You may be thinking that it's too early.

But, see it this way as you begin the week...

Let Christmas decorations and the thought of Christmas be a reminder of the joy of Jesus' first coming and anticipation (see definition above) of His second coming!
"And an angel of the Lord appeared to them, and the glory of the Lord shone around them, and they were filled with great fear. And the angel said to them, 'Fear not, for behold, I bring you good news of great joy that will be for all the people. For unto you is born this day in the city of David a Savior, who is Christ the Lord. And this will be a sign for you: you will find a baby wrapped in swaddling cloths and lying in a manger.' And suddenly there was with the angel a multitude of the heavenly host praising God and saying, 'Glory to God in the highest, and on earth peace among those with whom he is pleased!' When the angels went away from them into heaven, the shepherds said to one another, 'Let us go over to Bethlehem and see this thing that has happened, which the Lord has made known to us.'" (Luke 2:9-15)

"Behold, I am coming soon, bringing my recompense with me, to repay each one for what he has done. I am the Alpha and the Omega, the first and the last, the beginning and the end." (Revelation 22:12-13)

"He who testifies to these things says, 'Surely I am coming soon.' Amen. Come, Lord Jesus! The grace of the Lord Jesus be with all. Amen." (Revelation 22:20-21)

Anticipate Jesus' second coming at any moment. Live in such a way that you don't waste a single moment. Live for Him, tell others about Him, honor Him.

Don't worry about the future...Anticipate what He has in store for you today, this week, and the rest of your life. Anticipate with joy!

-427-

11/20

Hello Everyone,

Two phrases for today:
Jesus loves me
Jesus loves you

Know and believe the first in order to share the second to each person you come across…through your actions and words.

May seem simple, but the simple things we overlook at times and don't really dwell upon.

His love for you.
Your love for Him.
For others to hear and be shown.

Two phrases!

11/21

Jesus loves you.

He knows you and loves you.

I hope you hold to the unending truth of those statements: Jesus loves you. He knows you and loves you.

"A new commandment I give to you, that you love one another: just as I have loved you, you also are to love one another. By this all people will know that you are my disciples, if you have love for one another." (John 13:34-35)

Are you a follower of Jesus Christ? Love everyone.
Yes...everyone. The terrorist? Yes. The rapist? Yes. The child molester? Yes.

Jesus never said there should not be consequences to wrong actions. But...
"A new commandment I give to you, that you love one another: just as I have loved you, you also are to love one another."

And then...
"By this all people will know that you are my disciples, if you have love for one another."

The annoying co-worker? Yes.
The power-hungry boss? Yes.
The family member that never changes? Yes.

Every single person that you will ever come into contact with while you still have breath in your lungs? Yes.

"A new commandment I give to you, that you love one another: just as I have loved you, you also are to love one another. By this all people will know that you are my disciples, if you have love for one another."

This very moment, pause and ask God to help you show His love to every single person you ever come into contact with. Ask Him to help you move past any hurts that have prevented you from loving and ask Him to help you forgive.

Love others. Jesus loves you. Jesus knows you and loves you. Love others. Only by His love!

11/22

Good Greetings,

"Rejoice in hope, be patient in tribulation, be constant in prayer." (Romans 12:12)

These words were written by Paul, a man well acquainted with trials and tribulations. Yet, he wrote this verse, which was inspired by God.

The first portion: find joy in the hope you have in Jesus Christ. Remember, joy is the soul smiling in the midst of a frowning world. You have a hope that will never fail because the Author of that hope can never be defeated.

The second portion: when you are going through tough times, it is easy to become anxious. Ask Christ to give you patience, knowing that He will conform you more to His likeness through the trial. Ask Christ to help you not focus on the trial itself, but on what He is teaching you through it and how you can, in the midst of even dire circumstances, reflect Him to others.

The third portion: never stop praying. The enemy knows that prayer is your lifeline and will seek to distract you from it or try to convince you it is of no worth or value anymore. Don't believe him for one second. Ask Christ to keep your mind upon Him, always dwelling upon Him, and ever in conversation with Him. You don't have to be in a certain physical spot or location to pray and your prayer does not have to be a specific length or time. Keep open communication and in constant communication with your Savior throughout the day.

RHPTCP
Rejoice in hope, patient in tribulation, constant in prayer
RHPTCP

Oh...and enjoy the snow and remember He has washed your sin as white as snow. Amen!

11/23

Good Day,

Thanksgiving is closely coming upon us.

"Give thanks to the Lord, for he is good, for His steadfast love endures forever. Give thanks to the God of gods, for His steadfast love endures forever. Give thanks to the Lord of lords, for His steadfast love endures forever." (Psalm 136:1-3)

I encourage you to take time this week to read the complete chapter of 136.

Our mere mortal words fall into an inadequacy chasm
For how can we express thanks for a love we cannot fathom

Our souls were sentenced to eternal damnation
For we were enemies of God's heavenly nation

Our Christ, He came and dwelt among men
For to pay our penalty for our sin He left heaven

Our hearts He calls to and desires to live in
For thus let us forever give thanks for our salvation He did win

Don't allow Thanksgiving to simply be for one Thursday in November.
Let Thanksgiving be your life's song you sing to Jesus Christ!

Enjoy His bounty!

11/24

Hello and good greetings,

Have you ever longed to hear the voice of God and it just seemed like it was impossible? Maybe it seemed as if God had specifically chosen you as the one person He would not allow to hear Him speak.

If you have felt that way, take heart. He speaks and longs for you to listen. You can hear God's voice. His very voice!

But, you must come to understand that God does not always speak in the most obvious and boisterous ways. We must be ever alert, through the power of the Holy Spirit, to discern God's voice throughout the day.

"And He said, "'Go out and stand on the mount before the Lord.' And behold, the Lord passed by, and a great and strong wind tore the mountains and broke in pieces the rocks before the Lord, but the Lord was not in the wind. And after the wind an earthquake, but the Lord was not in the earthquake. And after the earthquake a fire, but the Lord was not in the fire. And after the fire the sound of a low whisper."
(1 Kings 19:11-12)

Ask the Holy Spirit to make your heart attentive to God's gentle whisper. There are many "loud noises" throughout the day that would seek to distract you or deceive you into thinking they are the voice of God. Pray that you may not fall to them.

God speaks through many avenues: the Bible, music, people, nature, and any other avenue He desires.

God speaks.
He speaks to you.
Will you listen?

He loves you.

Have a wonderful day listening!

11/25

Good greetings to you all,

There are many areas of interest that fight for one's attention during the weekend. They can and many of them are good areas of interest. But good things can often times become elevated by our own hands to too lofty of a shelf.

"You shall not make for yourself a carved image, or any likeness of anything that is in heaven above, or that is in the earth beneath, or that is in the water under the earth. You shall not bow down to them or serve them, for I the LORD your God am a jealous God..." (Exodus 20:4-5a)

The jealousy of God is all together pure, righteous and holy. He alone is deserving of our worship. Nothing should and nothing must take His place in our minds and hearts.

What have or what are you elevating above Him. To whom or to what are you giving your affection and attention in the place of which should belong to God? Again, things can be good in and of themselves, but when we elevate them above God, we have sinned and must repent (do an about-face and walk again in His paths).

Watching sports? Your children's sporting interests?
Your spouse? Your children?
Food? Shopping?
Christmas decorations? Politics? Facebook?
Work? Exercise? Hobbies?
Etc, Etc, Etc
It can be anything or anyone...literally anything or anyone!

Pray to the God of your soul that He would aid you in not elevating anything or anyone to a place that should and must be reserved for Him alone. He will honor that prayer.

Worship Him!
Enjoy Him!

Revere Him!

11/26

Hello,

Have you ever felt weary of standing for biblical truth? Is it even worth it anymore? There are so many different versions of truth nowadays and so many different avenues of so-called enlightenment, peace and purpose.

But, they are not truth. Remember and hold to the Truth.

"For the time is coming when people will not endure sound teaching, but having itching ears they will accumulate for themselves teachers to suit their own passions, and will turn away from listening to the truth and wander off into myths. As for you, always be sober-minded, endure suffering, do the work of an evangelist, fulfill your ministry." (2 Timothy 4:3-5)

We live in such a time. Think clearly with the Holy Spirit guiding your thoughts. Don't give up when you are persecuted for holding on to the truth. Spread the truth about the Gospel.
Do what God has called you to do.

Reflect upon these lyrics from a song sung by Geoff Moore:

Tell me again of the Gospel story
Tell me again how the whole world was lost
How the Only Begotten with grace so amazing
Gave up His life on an old rugged cross
I don't want to forget so please, tell me
Tell me again of the old, old stories
Tell me again of the faithful who walked
How the Only Begotten, with grace so amazing
Gave up His life on an old rugged cross
I don't want to forget so please, tell me again
I don't want to forget, so please, tell me again

Don't forget. Ask God to tell you again each and every day.

Because of Jesus' death on that old rugged cross and His resurrection, go in Him!

11/27

Happy Greetings,

My wife, Katie, was in the hospital on two separate visits and in the midst of that period of our lives, we witnessed the outpouring of the family of God.

From phone calls to texts to visits…prayers being offered from God's people as they entered His throne room…these people were from different states, friends and family, from the present church we are serving at to the church we came from. They were the hands and feet of Jesus...

"Little children, let us not love in word or talk but in deed and in truth." (1 John 3:18)
These people were a reflection of Jesus to us. They lived out their faith..."in deed and in truth."

From this I offer some bits of reflection: If you don't have a church family that you are active in, I deeply encourage you to find one that God leads you to. It won't be perfect, but then again, neither are you. Neither am I. Neither is anyone. If you do have a church, but are not active, please become active. This is Jesus' desire for all of His followers!

"For just as the body is one and has many members, and all the members of the body, though many, are one body, so it is with Christ. For in one Spirit we were all baptized into one body—Jews or Greeks, slaves or free—and all were made to drink of one Spirit. For the body does not consist of one member but of many. If the foot should say, 'Because I am not a hand, I do not belong to the body,' that would not make it any less a part of the body. And if the ear should say, 'Because I am not an eye, I do not belong to the body,' that would not make it any less a part of the body. If the whole body were an eye, where would be the sense of hearing? If the whole body were an ear, where would be the sense of smell? But as it is, God arranged the members in the body, each one of them, as he chose. If all were a single member, where would the body be? As it is, there are many parts, yet one body." (1 Corinthians

12:12-20)

Each believer has a God-given role to play in the adventure God has placed him or her in! Take a moment and reflect upon God's character. Meditate upon who He is. This verse reveals who God is...the God that created you and whom you believe in!

"The LORD your God is in your midst, a mighty One who will save; He will rejoice over you with gladness; He will quiet you with His love; He will exult over you with loud singing." (Zephaniah 3:17)

Remember and thank Him for who He is!

11/28

Happy Hello!

God is good, all the time!
All the time, God is good!

Thanksgiving is a day that may find you enjoying exactly what is taking place in life. Or, this day may find you going through trials and tribulations. This day may find you alone or it may find you surrounded by friends and family.

God is with you no matter what your circumstances!

Whatever your lot may be, "give thanks in all circumstances; for this is the will of God in Christ Jesus for you." (1 Thessalonians 5:18)

Jesus Christ came, died and rose again in order to save our souls. He gave up His life for you. He loves you. God is love. Be thankful for who God is!
Be thankful to God not only for the tangible things in your life that He has given you, but for who He is.

I leave you with these lyrics from a Mark Schultz song, "I AM"...

I am the maker of the heavens
I am the bright and morning star
I am the breath of all creation
Who always was
And is to come
I am the One who walked on water
I am the One who calmed the seas
I am the miracles and wonders
So come and see
And follow me
You will know
I am the fount of living water
The risen Son of Man

The healer of the broken
And when you cry
I am your Savior and Redeemer
Who bore the sins of man
The author and perfecter
Beginning and the end
I am
I am the Spirit deep inside you
I am the Word upon your heart
I am the One who even knew you
Before your birth
Before you were
Before the Earth (I am)
The universe (I am)
In every heart (I am)
Oh, where you are (I am)
The Lord of love (I am)
The King of Kings (I am)
The Holy Lamb (I am)
Above all things
Yes, I am almighty God your Father
The risen Son of Man
The healer of the broken
And when you cry
I am your Savior and Redeemer
Who bore the sins of man
The author and perfecter
Beginning and the end
I am

God is all these things! Let us be thankful to Him for who He is this and every day!

Happy Thanks-living!

11/29

Good greetings to you,

The day after Thanksgiving is a national day of spending money... lots of money. In fact, take a read below:

"Black Friday 2018 is expected to be bigger than ever, with 74% of Americans planning to open their wallets on either Black Friday and Cyber Monday, according to the latest research from finder.com.
The average adult is expected to drop $483.18 on the shopping holiday of holidays, which equates to $90.14 billion—up $30.57 billion from 2017's projected spend of $59.57 billion." (https://www.finder.com/black-friday-statistics)

Whoa!

Don't get me wrong, Christmas shopping is fun and something I have enjoyed for many years. Yes, I even enjoy wrapping Christmas presents. Yes, I even take note of what design of wrapping paper I like to use for people's gifts. I simply enjoy it!

But...

"Do not lay up for yourselves treasures on earth, where moth and rust destroy and where thieves break in and steal, but lay up for yourselves treasures in heaven, where neither moth nor rust destroys and where thieves do not break in and steal. For where your treasure is, there your heart will be also."
(Matthew 6:19-21)

I encourage you to not set the obtaining of material possessions as your goal, as your passion, as your false sense of joy.
Lay up eternal treasures...pursue the things of God, spend as He would have you spend, tell others about Him and live for Him.
How you spend reveals if your heart is focused on Christ or the world.

Now...

Is shopping for yourself and others wrong? No.

Is wrapping presents wrong? No.

Is our American culture of excessive shopping and spending wrong? Absolutely and unequivocally Yes.

"...the borrower is the slave of the lender." (Proverbs 22:7b

I encourage you to no go into debt trying to obtain all the perfect gifts for others or for yourself. Debt enslaves people.

If you are in serious debt, seek financial advice. God will walk with you through it!

11/30

Hello and Hi,

As Christians, shopping must not become our focus during the Christmas season. We must take a good hard look at our spending and see...

Am I spending more than is wise?
What am I identifying as my treasures?
Am I sacrificing the giving of my funds to my church? (This can be a touchy subject. But, it is a biblical question to be asked.)

"Who doesn't like a good deal? Anticipation of those deep price cuts and the rush to get there first heightens the excitement and increases the frenzy to GET THE DEAL, NOW! Excitement clouds this reality: even though you are getting great deals, you are still spending money." (Maggie Baker)

Ask God to not allow the "clouds of this reality" to develop over your heart this Christmas season. Ask God to give you discernment in your spending and a heart to spend your money in such a way that Christ would be evident within your spending...that HE would be glorified.

This Christmas season, anticipate more so all the ways He will grow your walk with Him and how He will use you to show Himself to others, than all the great shopping deals.

Christmas is a celebration of when God came to dwell with us. He is with you. And He's coming back again someday!

Live in anticipation this Christmas season and always!

12/1

Good Late Greetings,

Late...that actually is a word that describes how I and all of us sometimes feel God is in His timing. Although I am late in sending this devotional out, I and all of us must remember that God is never late and His timing is always perfect...no matter what our desires or emotions may lead or tell us.

One of J.R.R. Tolkien's characters, Gandalf, in The Lord of the Rings says that he "is never late, nor is he early. He arrives precisely when he means to." This character was the wise old sage in the series. Such a description is completely accurate way for our humans minds to better understand the character of our God. God is never late, nor early. God's timing is perfect!

"But do not overlook this one fact, beloved, that with the Lord one day is as a thousand years, and a thousand years as one day." (2 Peter 3:8)

"The Lord is good to those who wait for Him, to the soul who seeks Him. It is good that one should wait quietly for the salvation of the Lord." (Lamentations 3:25-26)

God's timing is far above ours. Trust His timing instead of yours.
God is good. He carries out His goodness to you as you wait for Him. Wait in patience for Him.

"...God, in His mercy, does not answer our prayers according to our understanding, but according to His wisdom." (Rich Mullins)

Trust God.
Trust that God is good.
Trust that God's timing is perfect.
By trusting, you will be able to rest in His peace.

Trust, rest, have peace.

From one sinner saved by the grace of Jesus Christ to another!

12/2

Good Greetings and Merry Christmas to you all,

The Christmas season is now upon us, which also means the advent season is upon us.

O come, O come, Emmanuel,
And ransom captive Israel,
That mourns in lonely exile here
Until the Son of God appears.
Rejoice! Rejoice!
Emmanuel shall come to thee, O Israel.

Hope allows us to trust in the promise that Jesus is coming back for His people.

Hebrews 6:18-20 states: "so that by two unchangeable things, in which it is impossible for God to lie, we who have fled for refuge might have strong encouragement to hold fast to the hope set before us. We have this as a sure and steadfast anchor of the soul, a hope that enters into the inner place behind the curtain, where Jesus has gone as a fore-runner on our behalf..."

The hope that is through Jesus Christ is a gift He gives you as an anchor for your soul through the many storms of life. Jesus will return again one day and take you to be with Him. Believe and rest in this hope.

"Hope, like faith, is nothing if it is not courageous; it is nothing if it is not ridiculous." -Thornton Wilder

Our hope and faith will seem ridiculous to the world. But Jesus will supply the courage to stand your ground and hold to the hope and faith you have in Him.

In John 14:3, Jesus states: "And if I go and prepare a place for you, I will come again and will take you to myself, that where I am you may be also."

He will bring you to that place. Trust and believe it! And what a wonderful place it will be!

Go forth this day, week, month, season and the rest of your days with this hope!

Merry, Merry Christmas in His hope!

12/3

Merry Christmas,

Reflect upon the following lyrics from the song "Go Tell It On The Mountain":

Down in a lowly manger
Our humble Christ was born
And God sent us salvation
That blessed Christmas morn

Go, tell it on the mountain
Over the hills and everywhere
Go, tell it on the mountain
That Jesus Christ is born!

Psalm 96:3
"Declare his glory among the nations, His marvelous works among all the peoples!"

Mark 16:15
"And he said to them, "Go into all the world and proclaim the gospel to the whole creation.""

Go forth this day, and each one God gives you, living out those lyrics and living out those verses!

Merry Christmas indeed!

12/4

Merry Christmas,

What makes this season, and actually what should be every day, merry?
Jesus, Jesus, Jesus!
Because He chose to have a relationship with you, this and every day can be merry! Not necessarily happy, for happiness depends upon circumstances. But joyful, for joy depends upon the holder of one's soul. For the Christian, the holder is Jesus Christ. With Jesus also as your example of how to live, you will know how to abide with a heart of joy, no matter what the circumstances. are in your life.

Hebrews 12:1-3
"Therefore, since we are surrounded by so great a cloud of witnesses, let us also lay aside every weight, and sin which clings so closely, and let us run with endurance the race that is set before us, looking to Jesus, the founder and perfecter of our faith, who for the joy that was set before Him endured the cross, despising the shame, and is seated at the right hand of the throne of God. Consider Him who endured from sinners such hostility against himself, so that you may not grow weary or fainthearted."

Jesus endured it all in obedience to the Father, for the glory of God, in order to save your soul from hell. Remember His endurance, call upon Him to help you endure and seek Him to replenish your joy even in the midst of the trials of life.

God sent His son, they called Him Jesus;
He came to love, heal and forgive;
He lived and died to buy my pardon,
An empty grave is there to prove my Savior lives!

Because He lives, I can face tomorrow,
Because He lives, all fear is gone;
Because I know He holds the future,
And life is worth the living,

Just because He lives!
(Gloria Gaither and William J. Gaither)

Because Jesus lives and lives in you, you can have joy this Christmas and every day!

Joy to the World, Jesus has come!

12/5

Good greetings and merry Christmas,
Go forth this day in the power of the Holy Spirit and make much of Jesus!

"I want to make much of You, Jesus
I want to make much of Your love
I want to live today to give You the praise
That You alone are so worthy of
I want to make much of Your mercy
I want to make much of Your cross
I give You my life
Take it and let it be used
To make much of You" (Much of You, sung by Steven Curtis Chapman)

Take a look at the story that is a prelude to the Christmas story... about Zechariah, his wife Elizabeth and their son John the Baptist. There is great worth in taking a look at this portion of God's Word during this wonderful time of year.

"And there appeared to him an angel of the Lord standing on the right side of the altar of incense. And Zechariah was troubled when he saw him, and fear fell upon him. But the angel said to him, 'Do not be afraid, Zechariah, for your prayer has been heard, and your wife Elizabeth will bear you a son, and you shall call his name John. And you will have joy and gladness, and many will rejoice at his birth...'" (Luke 1:11-14)

God heard Zechariah's prayer. God hears your prayers. God answers according to His will. Take comfort in these truths!

"...God, in His mercy, does not answer our prayers according to our understanding, but according to His wisdom." (Rich Mullins)
Take comfort in believing that God's answers are always better than your human desires.

When we desire for God's will to be done in our lives, we will have joy...unceasing joy. You may find yourself just beginning to pray for something. Or, you may find yourself in the midst of praying for something for many years. God hears you. God Almighty hears you. If you have trusted the eternal destination of your soul to Him, trust Him with the answers to your prayers. Trust and be merry in Him!

12/6

Merry Christmas through Jesus everyone!

How is your gift-giving going this Christmas season?
No no...not your Christmas shopping, but your gift-giving?

You may be asking yourself, "What in the name of jingle bells and deck the halls does he mean?"

What I mean by gift-giving is the words you are speaking to and about others. Those words are either beautifully wrapped presents or lumps of coal.

How would you describe your gift-giving thus far this Christmas season...or throughout this past year?

"Death and life are in the power of the tongue, and those who love it will eat of its fruits." (Proverbs 18:21)
Choose to give life-gifts through your words this Christmas season and every day of your life. Ask the Holy Spirit to give you His words to speak to others, in order that Jesus would be seen and honored through everything you say.

Also, the words you speak reveal your character to others...

"Better to remain silent and be thought a fool than to speak and remove all doubt." (Different attributions to this quote)

"Whoever restrains his words has knowledge, and he who has a cool spirit is a man of understanding. Even a fool who keeps silent is considered wise; when he closes his lips, he is deemed intelligent." (Proverbs 17:27-28)

Weigh your words before you allow them out of your mouth. Not simply profanity, but also the thoughts you express, the beliefs you state, and each and every sentence your tongue creates. Make sure they all bring honor to Jesus.

How's your gift-giving going? What is your character depiction you are giving others based upon the words your speak?

Seek God's grace, mercy, wisdom, and goodness...that your words may be gifts and that your character may reflect that of Jesus Christ... this Christmas season and every day of your life!

12/7

Greetings on this 7th day of December.

On this day, years ago, our country found itself under attack at Pearl Harbor. This day, so many years ago, became the trigger for our entry into WW2. This day, take pause to remember that day.

"December 7, 1941—a date which will live in infamy..." (President Franklin D. Roosevelt) Our country chose to ban together in order to fight for their very freedom and the freedom of others. Bravery, courage and honor were their character traits. My wife's grandfather, fought in WW2 and exhibited these traits during the course of his life.

Ultimately, it was by God's good grace and through Him alone, that the allies journeyed through to victory. Yet, there is an even greater battle that I hope you will dwell upon today and every day. Paul writes, "For we do not wrestle against flesh and blood, but against the rulers, against the authorities, against the cosmic powers over this present darkness, against the spiritual forces of evil in the heavenly places." (Ephesians 6:12)

There are physical battles and wars that begin and cease. But, the spiritual realm is always in the midst of warfare. We must not become blind to this reality...this very real reality. Satan and demons are not made up characters. Yet, neither are angels! God Almighty is, and will forever remain, more powerful than the devil. Still, the enemy fights against us humans (Christians and non-Christians) each day and every day.

You will fail in your fight against the devil if you choose to fight by the failing strength of your own self. Should you choose to fight through Jesus, standing upon Him, you shall not fail. Yes, you will fall (you're still imperfect and will sin), but the end result will not be one of failure, but of victory in Jesus.

Addictions, anger, lust, lies, family troubles, work troubles, bad habits...whatever is drawing you away from Christ or whatever the enemy is using as fiery arrows to shoot towards your heart...are battles in the spiritual realm. "The LORD will fight for you, and you have only to be silent." (Exodus 14:14) Read God's Word, the Bible. Fellowship with believers (yes, witness to and hang out with unbelievers, but have a core group of Christians). Pray through and in the power of Jesus Christ. Spiritual warfare is real. Let Jesus fight for you! He loves you and fights for you. Stand in Jesus alone!

12/8

Good Afternoon and Merry Christmas!

Katie and I purchased our first Christmas tree as a married couple yesterday. We decided to go with a real tree. It's full, rich green, fresh, and something that brings a smile to our hearts. Gotta love the sap that one gets on the hands though...but I digress!

"O Christmas Tree! O Christmas Tree!
Thy leaves are so unchanging;
O Christmas Tree! O Christmas Tree!
Thy leaves are so unchanging;
Not only green when summer's here,
But also when 'tis cold and drear.
O Christmas Tree! O Christmas Tree!
Thy leaves are so unchanging!"

There is another tree...one that our Jesus died upon. A tree that the only One that is unchanging bled upon and died for you and me. A tree that the One whose love for you and me is constant through any season of life we may find ourselves. "And when they came to the place that is called The Skull, there they crucified him, and the criminals, one on his right and one on his left. And Jesus said, 'Father, forgive them, for they know not what they do.' And they cast lots to divide his garments." (Luke 23:33-34)

Remember the path that Jesus would take, from the stable to the hill, to win freedom for your soul.
"O Christmas Tree! O Christmas Tree!
How richly God has decked thee!
O Christmas Tree! O Christmas Tree!
How richly God has decked thee!
Thou bidst us true and faithful be,
And trust in God unchangingly.
O Christmas Tree! O Christmas Tree!
How richly God has decked thee!"

"When Jesus had received the sour wine, he said, 'It is finished,' and he bowed his head and gave up his spirit." (John 19:30) Three words... It is finished.

Remember them. Live in light of them. His death and resurrection forever defeated death. The sacrifice is finished. Live out the lyrics of that stanza: "Thou bidst us true and faithful be, And trust in God unchangingly." Every time you see a Christmas tree, remember the cross and remember your Savior. And may Christmas lights spur you on to shine the light of Christ in a dark world!

12/9

Good Greetings and Merry Christmas!

"But when the fullness of time had come, God sent forth his Son, born of woman, born under the law, to redeem those who were under the law, so that we might receive adoption as sons. And because you are sons, God has sent the Spirit of his Son into our hearts, crying, "Abba! Father!" So you are no longer a slave, but a son, and if a son, then an heir through God."
(Galatians 4:4-7)

God's timing was and is perfect!
Upon receiving Christ, God becomes your Heavenly Father!
Sin is no longer your master and you are an heir of heavenly things and an heir of righteousness through God!

"The Son of God became a man to enable men to become sons of God."
(C.S. Lewis)
Meaning that Jesus came to earth in order to save us...in order for us to become children of God and have eternal life by believing in Jesus.
Everyone is a creation of God, but not everyone is a child of God. A person becomes a child of God as soon as he or she accepts Jesus Christ as their Lord and Savior.

Contemplate the amazingness of Jesus choosing to dwell among us!

Let the following be your response this Christmas season and every day of your life...
"What can I give Him, poor as I am?
If I were a shepherd, I would bring a lamb;
If I were a Wise Man, I would do my part;
Yet what I can I give Him: give my heart."
(Christiana Rossetti)

Merry Christmas!

12/10

Hello,

Take a moment and read the following, which was given as a eulogy in the movie Open Range:

"Woke with a smile, seemed like he could keep it there all day. Kind of a man that'd say 'good morning' and mean it, whether it was or not."

That's the kind of person I should be. That's the kind of person you should be.

That's the kind of person the world needs to see us Christians being!

Read the following Scripture and dwell upon the words that David prays to his King, God Almighty:

"Search me, O God, and know my heart! Try me and know my thoughts! And see if there be any grievous way in me, and lead me in the way everlasting!" (Psalm 139:23-24)

David knew he was a mortal man and not above falling to wicked thoughts and actions. He also knew his God was the great and glorious Savior of his soul. Therefore, David prayed that anything in him that was not pleasing to God would be taken away. David yearned for his life to be led by God and God alone.

Take time right now and ask God to quiet your soul. Pray these verses to your Heavenly Father. Begin each day with this prayer and let it be an anthem of your soul.

Merry Christmas!

12/11

Merry Christmas Greetings Everyone,

Are you wishing people a Merry Christmas'?
Don't lose heart in being a light for all to see Jesus! Let us now turn to a Christmas carol...not the movie...but a song that has been around for many years: God Rest You Merry, Gentlemen.

I did some research into this song and the term "rest," in this case, means to keep something going and to have it remain. Thus, the song is singing out for God to keep people merry (full of cheer).

Here is one version of some of the lyrics:
God rest you merry, gentlemen
Let nothing you dismay
For Jesus Christ, our Saviour
Was born upon this day,
To save us all from Satan's power
When we were gone astray.

There is rich meaning...very rich and deep meaning in these lyrics.
"For while we were still weak, at the right time Christ died for the ungodly. For one will scarcely die for a righteous person—though perhaps for a good person one would dare even to die—but God shows his love for us in that while we were still sinners, Christ died for us." (Romans 5:6-8)

Christ, in His perfect timing, died for you and me. Rarely will a person for die another good person. We are not good people apart from Christ. No, people are not good at heart. The Bible is clear on this subject:

"And you were dead in the trespasses and sins in which you once walked, following the course of this world, following the prince of the power of the air, the spirit that is now at work in the sons of disobedience—among whom we all once lived in the passions of our flesh, carrying out the desires of the body[a] and the mind, and were by nature children of wrath, like the rest of mankind. But God, being rich in mercy, because of the great love with which he loved us, even when we were dead in our trespasses, made us alive together with Christ—by grace you have been saved..." (Ephesians 2:1-5)

Two sides to the cross: wrath/judgement and grace/mercy, enveloped in love. That is something to be merry about. Ask God to keep you merry in the midst of an ever changing world. Remember both sides of the cross and be merry in Jesus!

12/12

Merry Christmas,

"And the angel said to them, 'Fear not, for behold, I bring you good news of great joy that will be for all the people." (Luke 2:10)

I was looking at what Christmas, the word, means. The first part of this greeting, merry, means lively or cheerful. The second part of the phrase is broken down into two components: "Christ", is translated from a word in Greek, which is a translation from the Hebrew language for the word that is Messiah; the next part, "mas," comes from missa, which in Latin is the Lord's Supper.

In other words, when you say "Merry Christmas!" you're expressing a cheerful heart at the remembrance of Jesus' sacrifice for you and the world on the cross!

"And he took bread, and when he had given thanks, he broke it and gave it to them, saying, 'This is my body, which is given for you. Do this in remembrance of me.' And likewise the cup after they had eaten, saying, 'This cup that is poured out for you is the new covenant in my blood.'"
(Luke 22:19-20)

Puts a different impact behind such a well-known phrase. When you say it (and say it often!), remember what you are saying, share Jesus with all who will listen, and let it be a reminder to you own soul as well.

"Though you have not seen him, you love him. Though you do not now see him, you believe in him and rejoice with joy that is inexpressible and filled with glory..." (1 Peter 1:8)

Merry may your heart be at the remembrance of Christ your King!

12/13

Top of the Christmas season to you all,

How do you react to the wonderful works of God within your life and around you each and every day? Do you take time to remember them, write them down, reflect upon them? Let's turn to Mary and see her response...

"But Mary treasured up all these things, pondering them in her heart." (Luke 2:19)

Put yourself in Mary's shoes and contemplate what she has seen and experienced up to this point. I would describe her experiences as pretty bland and common-day.

Gotcha! What Mary had seen and experienced was anything but bland or common-day! They were supernatural!

She took time to treasure these sweet and amazing moments that God had blessed her with and allowed her to experience. She thought back upon them and dwelt upon them. She wondered at what God's meaning was through them.

Do you do the same?

Take time right now, today, and each day of your life to call to memory and to dwell and reflect upon the provisions of God in your life, His wonderful blessings, His answers to prayer (when they were yes, when they were no, when they were maybe), and all the miraculous ways He has moved in your life and grown you. His grace, love, mercy, peace, and hope are all worth recalling and dwelling upon. Ask Him to show you what He wants to teach you through past events and move forward in His mighty power for His glory and to tell others about Him!

Merry Christmas!

12/14

Greetings,

How would others describe your "greeting" character? Hm-mmmm...you may be thinking to yourself at this very moment, "What in the name of Rudolph the Red Nosed Reindeer does he mean?"

I'm not sure actually.

Just kidding. What I mean is...when you come into contact with others throughout your day (whether in person, over the phone, through texting, or through email), how do you greet them?
Is it with...
Haste or Patience?
Disgust or Joy?
With a Smile, Frown, or Simply Zero Emotion?
Peace or Anxiousness?
Love or Hate?
With Eternal Things in Mind or Temporary Things in Mind?
With the Love of Jesus or the Love of Self?

Take pause and really think how others would describe your greeting towards them (those you've never met or those closest in your life).

Dr. Jerry Vines mentioned before that as Christians, we do not have the luxury of being unkind.

"Therefore welcome one another as Christ has welcomed you, for the glory of God."
(Romans 15:7)
"We love because He first loved us. If anyone says, 'I love God,' and hates his brother, he is a liar; for he who does not love his brother whom he has seen cannot love God whom he has not seen. And this commandment we have from Him: whoever loves God must also love his brother."
(1 John 4:19-21)

Go forth today and may everyone you come into contact with (whether in person, over the phone, through texting, or through email) see Jesus and feel His love as the Holy Spirit works through you.

As Jesus greeted you, go greet others!

12/15

Good Hello Everyone,

"And an angel of the Lord appeared to them, and the glory of the Lord shone around them, and they were filled with great fear. And the angel said to them, 'Fear not, for behold, I bring you good news of great joy that will be for all the people. For unto you is born this day in the city of David a Savior, who is Christ the Lord.'" (Luke 2:9-11)

The fear and anxieties of the world cave in
No light of hope seems to shine from within

Cease searching for joy in a world of unbelief
For that will never assuage your heartache and grief

Call to mind the message the shepherds received
In that field, long ago, the angel spoke and they believed

Go forth today in the strength of the Lord
Jesus has come and joy to you, He will restore

Enjoy living in His joy!

12/16

Merry Christmas,

Where do you seek help from? What avenues in the world advertise to you, seeking to have you buy into their schemes?

Is it...
Food
Relationships
Money
Sports
TV
Reading
Movies
Work
Family
Christmas or other holidays
Is it one of these?

You see, none of these are bad in and of themselves. But, when we switch the order and place these things above God Almighty, then we sin...plain and simple. We sin. Our true and lasting help does not come from any of these.

"I lift up my eyes to the hills. From where does my help come? My help comes from the Lord, who made heaven and earth. He will not let your foot be moved; He who keeps you will not slumber. Behold, He who keeps Israel will neither slumber nor sleep. The Lord is your keeper; the Lord is your shade on your right hand. The sun shall not strike you by day, nor the moon by night. The Lord will keep you from all evil; He will keep your life. The Lord will keep your going out and your coming in from this time forth and forevermore." (Psalm 121)

Study and meditate upon God's Word. Dwell upon it. It will nourish your soul.

Ask God to bring to mind things you have replaced Him with. Again, they may be good things in and of themselves, but must not be elevated above your Creator, God All Powerful and All Saving.

Elevate Him alone today and everyday!

-470-

12/17

Merry Christmas,

Have you ever felt that standing for your faith is rough, tough, fatiguing...the opposite of the feeling a beautifully decorated Christmas tree gives you?

Don't lose heart. Don't give up.
"Never give in--never, never, never, never, in nothing great or small, large or petty, never give in except to convictions of honor and good sense. Never yield to force; never yield to the apparently overwhelming might of the enemy." (Sir Winston Churchill)

Today and everyday, remember that living for Christ will bring you under attack. Jesus said it Himself...

"If the world hates you, know that it has hated me before it hated you. If you were of the world, the world would love you as its own; but because you are not of the world, but I chose you out of the world, therefore the world hates you." (John 15:18-19)

Scriptures says that Jesus Christ chose you and therefore, as you live for Him and stand for the truths found in His Word, you will face persecution from the world...for the world does not know Jesus and thus, does not stand for the truths He has given us.

Always remember, know and believe...
"In the world you will have tribulation. But take heart; I have overcome the world." (John 16:33b)

As you rejoice this Christmas season for the blessings God has bestowed upon you, rejoice also in being hated for walking according to Jesus' example. Love, in and through Jesus, everyone that hates you, dislikes you, or simply chooses to not agree with your beliefs!

Keep on lovin'!

12/18

Good Christmas Greetings Everyone,

"As each has received a special gift, employ it in serving one another as good stewards of the manifold grace of God." (1 Peter 4:10)

Today, even right now, seek to make someone else's Christmas merry by sharing with them the love of Jesus Christ through your words and actions...however God leads you. Be intentional to be His vessel!

You have received God's grace, but He did not intend for you to receive His gift and not reflect Him with your life in serving others.

Stop right now and pray for God to lead you in how to make someone's Christmas merry for His namesake!

Make much of Jesus!

12/19

Merry Christmas!

"O little town of Bethlehem
How still we see thee lie
Above thy deep and dreamless sleep
The silent stars go by
Yet in thy dark streets shineth
The everlasting Light
The hopes and fears of all the years
Are met in thee tonight"

"But you, O Bethlehem Ephrathah, who are too little to be among the clans of Judah, from you shall come forth for me One who is to be ruler in Israel, whose coming forth is from of old, from ancient days." (Micah 5:2)

Have you ever felt insignificant? Maybe felt that God could never work through you for any of a plethora of reasons?
Truth is...God chooses to work through people, out of His grace and for His glory, that feel insignificant.

Bethlehem was not the "powerful" city that one would expect the Savior of the world to be born in. God goes against "norms" in order to demonstrate who He is and what His character is.

"But the Lord said to Samuel, 'Do not look on his appearance or on the height of his stature, because I have rejected him. For the Lord sees not as man sees: man looks on the outward appearance, but the Lord looks on the heart.'" (1 Samuel 16:7)

Ask Jesus today how He wants to work through you. Surrender your will to His. Take heart, the Savior of the world loves you and desires to use willing vessels.

Remember Bethlehem!

12/20

Good greetings and Merry Christmas!

Katie and I visited Arlington National Cemetery yesterday. It was my first time to walk upon those hallowed grounds.

If we take pause during the business of our lives, we can take lessons from those that have gone before us.

These men and women who lie in military honor for the service given to their country, have procured a legacy for future generations to follow...one of self-sacrifice, duty, courage, honor and loyalty.

Take a lesson from these hallowed grounds...
What will your legacy be?
What will be your epitaph?

We see a description in 2 Timothy 4:7 of the ultimate legacy to leave behind, one that reflects a life lived in faith and passionate love for Jesus Christ: "I have fought the good fight, I have finished the race, I have kept the faith."

Paul took a stand for Jesus and strove to tell as many people as he could about his Savior. Paul was not perfect, but he strove to live a life that was faithful to Christ.

This was Paul's legacy and may it be ours...all in order to glorify Jesus and point future generations to Him!

Merry Christmas!

12/21

Good Greetings and Good Greetings,

Today is my brother's birthday! He is a man of many talents and most importantly, a godly man. I am proud to be his brother and am blessed beyond words.

He loves to sing and has a good voice. Papa Jack, our grandfather on our mom's side, also loved to sing. At Papa Jack's funeral in 2009, Jonathan sang a song he loved...

Be Thou my Vision, O Lord of my heart
Naught be all else to me, save that Thou art
Thou my best Thought, by day or by night
Waking or sleeping, Thy presence my light

Be Thou my Wisdom, and Thou my true Word
I ever with Thee and Thou with me, Lord
Thou my great Father, I Thy true son
Thou in me dwelling, and I with Thee one

Riches I heed not, nor man's empty praise
Thou mine Inheritance, now and always
Thou and Thou only, first in my heart
High King of Heaven, my Treasure Thou art

High King of Heaven, my victory won
May I reach Heaven's joys, O bright Heav'n's Sun
Heart of my own heart, whate'er befall
Still be my Vision, O Ruler of all

God's Word says:
"The steps of a man are established by the Lord, when he delights in his way; though he fall, he shall not be cast headlong, for the Lord upholds his hand." (Psalm 37:23-24)

Choose to ask God to be your vision in all things today and every day. He will not fail to guide you in all things. You will stumble at times due to your sinfulness, but God will hold you, shower you with grace, and continue to be your vision. Choose Him!

12/22

Merry Christmas,

Peace through Christ Jesus
For He promised He would never leave us
Joy during each tribulation
For Jesus showed His love for every nation
Hope against ever earthly odd
For Jesus Christ is the Son of God

"The Word became flesh and made his dwelling among us. We have seen his glory, the glory of the one and only Son, who came from the Father, full of grace and truth."
(John 1:14)

Take time this day and dwell upon the Christmas season...what Jesus did when He chose to come as a baby to dwell among us.

The Son of God chose to leave heaven for you.
He loves you that much!
Jesus Christ came to earth as 100% God and 100% man.

There is no other religion that has its god doing such a thing. But then again, Christianity is not a religion, but a relationship. And there is no other God besides Jesus Christ!

Don't let the world tell you there are other ways to heaven then the babe that came down at Christmas!

Rejoice!

12/23

Hello and Hello,

Get up early.
I like my bed.
Get up early.
I'm tired.
Get up early.
I like me.

I like sleep too, but it would behoove me and you to get up early before our day begins for the sake of…Jesus.

"And rising very early in the morning, while it was still dark, he departed and went out to a desolate place, and there he prayed." (Mark 1:35)

I would like to challenge you to begin making a habit of getting up early to spend time with God your Father.

He set the example for us in doing the same thing. If He did, we by allllllll means need to!

Ask God's help to do so and see what happens. You'll need to discipline yourself and, in a sense, suck it up. But it will be worth it! You get to spend time with your Creator, Savior and Lord. He will clothe you with His armor for the day.

Rise and rise early!

12/24

Merry Christmas!

That which you are willing to die for will reveal that which you are choosing to live for.

What are you living for? More importantly, who are you living for? Choose wisely.

"Never forget what Jesus did for you. Never take lightly what it cost Him. And never assume that if it cost Him His very life, that it won't also cost you yours." (Rich Mullins)

"...Some were tortured, refusing to accept release, so that they might rise again to a better life. Others suffered mocking and flogging, and even chains and imprisonment. They were stoned, they were sawn in two, they were killed with the sword. They went about in skins of sheep and goats, destitute, afflicted, mistreated—of whom the world was not worthy..." (Hebrews 11:35b-38a)

That which you are willing to die for will reveal that which you are choosing to live for.

Are you living for Jesus Christ?
Are you willing to be persecuted for your Jesus, your Savior?
Are you willing to be tortured for Jesus, your Strength?
Are you willing to die for Jesus, your Everlasting Prince of Peace?

Live in such a way that people know you are willing!

12/25

Merry Christmas!!!

"The Son of God became a man to enable men to become sons of God." (C.S. Lewis)

Jesus came to enable you and I to become a child of God. When a person is born, they are a creation of God. But, an individual is not a child of God until they accept Jesus Christ as their personal Lord and Savior.

"Once in our world, a stable had something in it that was bigger than our whole world." (C.S. Lewis)

Today is the day Christians remember the birth of the God-man... Jesus! He chose to leave heaven's celestial shores to dwell among mankind. He knew not everyone would choose to accept Him, yet He came anyway because He loved the world!

"Suddenly a great company of the heavenly host appeared with the angel, praising God and saying,
'Glory to God in the highest heaven, and on earth peace to those on whom his favor rests.'"
(Luke 2:13-14)

Rejoice in this amazingly wonderful news!
Rejoice and enjoy the gift of salvation Jesus has offered!
Rejoice in His peace, love, hope, joy and presence!

Rejoice and tell others!

Merry Christmas!

12/26

Greetings!

The day after Christmas can sometimes be tough and even depressing as the day which all the planning, activities and wishing led up to has come and gone.

Charles Dickens said, "I will honour Christmas in my heart, and try to keep it all the year."

You see, the foundation of Christmas is Christ and each day can be Christmas for the Christian! That doesn't mean the actual season is every day...with the decorations, parties and music. What it does mean is that Christians should practice generosity and good cheer towards their fellow man. It means that each day we as Christians should have the joy of Christmas...the joy of Christ!

Although...enjoying parties with friends and those you don't know well (maybe your neighbors) is something to do throughout the year. Fellowship with others and share the love of Christ with them! And... Christmas music can also be worship music when it tells of Jesus! Do both year round!!

"When the cares of my heart are many, Your consolations cheer my soul." (Psalm 94:19)

Be of good Christmas joy!

12/27

Merry Christmas!

"Now after Jesus was born in Bethlehem of Judea in the days of Herod the king, behold, wise men from the east came to Jerusalem, saying, 'Where is He who has been born king of the Jews? For we saw His star when it rose and have come to worship Him.'" (Matthew 2:1-2)

There is a saying that goes like this: "Wise men still seek Him."
Will this quote reflect you and I for the remainder of our days?

The wise men from the above passage pursued the One for whom the star was up in the sky. These men of nobility knew there was One above them. They knew and they pursued.

Know Jesus through the Bible.
Pursue Him in how you live, speak and think.
Follow after Jesus with every ounce of your being.

Let it be said that you were a man or woman that pursued Jesus Christ as the wise men did oh so many years ago.

Wise men sought Him.
Wise men and women seek Him still.

Seek Him!

12/28

Merry Christmas Greetings,

On this date in history, in the year 1945, the Pledge of Allegiance was officially recognized by Congress. That is a pledge for which men and women have died for, holding true to those words with an unwavering determination. We should approach this pledge with respect.

But, more importantly is the pledge of allegiance you give God Almighty. Are you holding true to the pledge you gave Him when you accepted Jesus Christ as your Lord and Savior? Yes, you will stumble, but God in His wonderful grace will lift you up.

"Only fear the Lord and serve Him faithfully with all your heart. For consider what great things He has done for you." (1 Samuel 12:24)

Do you have a reverence for God your Creator?
Do you strive to serve Him faithfully?
Have you called to mind all the great things He has done for you?

Take a moment to honestly answer these questions and talk to God about them. Seek His face.
He is faithful and will sustain you. He is mightily powerful and will help you.

He is worthy of your pledge of allegiance.

Go forth today honoring that pledge!

12/29

Hello Everyone,

Admiral Ackbar said, "It's a trap!"

Who?!
A character from Star Wars. But the same message would be said to you and me of moments throughout our days. The enemy is smart…not all-knowing, but smart. He will use things to trigger you into giving into the flesh and sin. Thoughts you may tend to think, words you may tend to say, actions you make tend to enact.

Know that you are at war and therefore, there are traps set for you each day…some you can see and others you can't.

Be aware with your spiritual eyes and armor.
God will grant you these, just ask Him!

Don't fall for the trap!

12/30

Good Greetings Everyone,

Please savor these three hearty pieces of nourishment throughout today and every day.

"Our worst days are never so bad that you are beyond the reach of God's grace. And your best days are never so good that you are beyond the need of God's grace." -Jerry Bridges

"Since then we have a great high priest who has passed through the heavens, Jesus, the Son of God, let us hold fast our confession. For we do not have a high priest who is unable to sympathize with our weaknesses, but one who in every respect has been tempted as we are, yet without sin. Let us then with confidence draw near to the throne of grace, that we may receive mercy and find grace to help in time of need." (Hebrews 4:14-16)

We don't need a human priest to be our connection to God, for Jesus Christ is our only way to God the Father. Through Jesus, grace and help is offered freely to you!

As the song goes...

Grace, grace, God's grace,

Grace that will pardon and cleanse within;

Grace, grace, God's grace,

Grace that is greater than all our sin!

Go forth today in God's grace!

12/31

Good Greetings and Happy New Year's Eve!

For some, 2018 was a fantastic year...a year that some would like to have duplicated and built upon in 2019. For some, 2018 was an extremely trying year...a year that some would like to forget and start from scratch in 2019. Maybe you simply feel numb, frozen, or indifferent because you are emotionally drained.

God sees you. God hears you. God loves you. God is with you. God has not relinquished His throne, nor has He quit on you.

"Remember not the former things, nor consider the things of old. Behold, I am doing a new thing; now it springs forth, do you not perceive it? I will make a way in the wilderness and rivers in the desert." (Isaiah 43:18-19)

View 2019, no matter how your 2018's whole scope and sequence transpired, through the lens of the above verses. Trust the One who has proven through His Word that He can be trusted. He has plans for you in 2019. He will make a way, even if you cannot presently see it.

"And I am sure of this, that He who began a good work in you will bring it to completion at the day of Jesus Christ." (Philippians 1:6)

Wow, what a promise! Take God at His word and see what happens! Believe it, hold onto it, dwell on it, hope in it, rejoice in it, and grow in it. Even if you feel 2018 was not a year you'd like to have duplicated, seek God and ask Him what He would have you learn from it, how He would have you live in light of it, and how He desires to use the experiences to grow you and bring Him glory!

Look forward into 2019 with eager anticipation of what God will do in you, through you, and for you...all for His glory!

"Because He lives, I can face tomorrow
Because He lives, all fear is gone

Because I know He holds the future
And life is worth the living
Just because He lives." (William J. Gaither and Gloria Gaither)

Go forth in faith today!

Author Bio

Reverend Nathan Kaspar is a wretch saved by Jesus, plain and simple. But the amazing sound of God's saving grace always plays! Nathan is married to the love of his life, Katie, who serves as a Pediatric Nurse Practitioner. Nathan's parents, Dan and Linda Kaspar, provided an amazingly undeserved homelife growing up for him and his brother, Jonathan, who is married to Maggie (they are expecting their first child!). Nathan currently serves as the Senior Pastor of Towne Baptist Church in Joppa, MD. Previously, he served as the Next Generation Pastor of Western Heritage Church in Irving, TX. Nathan is a graduate of Southwestern Baptist Theological Seminary where he obtained his Master of Divinity. He also holds a Bachelor of Science degree from Texas Christian University. Before entering vocational ministry, he served in various capacities within the social work field, assisting men and woman in gaining self-sufficiency and stability. Nathan and Katie both love sports (especially college football!), spending time with family and friends, being outdoors, and a variety of other things!

CPSIA information can be obtained
at www.ICGtesting.com
Printed in the USA
BVHW032350100321
602009BV00015B/50